"At last, a new edition of *Thoughts & Feelings*, chock full of systematic strategies for the treatment of a wide variety of psychological problems. This volume takes the readers through the step-by-step operations involved in overcoming their difficulties. It is eminently readable and helpful for professionals as well as patients."

—Aaron T. Beck, M.D.

"This is an outstanding book. I recommend it without reservation for both general readers and therapists who want to learn effective strategies for managing depression, stress, anxiety, panic, worry, anger, and similar problems we all experience. The book is straightforward and easy to read. It stands apart from other similar books in its reliance on scientific data, not fad, hype, or mysticism."

—Jacqueline B. Persons, Ph.D.
Director, Center for Cognitive Therapy,
Oakland, California
Associate Clinical Professor, Department of
Pyschiatry, University of California, San Francisco

"McKay, Davis, and Fanning have offered us a welcome update to their classic *Thoughts & Feelings*. The new edition will serve as an excellent resource, reference tool, treatment manual, therapy coach, and compendium of techniques. It has great value for the experienced clinician and for the novice therapist, as a guide and prompt for individuals in therapy, and as a self-help guide for individuals to use as an adjunct to therapy."

—Arthur Freeman, Ed.D., ABPP
Chair, Department of Psychology
Director, Doctoral Program in Clinical Psychology
Philadelphia College of Osteopathic Medicine

"The new edition of *Thoughts & Feelings* is one of the most comprehensive and empirically sound guidebooks in all of self-help literature. All of the major problems in living are covered. This book will be extremely valuable as a stand-alone guide for persons trying to change their lives on their own, as a centerpiece of therapy clients' bibliotherapy, and as a source of dozens of ideas for interventions and homework assignments for therapists."

—Cory F. Newman, Ph.D.
Clinical Director, Center for Cognitive Therapy
University of Pennsylvania
Co-author of *Choosing to Live*

"*Thoughts & Feelings* artfully organizes the best techniques and strategies for managing many of the emotional troubles that life may bring. For professionals and the public, this wonderful workbook, like a wise teacher, can help make a positive difference."

—Thomas F. Cash, Ph.D.
Professor of Psychology, Old Dominion University
Author of *The Body Image Workbook*

"This is a jewel of a book: while sensible and matter-of-fact, *Thoughts & Feelings* speaks in a supportive and empathic tone. Short on platitudes and long on practical applications, this book is chock-full of helpful information and practical exercises.. A must-buy for all cognitive-behavioral therapists."

> —Thomas E. Ellis, Psy.D., ABPP
> Associate Professor, Department of Behavioral
> Medicine and Pyschiatry
> West Virginia University School of Medicine
> Co-author of *Choosing to Live*

"This book is a state-of-the-art guide to cognitive-behavioral therapy that will be useful to both therapists and clients. The format, which matches interventions to specific problems, is especially helpful."

> —Edmund J. Bourne, Ph.D.
> Author of *The Anxiety & Phobia Workbook*

"This book is useful, well organized, thoughtful, and pragmatic. It's honest, too, with no irresponsible promises tht you can make real changes without working hard. I'll recommend *Thoughts & Feelings* to others because I will use it myself."

> —Ronald T. Potter-Efron, M.S.W., Ph.D.
> Author of *Angry All the Time* and *Letting Go of Anger*

"Long-standing negative thought patterns often make us feel anxious, depressed, and angry; they interfere with our happiness and well-being. This book helps us become aware of these thoughts and teaches us to find adaptive coping responses that truly work. This might be the most useful self-help book in the market since *The Feeling Good Handbook*. I strongly recommend it."

> —Elke Zuercher-White, Ph.D.
> Author of *An End to Panic*

"This book is an absolutely fantastic resource. I thought the first edition was an invaluable guide, but I think the second edition has far surpassed it. I'm looking forward to having it available so I can recommend it to the people I teach."

> —Mary Ellen Copeland, M.A., M.S.
> Author of *The Depression Workbook* and *Living without Depression and Manic Depression*

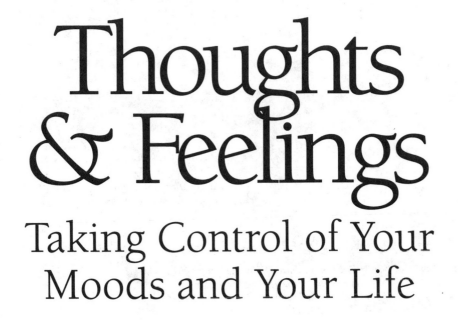

Thoughts & Feelings

Taking Control of Your Moods and Your Life

Matthew McKay, Ph.D.

Martha Davis, Ph.D.

Patrick Fanning

NEW HARBINGER PUBLICATIONS, INC.

Distributed in Canada by Raincoast Books.

Copyright © 1997 by   Matthew McKay, Patrick Fanning, and Martha Davis
New Harbinger Publications, Inc.
5674 Shattuck Avenue
Oakland, CA 94609

Cover design by SHELBY DESIGNS AND ILLUSTRATES
Edited by Carole Honeychurch
Text design by Michele Waters

Library of Congress Card Catalog Number: 97-69491
ISBN 157224-093-8 Paperback

Printed in the United States of America

New Harbinger Publications' Web site address: www.newharbinger.com

07   06

20   19   18   17   16   15

*Dedicated to all the researchers and
clinicians who have shown us what works.*

Table Of Contents

Preface to the Second Edition

The first edition of *Thoughts & Feelings* appeared in 1981 and sold 70,000 copies. It was an introduction to cognitive behavioral therapy that was used by general readers and therapists alike. It provided simple step-by-step instructions for a dozen specific techniques.

Over the years we came to realize the book's limitations. To begin with, some of the techniques had not stood the test of time. Later studies had shown them to be less effective than newer, more powerful interventions. Second, cognitive behavioral therapists were developing multistep protocols to treat many disorders. But the original *Thoughts and Feelings* didn't show how to link a series of techniques together into an integrated treatment plan for problems like depression, panic disorder, or anger.

This new edition of *Thoughts & Feelings* is 90 percent revised. In truth, it's more like a new book than a second edition. It has fourteen new chapters, and the remaining six chapters have been extensively revised to include more effective methodologies and changes in modern practice.

By far the most important change in the second edition is the development of multistep protocols to treat many mood-based problems. These protocols are outlined in chapter 1 and show you a sequence of relevant chapters and techniques for each disorder. This is consistent with the way cognitive behavioral treatments are conducted during therapy—you take a series of steps to acquire building-block skills to cope with your problem.

Our intention, as with the first edition, is for both the general reader and the therapist to use this book. The general reader will find that each treatment protocol has clear, easy-to-follow steps that provide tools for genuine self-help. Therapists will find the new *Thoughts & Feelings* to be a resource for the most effective treatment methods, as well as a helpful take-home manual for their clients.

To all those who used the original *Thoughts & Feelings*, we wish to express our thanks. We hope you'll find the second edition even more useful and effective. To our new readers, we hope you'll find here many helpful tools to take control of your moods and your life.

Matthew McKay
Patrick Fanning
Calistoga, California

Grateful acknowledgment is made to Norman Cavior, Ph.D., our teacher, and the one who first introduced us to cognitive behavioral techniques. He continues to be a source of wisdom and inspiration.

We also wish to acknowledge three fine writers who made significant contributions to this book: Mary Hills Hoffman, Dana Landis, and Susan Johnson.

How to Use this Book

These cognitive behavioral techniques are presented in a workbook format so you can practice them as self-help steps toward change. People in the helping professions—therapists, doctors, nurses, social workers, even teachers and supervisors—will find many of these techniques not only useful in their personal lives, but also of value to their clients, patients, students, or employees.

In chapter 1 you'll find a list of twelve major problems and a specific, step-by-step protocol to treat each of them. The protocol will give you the sequence in which to work through relevant chapters and techniques. At the end of chapter 1 is the Treatment Planner chart, showing which chapters you should read to treat many additional problems.

In most cases you'll find it helpful to read chapters 2, 3, and 4 first, because they represent the foundation of cognitive behavioral therapy. You'll learn how thoughts influence feelings and how habitual negative thoughts can impact your mood. You'll also find tools for changing your thoughts in order to relieve anxiety, depression, and anger.

The full benefits of cognitive behavioral therapy can be realized only through regular practice over time. Simply understanding a technique is of little value without first-hand experience. In other words, this is not a book for passive reading. You have to do the exercises, fill in the worksheets, and carry out real changes in how you think and behave.

The length of time required to practice a particular technique will vary. See the Time for Mastery sections for an idea of the time commitment necessary for each new skill. You should spend time doing the exercises daily because regular practice is the key to successful change. Some of the techniques will need to be "overlearned" to the point where they become automatic responses. The idea is to be able to use the techniques where and whenever you need to, without having to refer to the book.

If you feel you have limited self-discipline or are not highly motivated, try these two alternatives:

1. Make a contract with another person as described in chapter 20, or

2. Seek a consultation with a cognitive behavioral therapist to help you develop and monitor your treatment program.

Before undertaking any cognitive behavioral treatments for anxiety, you should get a complete physical checkup. Have your doctor rule out thyroid problems, hypoglycemia, mitral valve prolapse, and other cardiac arrhythmia problems. If you experience any prolonged physical effects while doing exercises in this book, consult your physician.

Chapter 1

Making Your Own
Treatment Plan

You have probably opened this book because you're feeling bad. You may be depressed, anxious, angry, worried, confused, frustrated, upset, ashamed—unfortunately, the list is very long. Please remember that you are not alone or unusual in your struggle with painful feelings and experiences. Everybody experiences emotional distress sometimes. It's normal.

When the pain becomes too strong and too enduring, it's time to do something about it. By reading this book, you are taking an important first step toward feeling better.

When you feel bad, you don't have the time and patience to wade through simplistic pep talks, unrealistic success stories, needless horror stories, or long-winded and obscure discussions of theory. Therefore, we have made this book as clear and as brief as possible.

On the other hand, when you feel bad, you don't have the energy to seek out partial fragments of the solution to your problem in widely scattered locations. So we also have made this book as complete as possible. Everything you need in order to learn the techniques in this book is presented in complete detail, proceeding logically, step-by-step.

If you are in pain, you also don't have any time to waste on unproven remedies of doubtful utility. Therefore we have included only techniques that have been proven over a long period of time, in many well-designed studies with many different types of people, to have strong therapeutic benefits.

Over the past twenty-five years, many new cognitive behavioral techniques have been developed and refined to relieve anxiety, lift depression, and calm anger. The best of these techniques are presented in this book. They offer you real promise that help is on the way. With patience and a little effort, you can start to feel better soon.

Why Cognitive Behavioral Therapy Works

Many people believe that painful feelings are caused by forgotten childhood experiences, and that the only way to relieve painful feelings is through long, difficult analysis that roots out unconscious memories and associations.

There is undoubtedly *some* connection between your distant past and painful feelings in the present. But modern cognitive behavioral therapists have discovered a much more immediate and accessible source of emotions: your current train of thought. It has been demonstrated over and over that most painful emotions are immediately preceded by some kind of interpreting thought.

For example, a new acquaintance doesn't telephone when he said he would. If your interpreting thought is, "He doesn't like me after all," you would feel sat at being rejected. If your thought was, "He's been in a car crash," you would feel anxiety for his well-being. If you thought, "He deliberately lied to me about calling," you might feel anger at his falsehood.

This simple insight forms the heart of cognitive behavioral therapy: You can change your feelings by changing your thoughts. Hundreds of studies over the last twenty-five years have proved that this simple insight can be applied to relieve a large variety of problems more easily and quickly than any other therapeutic technique.

Designing Your Treatment Plan

This is not the kind of book that you must read cover to cover. This chapter will help you assess your problem and plan which chapters you'll need to read to solve your problem.

Twelve major protocols are summarized below. A *protocol* is a set of techniques that has been shown to be effective in treating a specific problem, such as depression, worry, or phobia. Protocols follow a definite sequence, beginning with the most useful or general technique and proceeding to more specialized interventions.

Each protocol begins with a list of the symptoms characteristic of the problem. Then the pertinent chapters are listed in the order in which they should be read. Each section concludes with a brief description of the steps and rationale for the protocol.

If you would like an overview of the twelve protocols and all the additional problems this book treats, see the Treatment Planner chart at the end of this chapter. It breaks symptoms down into broad categories, provides cross references to help you identify your problem, and shows all the treatment options at a glance.

Worry

Worry is the main symptom of generalized anxiety disorder. You have a problem with worry if you have been excessively apprehensive, more days than not, for at least six months. Seriously anxious people find it difficult to control their worry and typically experience these symptoms:

- Restlessness
- Fatigue

- Difficulty concentrating
- Irritability
- Muscle tension
- Sleep disturbance

Treat worry by working through the following chapters in order:
Chapter 5, "Relaxation"
Chapter 6, "Worry Control"
Chapter 14, "Problem Solving"

Begin at chapter 5, "Relaxation," with an emphasis on cue-controlled relaxation. In chapter 6, "Worry Control," you'll learn how to make an accurate risk assessment, do worry exposure, and achieve worry behavior prevention. Because some worries can be addressed by a search for alternative solutions, chapter 14, "Problem Solving," can teach you skills to find new answers.

Panic Disorder

Panic is a period of intense fear. When you experience a panic attack, you feel some of the following symptoms very intensely, reaching a peak quickly—within ten minutes or less:

- Fast, pounding heart rate
- Sweating
- Trembling
- Shortness of breath
- Feeling of choking
- Chest pain
- Stomach pain or nausea
- Feeling "spacy"
- Fear of losing control, going crazy
- Fear of dying
- Numbness, tingling
- Chills or hot flushes

> **Treat panic disorder by working through the following chapters in order:**
> Chapter 9, "Coping with Panic"
> Chapter 11, "Stress Inoculation"
> Chapter 12, "Coping During Exposure"

You should follow the steps outlined in chapter 9, "Coping with Panic." You'll need to master breath control training, learn how to use a Probability Form, and practice interoceptive desensitization.

If you have not developed agoraphobia (fear of being away from a safe place) or significant avoidance because of the fear of panicking, you can stop here. However, if you've reached a point where you are avoidant or agoraphobic, you'll need to develop a fear hierarchy as explained in chapter 11, "Stress Inoculation," and begin exposing yourself in gradual steps to your feared situations.

Chapter 12, "Coping During Exposure," can help you create coping strategies to use while desensitizing yourself to real-life fears.

Perfectionism

When you struggle with perfectionism, nothing is ever good enough. Shades of gray disappear and you see only black and white—mostly black. You are your own harshest critic, constantly upbraiding yourself for failing to come up to the mark. You may spend hours checking and rechecking your figures, revising a paper, or sanding and polishing a craft project. But all this striving for perfection doesn't please you. It makes you all the more anxious about making mistakes and being criticized for them.

> **Treat perfectionism by working through the following chapters in order:**
> Chapter 2, "Uncovering Automatic Thoughts"
> Chapter 3, "Changing Patterns of Limited Thinking"
> Chapter 4, "Changing Hot Thoughts"
> Chapter 6, "Worry Control" (step 4, Worry Behavior Prevention, only)
> Chapter 15, "Testing Core Beliefs"

Begin with chapters 2, 3, and 4 to develop skills in using the Thought Journal. Pay particular attention to limited thinking patterns such as polarized thinking, catastrophizing, magnifying, and shoulds. You'll also need to learn in chapter 4 how to confront hot thoughts (the thoughts that trigger emotion) about the dire consequences of making mistakes.

The program for worry behavior prevention in chapter 6 is critical to limit the excessive checking and overworking that grow out of fears of making mistakes or being criticized.

Chapter 15, "Testing Core Beliefs," will give you tools to identify and change deeply held beliefs about unworthiness and incompetence that may fuel your perfectionism.

If serious problems persist at the end of this protocol, see chapter 11, "Stress Inoculation," to develop a hierarchy of feared mistakes, then expose yourself through imagery to each step of your hierarchy. You will also need to expose yourself to mistakes in real life by deliberately making mistakes in a series of planned experiments (see step 6, Testing Your Rules, in chapter 15).

Obsessional Thinking

Obsessional thinking consists of recurrent thoughts, impulses, or images that intrude on your consciousness. Obsessional thinking is not ordinary worry over a current problem—it's a disturbing, unwelcome train of thought that is excessive, unreasonable, and time-consuming. You try to stop obsessing, but the thoughts soon start up again. Obsessional thinking can significantly interfere with your normal routine at home, school, or work.

> **Treat obsessional thinking by working through the following chapters in order:**
>
> Chapter 7, "Thought Stopping"
> Chapter 8, "Flooding"
> Chapter 6, "Worry Control" (Worry Behavior Prevention only)

You start with chapter 7, "Thought Stopping," because it's simple and easy to learn. This technique will give you the skill to push away many unwanted thoughts. But there will be some thoughts—usually ones that trigger very high anxiety—that will require something more powerful to defeat. Chapter 8, "Flooding," shows you how to bombard yourself with images derived from your obsessional thoughts and in so doing take away their power.

The section on worry behavior prevention in chapter 6 helps you complete the treatment by stopping any checking and avoidance behaviors that reinforce your obsessions.

Phobia

Specific phobias include excessive or unreasonable fear of such things as flying, heights, animals, injections, blood, and so on. You avoid the object of your fear as much as possible. If you must fly or ascend heights or approach feared animals, it causes you intense anxiety, perhaps a full-blown panic attack. Specific phobias go beyond normal caution in risky situations. They seriously interfere with your relationships, daily routine, schooling, or career.

Agoraphobia is anxiety about or avoidance of public places. People with agoraphobia fear leaving a safe place such as their home. They don't want to be in a situation in which escape would be difficult or embarrassing. They are often concerned about having a panic attack someplace where help is not available. People with agoraphobia typically fear being outside their home alone, being in a crowd, standing in line, crossing a bridge, traveling in a bus or train, and so on.

Social phobia is a strong, persistent fear of being with unfamiliar people. If you have social phobia, you try to avoid situations in which you must meet new people, interact with those you don't know well, or be scrutinized by strangers. You're afraid you may behave awkwardly or embarrass yourself by showing how anxious you are. When you must function in social situations, you are very anxious, even though you realize that your fear is excessive. Social phobia seriously interferes with your life.

> **Treat phobia by working through the following chapters in order:**
> Chapter 5, "Relaxation"
> Chapter 11, "Stress Inoculation"
> Chapter 12, "Coping During Exposure"

The basic treatment protocol for all phobias is the same, with the exception of agoraphobia. Agoraphobia usually starts with untreated panic disorder. The panic disorder must be resolved first (see the panic disorder protocol), then you can continue with the regular phobia protocol.

Initially, read chapter 5, "Relaxation," then develop and expose yourself to a visualized fear hierarchy as explained in chapter 11, "Stress Inoculation." Once you've mastered relaxation and cognitive coping strategies in visualized fear scenes, you can read chapter 12, "Coping During Exposure." Now you'll practice your coping skills in real-life fear situations that range from very low to very high anxiety.

If stress inoculation doesn't work for you, an alternative phobia treatment is in chapter 8, "Flooding." Here the emphasis is on long periods of visualized exposure using an endless loop cassette tape.

If you are working through this protocol for a social phobia, you might also wish to explore chapter 18, "Covert Modeling," or chapter 10, "Coping Imagery," to develop and practice a specific plan to handle novel social situations.

Depression

When you're depressed, your mood is sad and nothing seems interesting or pleasurable. It can affect your appetite, causing you to lose or gain weight. You might sleep a lot more or less than usual. You feel restless and yet tired at the same time. It's hard to concentrate or make decisions, especially the decision to get up and do something. You feel worthless. Life seems hopeless. Thoughts of death are common and you may even think about suicide. Note: If you have serious thoughts of suicide, this book is not enough. You need to see a mental health professional.

> **Treat depression by working through the following chapters in order:**
> Chapter 13, "Getting Mobilized"
> Chapter 2, "Uncovering Automatic Thoughts"
> Chapter 3, "Changing Patterns of Limited Thinking"
> Chapter 4, "Changing Hot Thoughts"
> Chapter 14, "Problem Solving"

Since a major feature of depression is feeling tired and passive, you should start by reading chapter 13, "Getting Mobilized," so you can begin activity scheduling. The next step is to read chapters 2, 3, and 4 to become skilled in using the Thought Journal. The Thought Journal will give you a structure that enables you to explore, confront, and change patterns of negative thinking. Pay particular attention to limited thinking patterns such as filtering, polarized thinking, overgeneralization, and magnifying.

Finally, chapter 14, "Problem Solving," will provide a method for developing alternative solutions to interpersonal, job, financial, and other problems.

If depression persists after you work through this protocol, you may need to change specific core beliefs about competence, worth, and so on. See chapter 15, "Testing Core Beliefs," and then chapter 16, "Changing Core Beliefs With Visualization," to identify and change depression-generating core beliefs.

Low Self-Esteem

When you suffer from low self-esteem, you feel worthless, flawed, and incompetent. You are blind to your strong points and exaggerate your weak points. Your accomplishments in life seem trivial and your failures loom large. Your mood may be sad and depressed, or you may be irritable and aggressive to cover your feelings of low self-esteem. You are surprised and incredulous if someone claims to like you. You expect people to see through to your unworthy core. Low self-esteem keeps you from setting and achieving goals, forming meaningful relationships, trying for promotions, and taking other kinds of risks.

> **Treat low self-esteem by working through the following chapters in order:**
>
> Chapter 2, "Uncovering Automatic Thoughts"
> Chapter 3, "Changing Patterns of Limited Thinking"
> Chapter 4, "Changing Hot Thoughts"
> Chapter 15, "Testing Core Beliefs"
> Chapter 16, "Changing Core Beliefs with Visualization"

Begin with chapters 2, 3, and 4 to develop skills in using the Thought Journal. Pay particular attention to limited thinking patterns such as filtering, polarized thinking, overgeneralization, and magnifying.

Next, you'll need to work through chapter 15, "Testing Core Beliefs," to identify and change deep beliefs about worthiness. Chapter 16, "Changing Core Beliefs with Visualization," provides a way to strengthen this work by confronting childhood situations in which core beliefs were formed.

You may still have to work on remaining hot thoughts (thoughts that immediately precede a painful emotion). If one or two hot thoughts persist that undermine your self-esteem, you should try covert sensitization of hot thoughts in chapter 19, a difficult technique but effective in extinguishing disturbing thoughts.

Shame and Guilt

People who suffer from shame and excessive guilt often feel worthless and to blame for anything that goes wrong. Early sexual or physical abuse frequently contributes to a feeling of being "damaged goods," unworthy of any love or happiness in life. When tragedy strikes, pervasive shame and guilt make it seem like well-deserved punishment rather than simple bad luck.

Treat shame and guilt by working through the following chapters in order:

Chapter 2, "Uncovering Automatic Thoughts"

Chapter 3, "Changing Patterns of Limited Thinking"

Chapter 4, "Changing Hot Thoughts"

Chapter 7, "Thought Stopping"

Chapter 15, "Testing Core Beliefs"

Start your program by reading chapters 2, 3, and 4 to develop skills in using the Thought Journal. Pay special attention to limited thinking patterns such as magnifying, polarized thinking, overgeneralization, and shoulds.

You'll need the skills from chapter 7, "Thought Stopping," to interrupt key habitual thoughts that trigger shame or guilt. Most important, you'll need to work through chapter 15, "Testing Core Beliefs," to identify and change deep beliefs about worthiness, acceptability, and so on.

If your shame seems to arise out of childhood experiences of abuse, you should also work through the exercises in chapter 16, "Changing Core Beliefs with Visualization."

If one or two trigger thoughts persist that habitually trigger feelings of guilt or shame, you can try covert sensitization of hot thoughts in chapter 19.

Anger

You have a problem with anger if your frequent reaction to stress or frustration is to yell, hit, throw, or break things. You have a problem with anger when your temper negatively affects your intimate relationships, your family life, your work, or your friends and acquaintances.

Treat anger by working through the following chapters in order:

Chapter 2, "Uncovering Automatic Thoughts"

Chapter 3, "Changing Patterns of Limited Thinking"

Chapter 4, "Changing Hot Thoughts"

Chapter 5, "Relaxation"

Chapter 17, "Stress Inoculation for Anger Control"

The first step toward anger control is to read chapters 2, 3, and 4 to develop skill in using the Thought Journal. The Thought Journal will help you identify anger-triggering thoughts, then develop strategies to evaluate and challenge them.

Next, you'll need to learn all the relaxation skills in chapter 5, particularly cue-controlled relaxation. Chapter 17, "Stress Inoculation for Anger Control," will show you how to put your cognitive and relaxation skills together, practicing them in visualized anger-provoking situations.

If anger persists in specific, habitual situations, you should read chapter 18, "Covert Modeling." You'll develop a specific plan to change your behavior, and practice a sequence of new, more effective responses.

Mild Avoidance

Mild avoidance is a persistent fear of certain situations, people, or things. The fear is strong enough that you tend to avoid the feared situation when possible, but not so strong that you can't force yourself to deal with the situation if you must. For example, a mild avoidance of flying might mean you go by train or car when possible, but fly when there is no other option. Mild avoidance interferes moderately with your relationships, work, or education.

> **Treat mild avoidance by working through the following chapters in order:**
> Chapter 5, "Relaxation"
> Chapter 10, "Coping Imagery"

Because your avoidance is more on the level of procrastination and putting off rather than full phobia, you probably won't have to build a hierarchy and do stress inoculation to overcome it. Start with chapter 5, "Relaxation," and work to become skilled at deep breathing and cue-controlled relaxation. Then read chapter 10, "Coping Imagery," to gain practice relaxing and coping while imagining yourself handling the stressful situation.

Bad Habits

Bad habits range from excessive television watching to compulsive spending, from nail biting to driving too fast, from eating too much fat to letting the laundry and dishes pile up too long. A bad habit is any recurrent behavior that you can't seem to stop doing, even though you have come to realize that it has a negative impact on your life.

This book does not offer a strong protocol for treating consumptive, addictive bad habits such as smoking, alcoholism, or drug abuse, but less severe habits like the ones mentioned above can be improved significantly with the techniques offered here.

> **Treat bad habits by working through the following chapters in order:**
>
> Chapter 5, "Relaxation"
>
> Chapter 18, "Covert Modeling"
>
> Chapter 14, "Problem Solving"

Since many bad habits occur in response to stress, your first step is to read and master chapter 5, "Relaxation." You should be prepared to use cue-controlled relaxation whenever stress or anxiety begins to trigger your habit.

Next, you should work through chapter 18, "Covert Modeling," to develop alternative responses to replace your old habitual patterns. Finally, use chapter 14, "Problem Solving," to develop alternative solutions to difficult situations that have triggered your habit in the past.

Some persistent habits can be treated with a technique outlined in chapter 19, "Covert Sensitization," where you pair the habit with unpleasant stimuli and extinguish it.

Procrastination

In its most debilitating form, procrastination combines poor time management and problem solving skills with perfectionism and performance anxiety. You put off what you should be doing, waste time on low-priority distractions, let impossibly high standards keep you from starting, and fear failure or criticism once you do get started.

> **Treat procrastination by working through the following chapters in order:**
>
> Chapter 2, "Uncovering Automatic Thoughts"
>
> Chapter 3, "Changing Patterns of Limited Thinking"
>
> Chapter 4, "Changing Hot Thoughts"
>
> Chapter 14, "Problem Solving"

The first step should be reading chapters 2, 3, and 4 to develop skills in using the Thought Journal. Since procrastination often comes from a fear of failure or mistakes, pay special attention to limited thinking patterns such as catastrophizing, magnifying, and filtering. You'll need to confront and change trigger thoughts that define average performance or getting criticized as failure.

Next read chapter 14, "Problem Solving," to develop a plan to accomplish goals you've been avoiding. If procrastination persists, it is often due to deep beliefs about unworthiness or incompetence. You can identify and begin to change such beliefs by working through chapter 15, "Testing Core Beliefs."

Treatment Planner

This chart presents every treatment plan in the book at a glance. To use it, locate a problem in the left column. Reading to the right, a number "1" will be in the column corresponding to the chapter you should work through first. A number "2" indicates the chapter you should read second, and so on to the end of the numbers.

For some problems you may find columns marked with an "x." These are chapters that are not part of the core protocol for the problem, but contain additional procedures that may be applicable and useful if symptoms persist.

Some problems don't have a specific protocol. One or two chapters will be marked with an "x" to indicate suggested treatment options.

Don't be daunted—it only *looks* complicated. Take your time, work step-by-step. You can do it. Congratulations on embarking on this challenging voyage of self-discovery and healing.

Treatment

Problem	Uncovering Automatic Thoughts (2)	Changing Patterns of Limited Thinking (3)	Changing Hot Thoughts (4)	Relaxation (5)	Worry Control (6)	Thought Stopping (7)	Flooding (8)
Anxiety Disorders Worry				1	2		
Panic							
Perfectionism	1	2	3		4		
Obsessional Thinking					3	1	2
Phobia Specific				1			X
Agoraphobia				2			X
Social				1			X
Depressive Disorders Depression	2	3	4				
Low Self-Esteem	1	2	3				
Shame and Guilt	1	2	3			4	
Anger	1	2	3	4			
Physical Stress Muscular Tension				X			
Fight or Flight Symptoms				X			
Behavioral Problems Bad Habits				1			
Mild Avoidance				1			
Procrastination	1	2	3				
Aggression (see Anger)							
Immobilization							
Interpersonal Conflict							
Negative Thought Patterns Negative Core Beliefs							
Obsessions (see Anxiety) Worry (see Anxiety) Self-Criticism (see Self-Esteem)							

Planner

Coping with Panic (9)	Coping Imagery (10)	Stress Inoculation (11)	Coping During Exposure (12)	Getting Mobilized (13)	Problem Solving (14)	Testing Core Beliefs (15)	Changing Core Beliefs with Visualization (16)	Stress Inoculation for Anger (17)	Covert Modeling (18)	Covert Sensitization (19)
					3	X				
1		2	3							
		X				5				
		2	3							
1		3	4							
	X	2	3						X	
				1	5	X	X			
						4	5			
						5				
								5	X	
X										
					3				2	X
	2						.			
					4	X				
				X	X					
					X				X	
						X	X			

Chapter 2

Uncovering Automatic Thoughts

Thoughts cause feelings. This is the essential insight of cognitive therapy. All of the cognitive techniques that have been developed and refined in the last half of the twentieth century flow out of this one simple idea: that thoughts cause feelings, and many emotions you feel are preceded and caused by a thought, however abbreviated, fleeting, or unnoticed that thought may be.

In other words, events by themselves have no emotional content. It is your interpretation of an event that causes your emotions. This is often represented as the "ABC" model of emotions:

A. Event ⟶ B. Thought ⟶ C. Feeling

For example:

A. Event: You get into your car, turn the key, and nothing happens.

B. Thought: You interpret the event by saying to yourself, "Oh no, my battery's dead. This is awful; I'm stuck—I'll be late."

C. Feeling: You experience an emotion appropriate to your thoughts. In this case, you feel depressed and anxious about being late.

Change the thought and you change the feeling. If you had thought, "My son must have left the lights on all night again," you might have felt anger. If you had thought, "I'll have an extra cup of coffee, relax, and wait for a jump from the tow truck," you would have felt mild annoyance at most.

In this chapter you will learn how to uncover the automatic thoughts in this cycle. This is the basic skill you need to master in order to use cognitive therapy to reduce painful feelings.

Symptom Effectiveness

By itself, uncovering automatic thoughts is not considered a full-scale treatment. It is the first step in many different cognitive behavioral treatments. However, you may feel some immediate reduction in anxiety, depression, or anger as a result of exploring how you react to upsetting situations. This is a good sign that cognitive therapy is likely to help you quickly.

On the other hand, it is more likely that you will *not* experience any improvement in symptoms by the end of this chapter. In fact, some feelings may actually intensify as a result of exploring them. Don't worry. Remember that this is an early step along the way.

Time for Mastery

Most people make significant progress during the first week of faithfully keeping a Thought Journal. The longer you practice tuning into your automatic thoughts, the better you get at it. It's a skill like knitting, skiing, writing, or singing on key—practice makes perfect.

Instructions

Negative Feedback Loop

The Event ⟶ Thought ⟶ Feeling sequence is the basic building block of emotional life. But the building blocks can become very jumbled and confusing. The emotional life of real people is not always a simple series of ABC reactions, each with its discrete starting event, thought, and resultant feeling. More often a series of ABC reactions join in a feedback loop. The ending feeling from one sequence becomes the starting event for another sequence.

In the case of painful feelings, a negative feedback loop can be set up in which an uncomfortable feeling itself becomes an "event," the subject of further thoughts, which produce more painful feelings, which become a larger event inspiring more negative thoughts, and so on. The loop continues until you work yourself into a rage, an anxiety attack, or a deep depression.

Feelings have physiological components. When you experience emotions such as fear, anger, or joy, your heart speeds up, you breathe faster and less deeply, you sweat more, and your blood vessels contract and dilate in different parts of your body. "Quiet" emotions such as depression, sadness, or grief involve a slowing down of some of your physiological systems. Both your emotion and the accompanying bodily sensations trigger an evaluation process—you start trying to interpret and label what you feel.

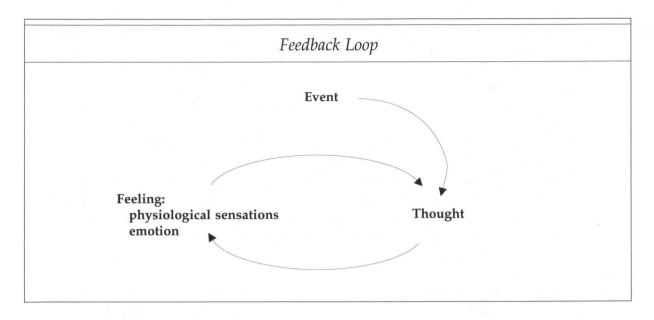

For example, if your car wouldn't start late at night when you were in a bad neighborhood, the negative feedback loop might go like this:

A. **Event:** Car doesn't start.

B. **Thought:** "Oh no, this is awful. I'll be late—and this is a dangerous street."

C. **Feelings:** Heart beating fast, feeling hot and sweaty, irritation, anxiety

B. **Thought:** "I'm scared . . . I could get mugged—this is really bad!"

C. **Feelings:** Stomach clenching, hard to breathe, dizzy, fear

B. **Thought:** "I'm freaking out . . . I'll lose control. . . . Can't move . . . can't get safe."

C. **Feelings:** Strong adrenalin rush, panic

The Nature of Automatic Thoughts

You are constantly describing the world to yourself, giving each event or experience some label. You automatically make interpretations of everything you see, hear, touch, and feel. You judge events as good or bad, pleasurable or painful, safe or dangerous. This process colors all of your experiences, labeling them with private meanings.

These labels and judgments are fashioned from the unending dialog you have with yourself, a waterfall of thoughts cascading down the back of your mind. These thoughts are constant and rarely noticed, but they are powerful enough to create your most intense emotions. This internal dialog is called *self-talk* by rational-emotive therapist Albert Ellis, and *automatic thoughts* by cognitive theorist Aaron Beck. Beck prefers the term automatic thoughts "because it more accurately describes the way thoughts are experienced. The person perceives these thoughts as though they are by reflex—without any prior reflection or reasoning; and they impress him as plausible and valid." (Beck 1976)

Automatic thoughts usually have the following characteristics:

1. **They often appear in shorthand,** composed of just a few essential words phrased in telegraphic style: "lonely . . . getting sick . . . can't stand it . . . cancer . . . no good." One word or a short phrase functions as a label for a group of painful memories, fears, or self-reproaches.

   An automatic thought needn't be expressed in words at all. It can be a brief visual image, an imagined sound or smell, or any physical sensation. A woman who was afraid of heights had a half-second image of the floor tilting and felt herself sliding down toward the window. This momentary fantasy triggered acute anxiety whenever she ascended above the third floor.

   Sometimes the automatic thought is a brief reconstruction of some event in the past. A depressed woman kept seeing the stairway in Macy's where her husband had first announced his plan to leave her. The image of the stairway was enough to unleash all the feelings associated with that loss.

   Occasionally an automatic thought can take the form of intuitive knowledge, without words, images, or sense impressions. For example, a chef who was plagued with self-doubt "just knew" that it was useless to try to get promoted to head chef.

2. **Automatic thoughts are almost always believed,** no matter how illogical they appear upon analysis. For example, a man who reacted with rage to the death of his best friend actually believed for a time that his friend deliberately died to punish him.

   Automatic thoughts have the same believable quality as direct sense impressions. You attach the same truth value to automatic thoughts as you do to sights and sounds in the real world. If you see a man getting into a Porsche and have the thought, "He's rich; he doesn't care for anyone but himself," the judgment is as real to you as the color of the car.

3. **Automatic thoughts are experienced as spontaneous.** You believe automatic thoughts because they are automatic. They seem to arise spontaneously out of ongoing events. They just pop into your mind and you hardly notice them, let alone subject them to logical analysis.

4. **Automatic thoughts are often couched in terms of** *should, ought,* **or** *must.* A woman whose husband had recently died thought, "You ought to go it alone. You shouldn't burden your friends." Each time the thought popped into her mind, she felt a wave of hopelessness. People torture themselves with "shoulds" such as "I should be happy. I should be more energetic, creative, responsible, loving, generous. . . ." Each ironclad "should" precipitates a sense of guilt or a loss of self-esteem.

   "Shoulds" are hard to eradicate, since their origin and function is actually adaptive. They are simple rules to live by that have worked in the past. They are templates for survival that you can access quickly in times of stress. The problem is that they become so automatic that you don't have time to analyze them, and so rigid that you can't modify them to fit changing situations.

5. **Automatic thoughts tend to "awfulize."** These thoughts predict catastrophe, see danger in everything, and always expect the worst. A stomachache is a symptom of cancer, the look of distraction in a lover's face is the first sign of withdrawal. "Awfulizers" are the major source of anxiety.

Awfulizers are also hard to eradicate because of their adaptive function. They help you predict the future and prepare for the worst-case scenario.

6. **Automatic thoughts are relatively idiosyncratic.** In a crowded theater a woman suddenly stood up, slapped the face of the man next to her, and hurried up the aisle and out the exit. The witnesses to this event reacted in different ways.

One woman was frightened because she thought, "She's really going to get it when they get home." She imagined the details of a brutal beating and recalled times when she had been physically abused. A teenager was angry because he thought, "That poor guy. He probably just wanted a kiss and she humiliated him. What a bitch." A middle-aged man became depressed when he told himself, "Now he's lost her and he'll never get her back." He could see his ex-wife's face set in angry lines. A social worker felt a pleasurable excitement as she thought, "Serves him right. I wish some timid women I know had seen that."

Each response was based on a unique way of viewing the stimulus event and resulted in a different strong emotion.

7. **Automatic thoughts are persistent and self-perpetuating.** They are hard to turn off or change because they are reflexive and plausible. They weave unnoticed through the fabric of your internal dialog and seem to come and go with a will of their own. One automatic thought tends to act as a cue for another and another and another. You may have experienced this chaining effect as one depressing thought triggers a long chain of associated depressing thoughts.

8. **Automatic thoughts often differ from your public statements.** Most people talk to others very differently from the way they talk to themselves. To others they usually describe events in their lives as logical sequences of cause and effect. But to themselves they may describe the same events with self-deprecating venom or dire predictions.

One executive calmly explained aloud, "Since I got laid off, I've been a little depressed." This matter-of-fact statement differed sharply from the actual thoughts that unemployment triggered in him: "I'm a failure . . . I'll never work again . . . My family will starve . . . I can't make it in this world." He had an image of himself spiraling down into a bottomless black pit.

9. **Automatic thoughts repeat habitual themes.** Chronic anger, anxiety, or depression results from a focus on one particular group of automatic thoughts to the exclusion of all contrary thoughts. The theme of anxious people is danger. They are preoccupied with the anticipation of dangerous situations, forever scanning the horizon for future pain. Depressed individuals often focus on the past and obsess about the theme of loss. They also focus on their own failings and flaws. Chronically angry people repeat automatic thoughts about the hurtful and deliberate behavior of others.

Preoccupation with these habitual themes creates a kind of tunnel vision in which you think only one kind of thought and notice only one aspect of your environment. The result is one predominant and usually quite painful emotion. Beck has used the term *selective abstraction* to describe this tunnel vision. Selective abstraction means looking at one set of cues in your environment to the exclusion of all others.

10. **Automatic thoughts are learned.** Since childhood people have been telling you what to think. You have been conditioned by family, friends, and the media to interpret events a certain way. Over the years you have learned and practiced habitual patterns of automatic thoughts that are difficult to detect, let alone change. That's the bad news. The good news is that what has been learned can be unlearned and changed.

Listening to Your Automatic Thoughts

Hearing your automatic thoughts is the first step in gaining control of unpleasant emotions. Most of your internal dialog is harmless. The automatic thoughts that cause harm can be identified because they almost always precede a continuing painful feeling.

To identify the automatic thoughts that are causing a continued painful feeling, try to recall the thoughts you had just prior to the start of the emotion and those that go along with the sustained emotion. You can think of it as listening in on an intercom. The intercom is always on, even while you are conversing with others and going about your life. You are functioning in the world and you are also talking to yourself at the same time. Listen in on the intercom of your internal dialog, and hear what you are telling yourself. Your automatic thoughts are assigning private, idiosyncratic meanings to many external events and internal sensations. They are making judgments and interpretations of your experience.

Automatic thoughts are often lightning fast and very difficult to catch. They flash on as a brief mental image, or are telegraphed in a single word. Here are two methods for coping with the swiftness of your thoughts:

1. Reconstruct a problem situation, going over it again and again in your imagination until the painful emotion begins to emerge. What are you thinking as the emotion comes up? Regard your thoughts as a slow-motion film. Look at your internal dialog, frame by frame. Notice the millisecond it takes to say, "I can't stand it," or the half-second image of a terrifying event. Notice how you are internally describing and interpreting the actions of others: "She's bored. . . . He's putting me down."

2. Stretch out the shorthand statement into the original statement from which it was extracted. "Feeling sick" is really "I'm feeling sick and I know I'm going to get worse. . . . I can't stand it." "Crazy" means "I feel like I'm losing control, and that must mean I'm going crazy. . . . My friends will reject me."

   Hearing the shorthand isn't enough. It is necessary to listen to your entire interior argument in order to understand the distorted logic from which many painful emotions bloom.

Recording Your Thoughts

To appreciate the power of your automatic thoughts and the part they play in your emotional life, keep a Thought Journal. As soon as possible after you experience an unpleasant feeling, record it on the form that follows.

Situation *When? Where? Who?* *What happened?*	Feelings *One-word summaries* *Rate 0-100.*	Automatic Thoughts *What you were thinking just before and* *during the unpleasant feeling*

Thought Journal

Example

A bookkeeper made the following entries on a very busy Friday.

Thought Journal		
Situation *When? Where? Who?* *What happened?*	**Feelings** *One-word summaries* *Rate 0-100.*	**Automatic Thoughts** *What you were thinking just before* *and during the unpleasant feeling*
Stuck on freeway.	anger 80	Late. Boss angry. Last one in. Have to rush all day.
Given extra work.	anxiety 90	I'll be here all night. Can't stand it. Jenny will be mad if I'm late.
Given extra work.	resentment 75	They always dump on me. It's not fair.
Have to work through lunch.	anxiety 85	I'm hungry, I'm tired. I can't stand this.
Have to work through lunch.	anger 65	Why don't they get enough staff to help? This is ridiculous.
Working late, have to call wife.	anxiety 75	She's really going to blow up.
Driving home.	depression 80	This is my whole life. There's no way out of this.
Watching TV with kids.	depression 90	They never talk to me. They hardly know me. They don't care.
Wife goes to bed early.	depression 75	She's really mad. She's disgusted with me.

The form is self-explanatory, except for how to rate your feelings. The Thought Journal allows you to assess your distress level with a scale running from 0 (the feeling causes no distress) to 100 (the most distressing emotion you have ever felt).

Make several copies of this journal and carry one with you at all times. You will use the material you generate in your Thought Journal in the next two chapters.

Use your Thought Journal for one week, making an entry only when you feel a painful emotion. You may find that concentrating on your automatic thoughts makes the feelings worse for a while. Keep working on it—it's normal to feel worse before you start to feel better.

The process of uncovering automatic thoughts may also make you begin to distrust these thoughts and begin questioning and disputing them as they pop up. The next chapter, on changing patterns of limited thinking, will give you specific tools for disputing automatic thoughts.

At this point it is important for you to recognize that thoughts create and sustain emotions. To reduce the frequency of painful emotions, you will first need to listen to what you think, then ask how true it is. What you think will ultimately create what you feel.

Special Considerations—Thought Counting

Sometimes automatic thoughts come so quickly and in such abbreviated form that you can't identify them, even though you know you just had some. In that case, you can simply count your thoughts.

Each time you notice that you've had an automatic thought, make a mark on a three-by-five card you carry with you. You can also keep track of the number of your automatic thoughts on a golf wrist-counter or a knitting stitch-counter.

Counting your automatic thoughts helps get some distance from them and a feeling of control. Rather than assuming that your automatic thoughts are an accurate assessment of events, you are noting them and letting them go. Once you've counted a thought, you needn't dwell on it.

This process will eventually slow your thoughts and sharpen your attention so that the actual content of the thoughts starts to become clear. When that happens, you may want to continue counting, this time categorizing your thoughts and counting how many you have of various types: catastrophic thoughts, loss thoughts, insecure thoughts, and so on.

If you forget to count your thoughts, set your watch alarm or a timer to go off every twenty minutes. When the alarm or timer goes off, stop what you're doing and look inside yourself. Count any negative thoughts you notice.

Chapter 3

Changing Patterns of Limited Thinking

A man walks up to a drugstore counter and asks for a particular brand of dental floss. The clerk says it's out of stock. The man concludes that the clerk has the dental floss, but just wants to get rid of him because she doesn't like his looks. This logic seems obviously irrational and paranoid.

But consider the case of the woman whose husband comes home with a cloudy look on his face. She immediately concludes that he is angry because she was too tired to make love the previous night. She expects to be hurt by some sort of retaliation and responds quickly by becoming peevish and defensive. This logic makes perfect sense to her and she does not question her conclusion until she learns that her husband had a minor auto accident on the way home.

The progression of logic she used goes like this:

1. My husband looks upset.

2. My husband often gets upset when I disappoint him.

3. Therefore, he's upset with me for disappointing him.

The problem with this logic lies in her assumptions that her husband's moods must all relate to her and that she is the prime cause of his ups and downs. This pattern of limited thinking is called *personalization,* the tendency to relate all the objects and events around you to yourself. Personalization limits you and causes pain because you consistently misinterpret what you see and then act on that misinterpretation.

This chapter will examine eight limited-thinking patterns and give you practice in identifying them. The chapter continues by teaching you to analyze the automatic thoughts you recorded in chapter 2, noticing which of the limited-thinking patterns you habitually employ in difficult situations. You'll learn how to compose balanced, alternative self-statements that will become more believable than your painful automatic thoughts.

Symptom Effectiveness

Challenging automatic thoughts is a powerful way to counter perfectionism, curb procrastination, and relieve depression and anxiety.

The techniques in this chapter are based on the cognitive therapy of Aaron Beck (1976), who pioneered this method of analyzing automatic thoughts and composing rational comebacks to refute and replace distorted thinking. This approach works well for abstract thinkers—people who can analyze their automatic thoughts to find thematic patterns of limited thinking.

Time for Mastery

You should begin to get results in one to four weeks of analyzing your automatic thoughts.

If you try all of the exercises in this chapter and still have difficulty picking out your limited-thinking patterns, don't give up hope. Go on to the next chapter, which will help you accomplish the same result by compiling the evidence for and against the thoughts that trigger your painful emotions.

Instructions

Eight Patterns of Limited Thinking

1. **Filtering** This pattern is characterized by a sort of tunnel vision—looking at only one element of a situation to the exclusion of everything else. A single detail is picked out and the whole event or situation is colored by this detail. For example, a computer draftsman who was uncomfortable with criticism was praised for the quality of his recent detail drawings and asked if he could get the next job out a little more quickly. He went home depressed, having decided that his employer thought he was dawdling. He filtered out the praise and focused only on the criticism.

   Each person looks through his or her own particular tunnel. Depressed people are hypersensitive to loss and blind to gain. For anxious people, the slightest possibility of danger sticks out like a barb in a scene that might otherwise be safe and secure. People who experience chronic anger look through a tunnel that highlights evidence of injustice and screens out fairness and equity.

   Memory can also be very selective. You may remember only certain kinds of events from your entire history and stock of experience. When you filter your memories, you often pass over positive experiences and dwell only on the memories that characteristically leave you angry, anxious, or depressed.

   The filtering pattern "awfulizes" your thoughts by pulling negative events out of context and magnifying them, while ignoring all your good experiences. Your fears, losses, and irritations become exaggerated in importance because they fill your awareness to the exclusion of everything else. Key words for the filtering pattern are *terrible, awful, disgusting, scary, horrendous,* and so on. A key phrase is "I can't stand it."

2. **Polarized Thinking** This is black-and-white thinking, with no shades of gray allowed. You insist on "either/or" choices, perceiving everything at the extremes with very little room for a middle ground. People and things are good or bad, wonderful or horrible, delightful or intolerable. Since your interpretations are extreme, your emotional reactions are extreme, fluctuating from despair to elation to rage to ecstasy to terror.

   The greatest danger in polarized thinking is its impact on how you judge yourself. You could believe that if you aren't perfect or brilliant, then you must be a failure or an imbecile. There's no room for mistakes or mediocrity. For example, a charter bus driver told himself he was a real loser when he took the wrong freeway exit and had to drive two miles out of his way. One mistake meant that he was incompetent and worthless. A single mother with three children was determined to be strong and "in charge." The moment she felt tired or nervous, she began thinking of herself as weak and falling apart, and she often criticized herself in conversations with friends.

3. **Overgeneralization** In this pattern, you make a broad, general conclusion based on a single incident or piece of evidence. One dropped stitch leads you to conclude: "I'll never learn how to knit." You interpret a rejection on the dance floor as: "Nobody would ever want to dance with me."

   This pattern can lead to an increasingly restricted life. If you got sick on a train once, you decide never to take a train again. If you got dizzy on a sixth floor balcony, you never go out there again. If you felt anxious the last time your husband took a business trip, you'll be a wreck every time he leaves town. One bad experience means that whenever you're in a similar situation you will repeat the bad experience.

   Overgeneralizations are often couched in the form of absolute statements, as if there were some immutable law that governs and limits your chances for happiness. Some of the cue words that indicate you may be overgeneralizing are *all, every, none, never, always, everybody,* and *nobody.* For example, you are overgeneralizing when you absolutely conclude: "*Nobody* loves me," "I'll *never* be able to trust anyone again," "I will *always* be sad," "I've *always* had lousy jobs," "*No one* would stay friends with me if they really knew me."

   Another hallmark of overgeneralization is the global label for persons, places, and things you don't like: Somebody who refused to give you a ride home is labeled a "total jerk." A quiet guy on a date is a "dull clam." Democrats are "knee-jerk liberals." New York City is "hell on earth." Television is an "evil, corrupting influence." You're "stupid" and "totally wasting your life."

   Each of these labels may contain a grain of truth, but it generalizes that grain into a global judgment. The overgeneralized label ignores all contrary evidence, making your view of the world stereotyped and one-dimensional.

4. **Mind Reading** When you mind read, you make snap judgments about others. You assume you know how others are feeling and what motivates them: "He's just acting

that way because he's jealous," "She's only interested in your money," "He's afraid to show he cares."

If your brother visits a new woman acquaintance three times in one week, you might conclude that he is (a) in love, (b) angry at his old girlfriend and hoping she'll find out, (c) depressed and on the rebound, or (d) afraid of being alone again. Without asking, you have no way of knowing which is true. Mind reading makes one conclusion *seem* so obviously correct that you assume it's true, act on it in some inappropriate way, and get into trouble.

As a mind reader, you also make assumptions about how people are reacting to you. You might assume what your boyfriend is thinking and say to yourself, "This close he sees how unattractive I am." If he is mind reading too, he may be saying to himself, "She thinks I'm really immature." You may have a casual encounter with your supervisor at work and come away thinking, "They're getting ready to fire me." These assumptions are born of intuition, hunches, vague misgivings, or a couple of past experiences. They are untested and unprovable, but you believe them nonetheless.

Mind reading depends on a process called projection. You imagine that people feel the same way you do and react to things the same way you do. Therefore you don't watch or listen closely enough to notice that they are actually different. If you get angry when someone is late, you imagine everyone feels that way. If you feel excruciatingly sensitive to rejection, you expect that most people are the same. If you are very judgmental about particular habits and traits, you assume others share your beliefs.

5. **Catastrophizing** If you "catastrophize," a small leak in the sailboat means it will surely sink. A contractor whose estimate gets underbid concludes he'll never get another job. A headache suggests that brain cancer is looming. Catastrophic thoughts often start with the words *what if*. You read a newspaper article describing a tragedy or hear gossip about some disaster befalling an acquaintance, and you start wondering, "What if it happens to me? What if I break my leg skiing? What if they hijack my plane? What if I get sick and have to go on disability? What if my son starts taking drugs?" The list is endless. There are no limits to a really fertile catastrophic imagination.

6. **Magnifying** When you magnify, you emphasize things out of proportion to their actual importance. Small mistakes become tragic failures. Minor suggestions become scathing criticism. A slight backache becomes a ruptured disk. Minor setbacks become cause for despair. Slight obstacles become overwhelming barriers.

Words like *huge, impossible,* and *overwhelming* are magnifying terms. This pattern creates a tone of doom and hysterical pessimism.

The flip side of magnifying is minimizing. When you magnify, you view everything negative and difficult in your life through a telescope that enlarges your problems. But when you view your assets, such as your ability to cope and find solutions, you look through the wrong end of the telescope so that everything positive is minimized.

7. **Personalization** There are two kinds of personalization. The first kind involves directly comparing yourself with other people: "He plays piano so much better than

I," "I'm not smart enough to go with this crowd," "She knows herself a lot better than I do," "He feels things so deeply while I'm dead inside," "I'm the slowest person in the office." Sometimes the comparison is actually favorable to you: "He's dumb (and I'm smart)," "I'm better looking than she." The opportunities for comparison never end. And, even when the comparison is favorable, the underlying assumption is that your worth is questionable. Consequently you must continue to test your value, constantly measuring yourself against others. If you come out better, you have a moment's relief. If you come up short, you feel diminished.

This chapter began with an example of the other kind of personalization—the tendency to relate everything around you to yourself. A depressed mother blames herself when she sees any sadness in her children. A businessman thinks that every time his partner complains of being tired, he means he's tired of him. A man whose wife complains of rising prices hears the complaints as attacks on his ability as a breadwinner.

8. **Shoulds**   In this pattern, you operate from a list of inflexible rules about how you and other people should act. The rules are right and indisputable. Any deviation from your particular values or standards is bad. As a result, you are often judging others and finding fault. People irritate you. They don't act correctly and they don't think correctly. They have unacceptable traits, habits, and opinions that make them hard to tolerate. They should know the rules, and they should follow them.

One woman felt that her husband should want to take her on Sunday drives. She decided that a man who loves his wife ought to take her to the country and then out to eat in a nice place. The fact that he didn't want to meant that he "only thought about himself." Cue words indicating the presence of this pattern are *should, ought,* or *must.* In fact, Albert Ellis (Ellis and Harper 1961) has dubbed this thinking pattern "musterbation."

Your shoulds are just as hard on you as they are on other people. You feel compelled to be or act a certain way, but you never ask objectively if it really makes sense. Psychiatrist Karen Horney (1939) called this the "tyranny of shoulds."

Here is a list of some of the most common and unreasonable shoulds:

- I should be the epitome of generosity, consideration, dignity, courage, and unselfishness.

- I should be the perfect lover, friend, parent, teacher, student, or spouse.

- I should be able to endure any hardship with equanimity.

- I should be able to find a quick solution to every problem.

- I should never feel hurt; I should always be happy and serene.

- I should know, understand, and foresee everything.

- I should always be spontaneous, but also always control my feelings.

- I should never feel certain emotions, such as anger or jealousy.

- I should love my children equally.

- I should never make mistakes.

- My emotions should be constant. Once I feel love, I should always feel love.

- I should be totally self-reliant.

- I should assert myself but I should never hurt anybody else.

- I should never be tired or get sick.

- I should always be at peak efficiency.

Summary

Eight Limited-Thinking Patterns

1. **Filtering:** You focus on the negative details while ignoring all the positive aspects of a situation.

2. **Polarized Thinking:** Things are black or white, good or bad. You have to be perfect or you're a failure. There's no middle ground, no room for mistakes.

3. **Overgeneralization:** You reach a general conclusion based on a single incident or piece of evidence. You exaggerate the frequency of problems and use negative global labels.

4. **Mind Reading:** Without their saying so, you know what people are feeling and why they act the way they do. In particular, you have certain knowledge of how people think and feel about you.

5. **Catastrophizing:** You expect, even visualize disaster. You notice or hear about a problem and start asking, "What if?" What if tragedy strikes? What if it happens to you?

6. **Magnifying:** You exaggerate the degree or intensity of a problem. You turn up the volume on anything bad, making it loud, large, and overwhelming.

7. **Personalization:** You assume that everything people do or say is some kind of reaction to you. You also compare yourself to others, trying to determine who is smarter, more competent, better looking, and so on.

8. **Shoulds:** You have a list of ironclad rules about how you and other people should act. People who break the rules anger you, and you feel guilty when you violate the rules.

Exercises

The following exercises are designed to help you notice and identify limited-thinking patterns. Work through the exercises one after another. Refer back to the above summary and carefully analyze how each statement or situation is based on one or more limited-thinking patterns.

Matching Exercise

Draw a line connecting the sentence in the first column and the pattern it exemplifies in the second column.

Statement	Pattern
1. Ever since Lisa, I've never trusted a redhead.	Filtering
2. Quite a few people here seem smarter than me.	Polarized Thinking
3. You're either for me or against me.	Overgeneralization
4. I could have enjoyed the picnic, but the chicken was burnt.	Mind Reading
5. He's always smiling, but I know he doesn't like me.	Catastrophizing
6. I'm afraid the relationship's over because he hasn't called for two days.	Magnifying
7. You should never ask people personal questions.	Personalization
8. These tax forms are impossible—I'll never get finished.	Shoulds

Multiple Choice

In this exercise, circle the limited-thinking pattern(s) present in each example. There may be more than one right answer.

1. The washing machine breaks down. A mother with twins in diapers says to herself, "This always happens. I can't stand it. The whole day's ruined."

   a. Overgeneralization   c. Shoulds   e. Filtering
   b. Polarized Thinking   d. Mind Reading

2. "He looked up from across the table and said, 'That's interesting.' I knew he was dying for breakfast to be over so he could get away from me."

    a. Magnifying   c. Shoulds   e. Personalization
    b. Polarized Thinking   d. Mind Reading

3. A man was trying to get his girlfriend to be warmer and more supportive. He got irritated every night when she didn't ask him how his day was or failed to give him the attention he expected.

    a. Shoulds   c. Overgeneralization   e. Magnifying
    b. Personalization   d. Catastrophizing

4. A driver feels nervous on long trips, afraid of having car trouble or getting sick and being stranded far from home. Faced with having to drive 500 miles to Chicago and back, he tells himself, "It's too far. My car has over 60,000 miles on it—it'll never make it."

    a. Overgeneralization   c. Filtering   e. Mind Reading
    b. Catastrophizing   d. Magnifying

5. Getting ready for the prom, a high school student thinks, "I've got the worst hips in my homeroom, and the second-worst hair. . . . If this French twist comes undone, I'll just die. I'll never get it back together and the evening will be ruined. . . . I hope Ron gets his Dad's car. If only he does, everything will be perfect."

    a. Personalization   c. Filtering   e. Catastrophizing
    b. Polarized Thinking   d. Mind Reading

Answer Key
1. a, e
2. d
3. a
4. b, d
5. a, b, e

Circle the Pattern and Quote the Phrase

The following exercises require a little more work on your part. Read the statement and circle the applicable patterns in the list following the statement. Next to each pattern, write the phrase that contains it.

1. "Jim's so easily upset, you just can't talk to him. He blows up at everything. He just doesn't have my patience. What if he blows up at work? He'll lose his job and we'll be homeless in about two weeks."

Pattern	Phrase Containing the Pattern
Filtering	
Polarized Thinking	
Overgeneralization	
Mind Reading	
Catastrophizing	

Magnifying   _____

Personalization   _____

Shoulds   _____

2. "One time she came up to me and said, 'This nursing station looks like a cyclone hit it. Better clean up the mess before the shift is over.' Well, I said, 'This was a mess when I got here. It's not my fault. The night shift shouldn't be allowed to punch out unless all the charts are filed.' She knew it wasn't my mess. She wants to fire me and she's just looking for an excuse."

Pattern	Phrase Containing the Pattern
Filtering	_____
Polarized Thinking	_____
Overgeneralization	_____
Mind Reading	_____
Catastrophizing	_____
Magnifying	_____
Personalization	_____
Shoulds	_____

3. "A lot of the time I feel nervous when I'm out with Ed. I keep thinking how smart he is, how sophisticated, and that I'm just a hayseed by comparison. He cocks his head and he looks at me and I know he's thinking how dumb I am. He's really sweet and we have a good time talking. But when he cocks his head, I feel like I'll be dumped. One time he kind of wrinkled up his face when I said something a little critical about his jacket. Now I'm afraid to say anything for fear of hurting him.

"Usually I think Ed is completely wonderful. But last week he made me take the bus to his house instead of picking me up. I suddenly felt he didn't give a damn, that he was just another jerk. That was a passing thing, and now he's wonderful again. My only problem is this business of being nervous when he cocks his head."

Pattern	Phrase Containing the Pattern
Filtering	_____
Polarized Thinking	_____
Overgeneralization	_____
Mind Reading	_____
Catastrophizing	_____
Magnifying	_____

Personalization _____

Shoulds _____

4. "There are three ways to make a magazine go: work, work, and more work. If you have to work sixteen hours a day to get it out, then that's what you have to do. These kids today want to go home at five o'clock. If they're too lazy to work, I say get rid of them. Profits get slimmer every year because of total laziness. It's the way they're raised—the way the whole damn country is falling apart. In five years it'll drive me under. There are just two kinds of editors: the ones who get the job done and the nine-to-fivers. It's the nine-to-fivers who will put me under. I can't fight the whole world."

Pattern	**Phrase Containing the Pattern**
Filtering	_____
Polarized Thinking	_____
Overgeneralization	_____
Mind Reading	_____
Catastrophizing	_____
Magnifying	_____
Personalization	_____
Shoulds	_____

Answer Key

1. Overgeneralization: "He blows up at everything."
   Catastrophizing: "He'll lose his job and we'll be homeless."
2. Mind Reading: "She knew . . . She wants . . . she's just looking . . ."
   Shoulds: "The night shift shouldn't . . ."
3. Mind Reading: "I know he's thinking how dumb I am."
   Personalization: "I feel nervous when I'm out with Ed." (assuming all Ed's behavior relates to her)
   Polarized Thinking: "he was just another jerk . . . now he's wonderful again."
4. Shoulds: "that's what you have to do."
   Filtering: "Profits get slimmer . . . total laziness" (sees laziness only)
   Polarized Thinking: "There are just two kinds of editors."
   Magnifying: "I can't fight the whole world."

Thought Journal

Now that you have learned to identify limited-thinking patterns, it's time to apply your new skill to the Thought Journal you started in the previous chapter. Three new columns have been added to the blank form that follows. You now have space to fill in your limited-thinking patterns, balanced or alternative thoughts, and a re-rating of your feelings.

Thought Journal

Situation *When? Where? Who? What happened?*	Feelings *One-word summaries. Rate 0-100.*	Automatic Thoughts *What you were thinking just before and during the unpleasant feeling.*	Limited-Thinking Pattern	Balancing or Alternative Thoughts *Circle possible action plans.*	Re-rate Feelings *0-100.*

Start by analyzing your most distressing automatic thoughts to see which limited-thinking pattern each one fits best. You may find evidence of more than one limited-thinking pattern, so write down all that apply.

In the next column, rewrite your automatic thoughts in a more balanced way, or compose an alternative thought that refutes the automatic thought. You can refer to the section that follows for help in countering the limited-thinking patterns.

In the last column, re-rate your bad feeling now that you have worked on your automatic thoughts. The feeling should be less intense after this work.

Composing Balancing or Alternative Thoughts

Listed below are alternative responses to the eight limited thinking patterns. It isn't necessary to read through the list from beginning to end. Use it as a reference when you are having problems with a particular pattern.

1. Filtering

Pattern Summary	Key Balancing Statement
• Focusing on the negative	• Shift focus
• Filtering out the positive	

You have been stuck in a mental groove, focusing on things from your environment that typically frighten, sadden, or anger you. In order to conquer filtering you will have to deliberately shift focus. You can shift focus in two ways: First, place your attention on coping strategies for dealing with the problem rather than obsessing about the problem itself. Second, focus on the opposite of your primary mental theme. For example, if you tend to focus on the theme of loss, instead focus on what you still have that is of value. If your theme is danger, focus instead on things in your environment that represent comfort and safety. If your theme is injustice or stupidity or incompetence, shift focus to what people do that *does* meet with your approval.

2. Polarized thinking

Pattern Summary	Key Balancing Statements
• Seeing everything as awful or great, with no middle ground	• No black-or-white judgments
	• Think in percentages

The key to overcoming polarized thinking is to stop making black-or-white judgments. People are not either happy or sad, loving or rejecting, brave or cowardly, smart or stupid. They fall somewhere along a continuum. They are a little bit of each. Human beings are just too complex to be reduced to either/or judgments.

If you have to make these kinds of ratings, think in terms of percentages: "About 30 percent of me is scared to death, and 70 percent is holding on and coping," "About 60 percent of the time he seems terribly preoccupied with himself, but there's the 40 percent when he can be really generous," "Five percent of the time I'm an ignoramus; the rest of the time I do all right."

3. Overgeneralization

Pattern Summary	Key Balancing Statements
• Making sweeping statements based on scanty evidence	• Quantify • What's the evidence? • There are no absolutes • No negative labels

Overgeneralization is exaggeration—the tendency to take a button and sew a vest on it. Fight it by *quantifying* instead of using words like *huge, awful, massive, minuscule,* and so on. For example, if you catch yourself thinking, "We're buried under massive debt," rephrase with a quantity: "We owe $27,000."

Another way to avoid overgeneralization is to examine how much evidence you really have for your conclusion. If the conclusion is based on one or two cases, a single mistake, or one small symptom, then throw it out until you have more convincing proof. This is such a powerful technique that most of the next chapter is devoted to amassing evidence for and against your hot thoughts.

Stop thinking in absolutes by avoiding words such as *every, all, always, none, never, everybody,* and *nobody.* Statements that include these words ignore the exceptions and shades of gray. Replace absolutes with words such as *may, sometimes,* and *often.* Be particularly sensitive to absolute predictions about the future such as "No one will ever love me." They are extremely dangerous because they can become self-fulfilling prophecies.

Pay close attention to the words you use to describe yourself and others. Replace frequently used negative labels with more neutral terms. For example, if you call your habitual caution *cowardice,* replace it with *care.* Think of your excitable mother as *vivacious* instead of *ditzy.* Instead of blaming yourself for being *lazy,* call yourself *laid-back.*

4. Mind Reading

Pattern Summary	Key Balancing Statements
• Assuming you know what others are thinking and feeling	• Check it out • Evidence for conclusions? • Alternative interpretations?

In the long run, you are probably better off making no inferences about people at all. Either believe what they tell you or hold no belief at all until some conclusive evidence comes your way. Treat all of your notions about people as hypotheses to be tested and checked out by asking them.

Sometimes you can't check out your interpretations. For instance, you may not be ready to ask your daughter if her withdrawal from family life means she's pregnant or taking drugs. But you can allay your anxiety by generating alternative interpretations of her behavior. Perhaps she's in love. Or premenstrual. Or studying hard. Or depressed about something. Or deeply engrossed in a project. Or worrying about her future. By generating a string of possibilities, you may find a more neutral interpretation that's as likely to be true as your direst suspicions. This process also underlines the fact that you really can't know accurately what others are thinking and feeling unless they tell you.

5. Catastrophizing

Pattern Summary

- Assuming the worst will happen

Key Balancing Statement

- What are the odds?

Catastrophizing is the royal road to anxiety. As soon as you catch yourself catastrophizing, ask yourself, "What are the odds?" Make an honest assessment of the situation in terms of odds or percent of probability. Are the chances of disaster one in 100,000 (.001 percent)? One in a thousand (.1 percent)? One in twenty (5 percent)? Looking at the odds helps you realistically evaluate whatever is frightening you.

6. Magnifying

Pattern Summary

- Enlarging difficulties
- Minimizing the positive

Key Balancing Statements

- Get things in proportion
- No need to magnify

To combat magnifying, stop using words like *terrible, awful, disgusting, horrendous,* etc. In particular, banish phrases like: "I can't stand it," "It's impossible," "It's unbearable." You can stand it, because history shows that human beings can survive almost any psychological blow and can endure incredible physical pain. You can get used to and cope with almost anything. Try saying to yourself phrases such as "I can cope" and "I can survive this."

7. Personalization

Pattern Summary

- Assuming the reactions of others always relate to you
- Comparing yourself to others

Key Balancing Statements

- Check it out
- We all have strong and weak points
- Comparison is meaningless

When you catch yourself comparing yourself to others, remind yourself that everyone has strong and weak points. By matching your weak points to others with corresponding strong points, you are just looking for ways to demoralize yourself.

The fact is, human beings are too complex for casual comparisons to have any meaning. It would take you months to catalog and compare all the thousands of traits and abilities of two people.

If you assume that the reactions of others are often about you, force yourself to check it out. Maybe the reason the boss is frowning *isn't* that you're late. Make no conclusion unless you are satisfied that you have reasonable evidence and proof.

8. Shoulds

Pattern Summary

- Holding arbitrary rules for behavior of self and others

Key Balancing Statements

- Flexible rules
- Values are personal

Reexamine and question any personal rules or expectations that include the words *should, ought,* or *must.* Flexible rules and expectations don't use these words because there are always exceptions and special circumstances. Think of at least three exceptions to your rule, and then imagine all the exceptions there must be that you can't think of.

You may get irritated when people don't act according to your values. But your personal values are just that—personal. They may work for you, but, as missionaries have discovered all over the world, they don't always work for others. People aren't all the same.

The key is to focus on each person's uniqueness—his or her particular needs, limitations, fears, and pleasures. Because it is impossible to know all of these complex interrelations, even with intimates, you can't be certain whether your values apply to another. You are entitled to an opinion, but allow for the possibility of being wrong. Also, allow for other people to find different things important.

Example

On the next page is a portion of the Thought Journal from the previous chapter, showing how the bookkeeper completed it.

The bookkeeper felt better after identifying his limited-thinking patterns and composing his alternative thoughts. He realized that he had magnified the workload to the point that he had collapsed emotionally and was working inefficiently at low-priority tasks.

He went on to examine the depression he felt at home and found that he had been filtering and mind reading.

Action Plans

Your balancing or alternative thoughts may suggest actions you can take, such as checking out assumptions, gathering information, making an assertive request, clearing up misunderstandings, making plans, changing your schedule, resolving unfinished business, or making commitments. Circle those items and plan when you will put them into action.

In the example of the bookkeeper, he circled "I can prioritize the work" as an action plan to reduce anxiety on the job. He also circled "I should check it out" as an action plan to relieve the depression he felt when he assumed his wife was mad at him. It took him several days to work up the courage to ask his wife how she felt. It turned out she *was* angry, but she was mostly worried about him turning into a workaholic and getting an ulcer or having a heart attack.

It may be difficult, time consuming, or embarrassing to follow your action plan, You may have to break your plan down into a series of easier steps and schedule each step. But it's worth doing. Behavior that is inspired by your balancing or alternative thoughts will greatly reduce the frequency and power of your negative automatic thoughts.

For more on action plans, see the next chapter.

Thought Journal

Situation *When? Where? Who? What happened?*	Feelings *One-word summaries. Rate 0-100.*	Automatic Thoughts *What you were thinking just before and during the unpleasant feeling.*	Limited-Thinking Pattern	Balancing or Alternative Thoughts *Circle possible action plans.*	Re-rate Feelings 0-100.
Given extra work.	Anxiety, **90.**	I'll be here all night. Can't stand it. Jenny will be mad if I'm late.	Magnifying	Of course I can stand it. I've been standing it for twelve years. Jenny knows what's going on. She expects long hours this time of the year.	50
	Resentment, **75.**	They always dump on me. It's not fair.		I can prioritize the work and concentrate on one thing at a time.	40
Have to work through lunch.	Anxiety, **85.**	I'm hungry, I'm tired. I can't stand this.	Catastrophizing	It's always this way at tax time. It will be better in May.	30
Watching TV with kids.	Depression, **75.**	They never talk to me. They hardly know me. They don't care.	Filtering Overgeneralizing	They talk to me about baseball and trading cards and school stuff. It's the TV—they're engrossed in it and I'm not, so I sit there obsessing.	25
Wife goes to bed early.	Depression, **85.**	She's really mad. She's disgusted with me.	Mind reading	I have no evidence that she's mad or disgusted. I should check it out.	30

Continue for a week with your Thought Journal, identifying your automatic thoughts and analyzing them for limited-thinking patterns. After a week you should be adept at recognizing your habitual patterns of limited thinking. You will begin to notice your automatic thoughts popping up in stressful situations. Eventually you will recognize limited-thinking patterns in real life, and correct them with balancing or alternative thoughts as you go.

If you still have trouble spotting the limited-thinking patterns after a week of practice, go on to the next chapter and try the "evidence for/evidence against" approach. It may be a better alternative for you.

Chapter 4

Changing Hot Thoughts

If the techniques in the previous chapter, "Changing Patterns of Limited Thinking," worked well for you, this chapter may not even be necessary. This chapter presents an alternative approach based on evidence gathering and analysis that provides a powerful weapon against automatic thoughts.

This chapter is to be used in conjunction with chapter 2, "Uncovering Automatic Thoughts." It will give you skills to do three things: (1) identify the evidence that supports your hot (or trigger) thoughts, (2) uncover evidence that contradicts your hot thoughts, and (3) synthesize what you have learned into a healthier, more realistic perspective.

Gathering evidence on both sides of the question is crucial to reaching a clearer, more objective understanding of your experience. Albert Ellis (Ellis and Harper 1961) was the first to develop a method (rational-emotive therapy) to evaluate evidence for and against key beliefs. But by assuming that hot thoughts are always irrational, and focusing mostly on the evidence against them, his approach may not always feel objective. It also may alienate people who have solid evidence to support certain hot thoughts.

Christine Padesky (Greenberger and Padesky 1995), building on Beck (1976) and Ellis's work, developed the strategies for gathering and analyzing evidence used in this chapter. Padesky doesn't assume that hot thoughts are totally irrational. She focuses instead on looking at all the evidence and working toward a balanced position.

Thought and Evidence Journal

Situation When? Where? Who? What happened?	Feelings One-word summaries. Rate 0-100.	Automatic Thoughts What you were thinking just before and during the unpleasant feeling.	Evidence For	Evidence Against	Balanced or Alternative Thoughts Circle possible action plans.	Re-rate Feelings 0-100.

Based on the "Thought Record" developed by Christine Padesky and Dennis Greenberger, 1995.

Symptom Effectiveness

Thought Journals have been used effectively to treat depression, anxiety, and related problems. Numerous studies over the past twenty years demonstrate the usefulness of this technique.

Time for Mastery

Using the Thought and Evidence Journal described in this chapter, you can make significant changes in your moods in as little as one week. However, it will take from two to twelve weeks to consolidate some of these changes, allowing your new, more balanced thoughts to gain strength through repetition.

Instructions

In this chapter you'll be working on an extension of the Thought Journal you began in chapter 2. Photocopy the blank Thought and Evidence Journal on the opposite page so you can have a supply of pages to use whenever you need one.

Step 1: Select a Hot Thought.

Return to the Thought Journal that you began keeping in chapter 2 to select a hot thought from your record of automatic thoughts. Choose a thought that impacted your mood either because of its power or frequency. Rate each thought on a scale (0-100) that measures how strongly it contributed to your painful feelings. Circle the thought with the highest score—that's the hot one you'll work on now.

On the next page is a section in Len's Thought Journal that contains one of his most upsetting hot thoughts. Len is a rep for a large printing company. His customers are mostly publishers and advertising companies.

When Len rated all of his automatic thoughts on a scale measuring their impact on his mood, "I'm a first-class failure" turned out to be his hottest thought by far. By itself, the thought could hit Len hard enough to stir up strong feelings of inadequacy and depression.

Step 2: Identify Evidence that Supports Your Hot Thought.

Now is your chance to write down the experiences and the facts that would appear to support your hot thought. This is not the place to put your feelings, impressions, assumptions about the reactions of others, or unsupported beliefs. In the column marked "Evidence For," stay with the objective facts. Confine yourself to exactly what was said, what was done, how many times, and so on.

While it's important to stick with the facts, it's also important to acknowledge *all* the past and present evidence that supports and verifies your hot thought.

Len's Thought Journal		
Situation	**Feelings**	**Automatic Thoughts**
When? Where? Who? What happened?	*One-word summaries. Rate 0-100.*	*What you were thinking just before and during the unpleasant feeling.*
Sales figures for December were posted. I'm second from the bottom in sales out of nine reps.	Depression, **85**	I'm a stinko salesman. **70** They all think something's wrong with me. **40** Print buyers probably don't like me. **40** I'm a first-class failure. **95** Commissions will be way down—it's going to hurt. **65** I'm not working hard enough. **20**

Len identified five pieces of evidence that seemed to support the hot thought "I'm a first class failure." Here is what he wrote in his "Evidence For" column:

1. Only $24,000 in sales for December.

2. Couldn't close the Silex Corp. when they seemed almost ready to give me the contract.

3. Boss asked if I had any problems.

4. This is the third time in twelve months I've been below $30,000 in sales.

5. Had a disagreement with Randolph and he pulled his job.

Notice that Len doesn't talk about conjectures, assumptions, or a "feeling" that he's doing a bad job. He confines himself to the facts and an objective description of events.

Step 3: Uncover Evidence against Your Hot Thought.

You'll probably find this to be the hardest part of the technique. It's easy to think of things that support your hot thought, but you'll often draw a blank when it's time to explore evidence against it. You'll most likely need some help.

To assist you in the search for evidence against your hot thought, there are ten key questions you need to ask. Go through all ten questions for every hot thought you are analyzing—each of them will help you explore new ways of thinking.

Ten Key Questions

1. Is there an alternative interpretation of the situation, other than your hot thought?

2. Is the hot thought really accurate, or is it an overgeneralization? Is it true that ___(the situation)___ means ___(your hot thought)___? In Len's case, for example, do low sales figures in December mean that he's a failure?

3. Are there exceptions to the generalizations made by your hot thought?

4. Are there balancing realities that might soften negative aspects of the situation? In Len's case, for example, are there other things besides sales that he can feel good about in his job?

5. What are the *likely* consequences and outcomes of the situation? This question helps you differentiate what you fear might happen from what you can reasonably expect will happen.

6. Are there experiences from your past that would lead you to a conclusion other than your hot thought?

7. Are there objective facts that would contradict items in the "Evidence For" column? Is it really true, for example, that Len lost the Silex contract because he was a failure as a salesman? Are there facts at odds with this interpretation?

8. What are the real odds that what you fear happening in the situation will actually occur? Think like a bookmaker. Are the odds 1 in 2, 1 in 50, 1 in 1,000, 1 in 500,000? Think of all the people right now in this same situation, how many of them end up facing the catastrophic outcome you fear?

9. Do you have the social or problem-solving skills to handle the situation differently?

10. Could you create a plan to change the situation? Is there someone you know who might deal with this differently? What would that person do?

Write on a separate piece of paper your answers to all of the questions relevant to your hot thought. It may take some thinking: to find exceptions to the generalization created by your hot thought; to think objectively about the odds of something catastrophic happening; or to recall balancing realities that give you confidence and hope in the face of problems. The work you put into this step in the evidence-gathering process will directly impact your ability to challenge hot thoughts.

Len spent more than half an hour trying to answer the ten questions. Here's what they helped him develop in the "Evidence Against" column:

1. December's normally a low month. That might explain most of my drop-off in sales. (Question #1)

2. To be accurate: For the year I ranked fourth of the nine reps. That's not great, but it's not being a failure. (Question #2)

3. Some months have been good. I did $68,000 in August, and $64,000 in March. (Question #3)

4. I have many good relationships with customers; in some cases I have really helped them with major decisions. Most know they can trust me as an advisor. (Question #4)

5. My sales are good enough at number four in the company that they wouldn't fire me. (Question #5)

6. Five years ago I was ranked number two, and I'm always in the top half of the pack. There have been a lot of individual months over the years when I got the best-salesman award. (Question #6)

7. I was just outbid on Silex—it wasn't my fault. (Question #7)

8. Randolph said he wanted recycled paper and pulled the job when he didn't like the price. Not my fault. (Question #7)

9. I need to think about my relationship with each customer and less about the dollar worth of each contract. I know that works better for me. (Question #10)

Len found it particularly useful to look for objective facts that either counterbalanced or contradicted each item in the "Evidence For" column. He kept asking himself, "What in my experience balances out this piece of evidence?" and "What objective facts contradict this piece of evidence?" Len was surprised how much he discovered in the "Evidence Against" column, and he realized there were a lot of things he shut out of his awareness when he was feeling depressed.

Step 4: Write Your Balanced or Alternative Thoughts.

Now it's time to synthesize everything you've learned in both the "Evidence For" and "Evidence Against" columns. Read over both columns slowly and carefully. Don't try to deny or ignore evidence on either side. Now write new, balanced thoughts that incorporate what you've learned as you gathered the evidence. In your balanced thoughts it's OK to acknowledge important items in the "Evidence For" column, but it's equally important to summarize the main things you learned in the "Evidence Against" column.

Here's what Len wrote in the "Balanced or Alternative Thoughts" column in his Thought and Evidence Journal:

> *My sales are down, and I've lost two deals, but I have a solid sales record over the years, and I've had a lot of good months. I just need to focus on my customer relationships, and not the money.*

Notice that Len didn't ignore or deny that sales were down, but he was able to use items from his "Evidence Against" column to develop a clear, balanced statement that acknowledged his track record as a competent salesman.

Synthesizing statements don't have to be long. But they do need to summarize the main points on both sides of the question. Don't be afraid to rewrite your "Balanced or Alternative Thoughts" several times until the statement feels strong and convincing.

When you're satisfied with the accuracy of what you've written, rate your belief in this new balanced thought as a percentage ranging from 0 to 100. Len, for example, rated his belief in his new balanced thought as 85 percent. If you don't believe your new thought more than 60 percent, you should revise it further—perhaps detailing more items from the "Evidence Against" column. It's also possible that the evidence you've gathered isn't yet convincing enough, and you need to work further on developing ideas for your "Evidence Against" column.

Step 5: Re-rate Your Mood.

It's time to find out where all this work has gotten you. As part of your Thought Journal from chapter 2, you identified a painful feeling and rated its intensity on a 0-to-100 scale. Now you should rate the intensity of that same feeling again to see if anything has changed now that you've gathered evidence and developed a new balanced thought.

Len found that his depression had changed substantially following his efforts to gather evidence. His depression rating was now 30 on the 100-point scale. Most of the remaining depression seemed based on a realistic concern about reduced income from his low December sales.

Seeing your mood change can be a strong reinforcement for doing the Evidence work in your Thought and Evidence Journal. In the space of just a few minutes you can successfully confront powerful hot thoughts and make positive changes in how you feel.

Step 6: Record and Save Alternative Thoughts.

We encourage you to record what you've learned each time you complete the process of examining evidence and developing balanced or alternative thoughts. It's helpful to put this information on three-by-five file cards that you can keep with you and read whenever you wish. On one side of the file card write a description of the problem situation and your hot thought. On the opposite side of the card write your alternative or balanced thought. Over time, you will create a number of these cards. They can be a resource to remind you of your new, healthier thoughts when upsetting circumstances might induce you to forget them.

Step 7: Practice Your Balanced Thoughts.

You can use your completed file cards in a simple exercise that will give you practice with your balanced thoughts. Start by reading the side of the card that describes the trigger situation and your hot thought. Work at forming a clear visualization of the situation: Picture the scene, see the shapes and colors, be aware of who is there and what they look like. Hear the voices and other sounds that are part of the trigger scene. Notice the temperature. Notice if you're touching anything, and what it feels like.

When the image of the scene is very clear, read your hot thought. Try to focus on it to the point of having an emotional reaction. When you can picture the scene clearly and feel some of the emotions that go with it, it's time to turn the card over and read your balanced thoughts. Think of the balanced thoughts while continuing to visualize the scene, and continue to pair the balanced thoughts and the scene until your emotional reaction subsides.

Len did this exercise by picturing the monthly sales notice while thinking his hot thought, "I'm a first-class failure." After feeling a small surge in depression, he paired the image of the sales report with the balanced thoughts described earlier. It took several minutes of focusing on the balanced thoughts before his depression started to subside. One of the important things Len learned from this exercise was that he could both increase and decrease his depression by focusing on key thoughts.

Your Action Plan

Return your attention to the "Evidence Against" column in your Thought and Evidence Journal. Look for an item that involves using coping skills or implementing a plan to handle the situation differently. Circle the item(s) that suggest a plan of action. In the space below, write three specific steps you could take to implement your action plan in the problem situation.

1. _____

   _____

   _____

   _____

2. _____

   _____

   _____

   _____

3. _____

   _____

   _____

_____

Len's action plan focused on his decision to think about customer relationships rather than the dollar value of each contract. He decided to:

1. Send New Year's greetings to all of his regular customers.

2. Call each customer with a request for feedback about how he and his company could improve service.

3. Focus on enjoying his customers as people—for example, taking the time to chat instead of pushing quickly to business.

Example

Here is an example of the whole process in action. Take a look at how Holly implements the techniques in this chapter, paying special attention to the Thought and Evidence Journal and resulting action plan.

Holly was a modern-dance teacher. Her classes were offered on a drop-in basis, and she was paid per pupil. One of her seven classes had recently shown a sharp decline in attendance. To make matters worse, after class one night one of the remaining students had criticized Holly for giving little attention or feedback to individual dancers.

Holly felt like she'd been slapped. She went home wondering if she should—or would be allowed to—continue teaching. The following page shows how she completed her Thought and Evidence Journal:

Notice that Holly had two strong feelings: depression and anxiety. That's because thoughts such as "I'm a fraud" and "I'm no good at this" tended to make her feel bad about herself and depressed. On the other hand, a thought such as "I'll lose my job" was scary and anxiety-provoking. Under "Automatic Thoughts" Holly really had two hot thoughts. "I'm a fraud" and "I'll lose my job" were both rated eighty-five—major contributors to her bad feelings. Holly decided to work on "I'll lose my job" for the remainder of the journal because she was more anxious than depressed. Later, Holly went back and repeated her evidence gathering for the hot thought "I'm a fraud."

Notice under "Evidence For" that Holly focused on facts. She included evidence only for what had actually happened or what had actually been said. She didn't include any feelings, opinions, or assumptions as evidence—only the facts.

In the "Evidence Against" column Holly used the ten key questions to uncover evidence contrary to her hot thought. A few of the questions weren't relevant, but others helped her remember past and present experiences that made losing her job seem unlikely.

Because Holly's "Evidence Against" column was so substantial, she went through it carefully and underlined the items that seemed salient and convincing. To write her balanced thoughts, Holly acknowledged the truth of several problems in the "Evidence For" column but counterweighted it with strong evidence against. When Holly reevaluated her feelings, anxiety was down substantially—from eighty-five to twenty. But depression had improved only slightly. That's why Holly elected to do the Thought and Evidence Journal again, using "I'm a fraud" as her hot thought.

Recording Alternative Thoughts

Holly put a description of the situation and the hot thought "I'll lose my job" on one side of a file card. On the other side she wrote her balanced thoughts. Holly began by visualizing the problem situation while focusing on her hot thought. When she felt the first tinglings of anxiety, she turned the file card over and visualized the problem situation in conjunction with her new, balanced thoughts.

The exercise showed Holly that she could change her feelings by shifting from hot to balanced thoughts.

Holly's Thought and Evidence Journal

Situation When? Where? Who? What happened?	Feelings One-word summaries. Rate 0–100.	Automatic Thoughts What you were thinking just before and during the unpleasant feeling. Rate 0–100.	Evidence For	Evidence Against	Balanced or Alternative Thoughts How much do you believe this? 0–100%	Re-rate Feelings 0–100.
Class dwindling. Criticized for not giving individual attention.	Depressed, 65. Anxious, 80.	I'm turning off the class. **30** I'm no good at this. **50** I'm a fraud. **85** * I'll lose my job. **85** Stupid me—I never notice what's happening until it's too late. **50** I'll have to cancel the class. **20**	Class size dropped from 11 to 5. Complaint from dancer in class. Lost a few dancers from one or two of my other classes. Someone also complained a few months ago about my not giving feedback.	A popular Afro-Haitian instructor just started a class at the same time as mine. (Q-1) Classes fluctuate a lot, sometimes dwindle and get canceled. No one gets fired for it. (Q-2) Two of my classes are actually growing, the 6 p.m. on Tuesday had 23 dancers last week. (Q-3) Jill said I put together some lovely sequences, and several dancers standing around agreed. I'm good at choreographing teaching exercises. (Q-4) Most likely the class will stabilize at this number. At the worst I'll lose one of seven classes. (Q-5) Only one person has actually been fired—and that was for encouraging movements that risk injury. I doubt I'll be fired for a class with low attendance. (Q-6) The odds of being fired are less than 1 in 500. (Q-8) I can individually ask other dancers about their reactions to the class. Also I can focus on giving feedback to dancers in the back row, whom I often miss. (Q-10)	One class has dwindled, and I'm not great at giving feedback. But fluctuations are normal. No one gets fired except for risking injuries. Many dancers like my class, and I have a plan for improving feedback. **90%**	depressed, 50 anxious, 25

Holly's Action Plan

There were two parts to Holly's plan: (1) ask for feedback from certain dancers she knew in class, and (2) give more attention to the dancers in the back row. Holly decided to implement her plan with three specific steps:

1. Ask Maria, Eleanor, Michelle, and Farrin about my class in general and, specifically, find out what they've observed about the feedback I give dancers.

2. Bring the back row to the front row halfway through every class.

3. Try to find something to praise about each dancer.

Special Considerations

1. If you have more than one main hot thought, do a separate Thought and Evidence Journal for each hot thought.

2. If you have difficulty developing alternative interpretations to the hot thought, imagine how a friend or some objective observer might look at the situation.

3. If you have difficulty identifying exceptions, think of times you've been in the target situation without anything negative happening. Or perhaps when you experienced something positive. Was there a time when you handled the situation particularly well? Were you ever praised in the situation?

4. If you have difficulty remembering objective facts contrary to items in the "Evidence For" column, you might enlist a friend or family member to help you.

5. If you have difficulty assessing odds of a dangerous outcome, make an estimate of all the times in the last year someone in the United States has been in this same situation. How many times has the feared catastrophe occurred?

6. If you have difficulty making an action plan, imagine how a very competent friend or acquaintance would handle the same situation. What would he or she do, say, or try that might create a different outcome?

Chapter 5

Relaxation

Relaxation training differs from what we normally think of as "relaxing." It's more than seeing a movie to take your mind off things, or taking a long, quiet walk to unwind. When psychologists talk about "learning to relax," they are referring to the regular practice of one or more of a group of specific relaxation exercises. These exercises most often involve a combination of deep breathing, muscle relaxation, and visualization techniques which have been proven to release the muscular tension that your body stores during times of stress.

During your relaxation training sessions you will discover that your racing thoughts will start to slow, and your feelings of fear and anxiety will ease considerably. In fact, when your body is completely relaxed, it's impossible to feel fear or anxiety. In 1975, Herbert Benson studied how the body changes when a person is deeply relaxed. During the state that Benson termed the "relaxation response," he observed that the heart rate, breath rate, blood pressure, skeletal muscle tension, metabolic rate, oxygen consumption, and skin electrical conductivity all decreased. On the other hand, alpha brain wave frequency—associated with a state of calm well-being—increased. Every one of these physical conditions is exactly opposite to reactions that anxiety and fear produce in the body. Deep relaxation and anxiety are physiological opposites.

Symptom Effectiveness

When practiced regularly, relaxation training is effective in reducing general, interpersonal, and performance anxiety. The relaxation training outlined here is a key component in the protocols for treating phobias and chronic anger that appear later in the book. The training is also recommended to treat chronic muscular tension, neck and back pain, insomnia, muscle spasms, and high blood pressure.

Time for Mastery

In general, you can experience the benefits of deep relaxation within a session or two using any of the methods described below. Often two or more methods can be combined to deepen your sense of relaxation; for instance, you could visualize your peaceful scene while practicing deep breathing.

Abdominal breathing, progressive muscle relaxation, relaxation without tension, and cue-controlled relaxation should be learned in sequence. You cannot do cue-controlled relaxation (the quickest and easiest of all the methods) unless you've mastered the first three. The whole sequence will take two to four weeks to learn, depending on length and frequency of practice sessions.

Instructions

This chapter will focus on highly effective techniques which, when practiced regularly, can bring about deep states of relaxation.

Initially, you'll want to do your relaxation training in a quiet room where you won't be disturbed. Later, when you are more familiar with the exercises, you can try them in more distracting and public places. If you wish to, you can use white noise—the humming of an air conditioner or fan—to cover up sounds that you have no control over. Wear loose, nonbinding clothing. At the start of each exercise, assume a comfortable position, either lying down or sitting, in which your body feels well supported.

Abdominal Breathing

One group of muscles that commonly tense in response to stress are those located in the wall of your abdomen. When your abdominal muscles are tight, they push against your diaphragm as it extends downward to initiate each breath. This pushing action restricts the amount of air you take in and forces the air you do inhale to remain high in the top part of your lungs.

When your breathing is high and shallow, you will probably feel as though you aren't getting enough oxygen. This is stressful and sets off mental alarm bells that you are in danger. To make up for the lack of air, instead of relaxing your abdominal muscles and taking deeper breaths, you may take quick, shallow breaths. This shallow, rapid breathing can lead you to hyperventilate—one of the prime causes of panic.

Abdominal breathing reverses this process by relaxing the muscles that press against your diaphragm and slowing your breath rate. Three or four deep abdominal breaths can be an almost instant relaxer.

Abdominal breathing is usually easy to learn. Practice the following exercise for about three minutes.

1. Lie down and close your eyes. Take a moment to notice the sensations in your body, particularly where your body is holding any tension. Take several breaths and see what you notice about the quality of your breathing. Where is your breath centered?

Are your lungs filling all the way up? Does your chest move in and out when you breathe? Does your abdomen? Do both?

2. Place one hand on your chest and the other one on your abdomen, right below your waist. As you breathe in, imagine that you are sending your breath as far down into your body as it will go. Feel your lungs expand as they fill up with air. As you do this, the hand on your chest should remain fairly still, but the hand on your abdomen should rise and fall with each breath.

3. Continue to gently breathe in and out. Let your breath find its own pace. If your breathing feels unnatural or forced in any way, just maintain your awareness of that sensation as you breathe in and out. Eventually any straining or unnaturalness should ease up by itself.

   If you have difficulty getting the hand on your abdomen to move, or if both hands are moving, try pressing down with the hand on your abdomen. As you breathe, direct the air so that it pushes up against the pressure of your hand, forcing it to rise.

4. After breathing deeply for several breaths, begin to count each time you exhale. After ten exhalations, start the count over with one. When thoughts intrude and you lose track of the number you are on, simply return your attention to the exercise and start counting again from number one. Continue counting your breaths for ten minutes, making certain that the hand on your abdomen continues to rise with each breath.

Progressive Muscle Relaxation

Progressive muscle relaxation, or PMR, is a relaxation technique that involves tensing and relaxing all the various muscle groups in your body in a specific sequence. The technique was developed by Dr. Edmund Jacobson in 1929. Realizing that the body responded to anxious and fearful thoughts by storing tension in the muscles, Jacobson found that this tension could be released by consciously tightening the muscles beyond their normal tension point and then suddenly relaxing them. He discovered that repeating this procedure with every muscle group in the body could induce a deep state of relaxation.

Jacobson's original instructions for PMR were a complex routine, involving more than 200 different muscle relaxation exercises. Since then, researchers have discovered that a daily regimen of sixteen exercises can be equally effective. These exercises divide the body into four major muscle groups: the arms, the head, the midsection, and the legs.

If you practice PMR as outlined below, you will experience the physical benefits that Herbert Benson defined as the relaxation response. More importantly, if you continue to regularly practice the PMR exercises for several months, the amount of anxiety, anger, or other painful emotions that habitually come up in your life will significantly diminish.

Instructions for Practicing PMR

Practice the following exercise for about twenty or thirty minutes *daily*, whether you feel like it or not. You are developing a skill—the ability to relax. In the beginning, you may find that it takes you a long time to relax even a little bit. However, as you continue to practice, you will learn to relax more deeply and more rapidly.

As you go through the exercise, repeat the tensing and relaxing cycle once for each muscle group. Tighten each group for seven seconds, and relax for twenty seconds. Each time you tense a muscle group, tighten the muscles as hard as you can without straining. When it's time to release the tension, let go of it suddenly and completely. Notice the feeling of relaxation. Are your muscles heavy, warm, or tingly? Learning to recognize the physical signs of relaxation is a key part of the process.

The progression from one muscle group to another follows a logical sequence, and most people find that after practicing PMR a few times they can easily remember the sequence. If you do have trouble remembering the order, you may prefer to make a tape of the instructions or buy a professionally made tape.

Arms

1. Clench both hands tightly, making them into fists. Hold the tightness for seven seconds. Pay attention to the sensations in the muscles as they contract. Now let go of the tension and notice the difference. Stay focused on the sensations you are feeling. After twenty seconds of allowing the muscles to relax, clench your fists again. Hold the tension for seven seconds, then relax for twenty seconds.

2. Next, bend both elbows and flex your biceps. Hold this "Charles Atlas" pose for seven seconds, then let go of the tension. Flex a second time, then relax. Pay attention to the physical sensations of relaxation.

3. Tense your triceps—the muscles underneath your arms—by locking your elbows and stretching your arms as hard as you can down by your sides. Let go of the tension. Flex and release a second time. Notice the sensations of relaxation.

Head

1. Raise your eyebrows up as high as you can and feel the tension in your forehead. Hold this, then suddenly let your brow drop and become smooth. Repeat.

2. Squinch up your entire face as though you were trying to make every part of it meet on the tip of your nose. Feel where the strain is. Then release the tension and notice the feeling. Repeat.

3. Close your eyes tightly and smile, stretching your mouth as wide open as you can. Hold it, then relax. Repeat.

4. Clench your jaw and push your tongue up to the roof of your mouth. Hold, then release. Repeat. Notice how the sensations change. Open your mouth into a big, wide "O." Hold, then release so that your jaw goes back into a normal position. Feel the relaxation and notice the difference. Repeat.

5. Tilt your head back as far as you can until it presses against the bottom of your neck. Hold, then relax. Repeat. Stretch your head to one side so that it rests near your shoulder; hold, relax, then repeat. Now roll your head over to the other shoulder; hold, relax, then repeat. Lift your head to its natural resting position and feel the tension drain away. Let your mouth fall open slightly. Stretch your head forward until your head is resting on your chest. Release the tension as you return your head to the resting position. Repeat.

Midsection

1. Bring your shoulders up as high as you can—as though you are trying to touch your ears with them. Hold, then let them fall back down again. Feel the heaviness in the muscles as they relax. Repeat. Stretch your shoulders back—as though you were trying to touch your shoulder blades together. Hold the position, then let your arms drop by your sides. Repeat.

2. Bring your arms out straight in front of you, lifting from the shoulders so that your arms are parallel with each other. Then, while keeping them straight, cross one arm over the other at a point as high up on your arms as you can. Feel the stretch in your upper back. Hold the position. Now, let your arms drop down to your sides and notice the sensation of letting go. Repeat.

3. Take a deep breath. Before you exhale, contract all the muscles in your stomach and abdomen. Hold, then exhale and release the contraction. Repeat.

4. Gently arch your back. Hold the tension, then relax so your back is flat again on the floor, bed, or back of the chair. Repeat.

Legs

1. Tighten your buttocks and thighs. Increase the tension by straightening your legs and pushing down hard through your heels. Hold this position, then let go. Repeat.

2. Tense your inner thigh muscles by pressing your legs together as hard as you can. Release, and feel the sense of ease spread throughout your legs. Repeat.

3. Tighten your leg muscles while pointing your toes. Hold the position, then release as you return your toes to a neutral position. Repeat.

4. Flex your toes by drawing them up towards your head as you tighten your shin and calf muscles. Hold, and then release by letting your feet hang loosely. Repeat.

Shorthand Muscle Relaxation—Simultaneous Contractions

Although the basic PMR procedure is an excellent way to relax, it takes too long to go through all the different muscle groups sequentially to make it a practical tool for on-the-spot relaxation. To relax your body quickly, you will need to learn the following shorthand muscle relaxation method.

The key to shorthand PMR is learning to simultaneously relax the muscles in each of the four body areas. You will tense and hold each group for seven seconds, and then allow your muscles to relax for twenty seconds—just as you did in the full PMR exercise. As you become more adept, you may need less time for both the tensing and relaxing parts.

1. Make tight fists while flexing your biceps and forearms in a Charles Atlas pose. Or, if you would feel too conspicuous doing this in your current surroundings, simply tighten all the muscles in your arms as they hang straight by your sides. Hold the tension, then relax.

2. Press your head back as far as you can. Roll it clockwise in a complete circle, then roll it once counterclockwise. As you do this, wrinkle up your face as though you were

trying to make every part of it meet at your nose. Relax. Now tense your jaw and your throat muscles and hunch your shoulders up. Hold this position, then relax.

3. Gently arch your back as you take a deep breath. Hold this position, then relax. Take another deep breath, and this time push your abdomen out as you inhale. Then relax.

4. Point your toes up towards your face while tightening your calf and shin muscles. Hold the position, then relax. Now, curl your toes while tightening your calf, thigh, and buttock muscles. Hold this position, then relax.

Relaxation without Tension

Seven to fourteen PMR practice sessions should make you adept at recognizing and releasing tension in your muscles. By now you may not need to deliberately contract each muscle before you relax it. Instead, scan your body for tension by running your attention through the sequence of the four muscle groups. If you find any tightness, simply let go of it, just as you did after each contraction in the PMR exercises. Stay focused and really feel each sensation. Work with each of the four muscle groups until the muscles seem completely relaxed. If you come to an area that feels tight and won't let go, tighten that one muscle or muscle group and then release the tension. You will find this method faster than the PMR shorthand procedure. It also is a good way to relax sore muscles that you don't want to aggravate by overtensing.

Cue-Controlled Relaxation

In cue-controlled relaxation, you learn to relax your muscles whenever you want by combining a verbal suggestion with abdominal breathing. First, take a comfortable position, then release as much tension as you can using the relaxation without tension method. Focus on your belly as it moves in and out with each breath. Make breaths slow and rhythmic. With each breath let yourself become more and more relaxed. Now, on every inhalation say to yourself the words *breathe in,* and as you exhale, the word *relax.* Just keep saying to yourself, "Breathe in . . . relax, breathe in . . . relax," while letting go of tension throughout your body. Continue this practice for five minutes, repeating the key phrases with each breath.

The cue-controlled method teaches your body to associate the word *relax* with the feeling of relaxation. After you have practiced this technique for a while and the association is strong, you'll be able to relax your muscles anytime, anywhere, just by mentally repeating, "Breathe in . . . relax," and by releasing any feelings of tightness throughout your body. Cue-controlled relaxation can give you stress relief in less than a minute, and is a major component of the anxiety and anger management protocols.

Visualizing a Peaceful Scene

You have the ability to relax by mentally constructing a peaceful scene that you can enter whenever you feel stressed. Your peaceful scene should be a setting that you find interesting and appealing. It will be a place that will make you feel safe and secure when you imagine it—where you will be able to let your guard down and completely relax.

Finding Your Peaceful Scene

Find a comfortable position, either sitting or lying down, and take a few minutes to practice cue-controlled relaxation. Visualization is most effective when you are completely relaxed, so be sure to take enough time to relax thoroughly.

Now simply ask your unconscious to show you your peaceful scene. A picture may start to form in your imagination. Or, instead of an image, you may "hear" a word, phrase, or sound that will start to stir an image to life. However it happens, if an image does start to show itself, don't question it. Accept this as a setting that has a restful resonance for you.

If a scene doesn't start to appear to you, choose a place or an activity that appeals to you. Where would you like to be right now? Out in the country? The woods? A meadow? On a boat? In a cabin? The house where you grew up? A penthouse overlooking Central Park?

Once your imagination has settled on a scene, notice what objects you have around you in the scene. See their colors and shapes. What sounds do you hear? What scents are in the air? What are you doing? What physical sensations are you feeling? Try to notice everything about the scene. You may find that parts of your scene remain unclear or hazy no matter how hard you try. This is perfectly normal. Don't be disappointed if your scene doesn't appear in 3-D Technicolor right away. With practice, you'll be able to draw out the details and make your scene more vivid.

Visualization Skills

Visualization is a skill. Like many skills such as drawing, cabinet making, or sewing, some people are initially more adept at it than others. You may be a person who can sit down and re-create a scene so clearly that you feel like you're actually there. Or you might find it difficult to see anything at all.

Even if you aren't a natural at visualization, you can develop this skill with practice. The following guidelines will help you bring your visualizations to life.

1. Once an image appears, if there are any gaps in the scene—if one part seems hazy or void of any image at all—put all of your concentration on that area and ask, "What is it?" Hold your attention on that area and see if it starts to clear. Whatever appears in your imagination, even when the image is fuzzy or blank, watch it as intently as you can.

2. It is important to make your imagined scene as "real" as possible. One way to accomplish this is by adding as much detail as you can gather from at least three of your five senses. Visually, you can bring out the shapes in your scene by running your attention over the outline of the images as though you were tracing them with a pencil. Notice the colors in your scene. Are they vivid or faded? Locate the light source. How does light falling on an object affect its color? What areas are in shadow? Try to notice everything you could actually see if you were there.

3. Pay attention to the information you would gather through your other senses. What sounds would you hear if you were actually there? What would the environment smell like? What can you feel through your sense of touch? Are there areas that are hot or cold? Is a breeze blowing? If you are sitting or lying down in your scene, can you feel the pressure on the parts of your body that contact the ground? Run your

hand over various objects and notice their texture and the sensations this action creates in your body.

4. Pay attention to the perspective from which you are viewing the scene. Are you viewing it as though you are an outsider looking in? The clue to the "outside looking in" perspective is when you actually see an imagined "you" in your scene. If you do, you need to shift perspective so that your view is what you'd see if you were actually in the scene. For example, if you imagine yourself lying underneath some trees, instead of seeing a reclining "you" on the ground, shift your perspective so that you see only the branches of the trees against a clear blue sky. By seeing things from a perspective inside the scene, you will draw yourself completely into the image and make it easier to feel that you are living the scene rather than just viewing it.

5. When unrelated thoughts intrude, notice their content and then return your attention to the scene you are creating.

Examples of Peaceful Scenes

The following examples may give you an idea of how to put your scenes together.

The Beach. You have just descended a long flight of wooden stairs and now find yourself standing on a stretch of the most pristine beach you have ever seen. It is wide and stretches as far as you can see in either direction. You sit down on the sand and find that it's white and smooth, warm and heavy. You let the sand sift through your fingers and it seems almost liquid. You lie on your stomach, finding that the warm sand instantly conforms to the shape of your body. A breeze touches your face. The soft sand holds you. The surf rumbles as it rises into long white crests that break towards you, then dissolve on the sand's edge. The air smells of salt and sea life, and you breathe it in deeply. You feel calm and safe.

The Forest. You are in a forest, lying down in a circle of very tall trees. Underneath you is a cushion of soft, dry moss. The air is strongly scented with laurel and pine, and the atmosphere feels deep, still, and serene. You drink in the warmth of the sun as it streams through the branches, dappling the carpet of moss. A warm wind rises. The tall trees around you sway and bend, and the leaves rustle rhythmically with each gust. Each time the breeze swells, every muscle in your body becomes more and more relaxed. Two songbirds warble in the distance. A chipmunk chatters above. A sense of ease, peace, and joy spreads from head to toe.

The Train. You are riding in a private car at the very end of a long train. The entire ceiling of the car is a dome of tinted glass, and the walls of the car are glass, creating the illusion that you are out in the open, flying through the vast countryside. A plush couch sits at the far end, with two overstuffed chairs opposite and a coffee table in the middle—complete with your favorite magazines. You sink deeply into one of the chairs, push off your shoes, and put your feet on the table. Outside an ever receding panorama: mountains, trees, snowcapped peaks, a lake shimmering in the distance. The sun has almost set and the sky is washed in purples and reds, filled with towering red-orange clouds. And as you gaze, you ease into the rhythm of the clacking wheels and feel the lull of the rocking train.

Chapter 6

Worry Control

Everybody worries from time to time. It's a natural response to anticipated future problems. But when worry gets out of hand, it can become an almost full-time preoccupation. You have a serious problem with worry if you

- are chronically anxious about future dangers or threats.

- consistently make negative predictions about the future.

- often overestimate the probability or seriousness of bad things happening.

- can't stop repeating the same worries over and over.

- escape worry by distracting yourself or avoiding certain situations.

- find it difficult to use worry constructively to produce solutions to problems.

People who tell you to "just stop worrying" don't realize how the human mind works. It's like the famous philosophical puzzle: "I'll give you a thousand dollars if you can not think of a white bear for a full minute." You might go for months or years never thinking about a white bear, but as soon as you decide to *not* think about it, you can't get that damn bear out of your mind. Just try it.

This chapter will teach you to control worry in four ways. First, it will direct you to practice regularly the relaxation techniques you learned in chapter 5. Second, it will teach you to conduct accurate risk assessments to counter any tendency to overestimate future danger. Third, it will teach you *worry exposure*. In simplest terms, worry exposure means scheduling a thirty-minute period each day for full-scale, concentrated, organized worrying. You'll do all of your worrying then. If you're tempted to worry at any other time of the day, you can postpone it until your next scheduled worry exposure session. Worry exposure makes worrying less distressing and more productive.

Finally, this chapter also teaches worry behavior prevention, a technique for controlling the ineffective strategies you may use now, strategies that reduce your worries somewhat in the short term but perpetuate them in the long term. For example, you'll discover ways to get places on time without obsessively checking your watch or circling the block because you're too early. You can learn to stop calling to check up on loved ones about whom you worry too much.

Symptom Effectiveness

Relaxation, risk assessment, and worry exposure have been found to be effective in reducing the excessive worry that is the chief feature of Generalized Anxiety Disorder (O'Leary et al. 1992). Worry behavior prevention has also been found to be helpful in curbing ritual, preventive, and corrective behaviors that tend to perpetuate worry.

Considering the superiority of cognitive behavioral techniques in the treatment of panic attacks, you would expect success in treating worry with similar techniques. However, studies to date show cognitive behavioral techniques to work only about as well as other interventions to control or diminish worry (Brown et al. 1992). This may be because clinicians haven't hit upon just the right combination of techniques, because of unclear diagnostic categories and treatment protocols in some early studies, or because we simply don't understand what makes worry so persistent.

Time for Mastery

It will take you one or two weeks to learn to relax using deep breathing, pleasant imagery, and cue-controlled relaxation. At the same time, you can begin the process of assessing risks. Then you can begin worry exposure and should notice improvements by your second or third exposure session.

Worry prevention takes only an hour or two to put into practice, and its benefits can be felt immediately. All told, you can expect to see positive progress in about a month.

Instructions

Worry is not just a mental process. When you worry, you enter into a cyclical pattern that involves your thoughts, your body, and your behavior. On the following page is a diagram of the worry system.

An event—for example, the sight of an ambulance or the thought of a loved one getting hurt—starts worry thoughts going, and you start feeling anxious.

On the physical level, your heart starts beating faster, breathing quickens, your skin gets sweaty, your muscles tense, and you may have other physical symptoms associated with the flight-or-fight response.

On the behavioral level, you may take action to avoid the upsetting situation or place. Or you may begin "checking" behavior, such as calling to see if a loved one is all right or proofreading a report for the fifth time.

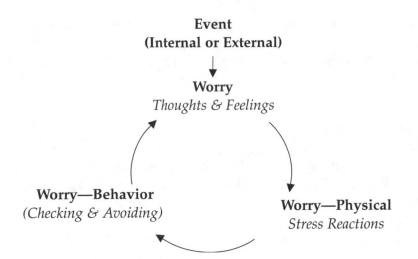

To control worry, you need to approach it on all these levels. The first step is to deal with physical stress reactions by practicing relaxation exercises. To address the cognitive features of worry, you'll take two more steps: risk assessment and worry exposure. Then you'll get the behavioral problems under control with the fourth and last step, worry behavior prevention.

Step 1. Relaxation

If you haven't learned relaxation skills in the previous chapter, go there first. You should master progressive muscle relaxation and cue-controlled relaxation. Chronic worry creates chronic muscular tension. By practicing relaxation daily, you can provide crucial breaks in the cycle of flight/fight reactions that worry causes.

Take the time once a day to perform the full progressive muscle relaxation procedure. Set aside an inviolate time each day when, no matter what else is going on, you will do your relaxation exercise. It's important that you practice daily and don't skip or shorten your practice sessions. Reaching a profound level of deep relaxation once a day is an important part of worry control that cannot be postponed or "made up" the next day if you skip it today.

Five times a day, at more or less regular intervals, do a quick cue-controlled relaxation. This only takes a moment and you can do it anywhere. Frequent relaxing moments will keep your overall level of physical stress under control.

Step 2. Risk Assessment

If worry is a problem for you, you probably have not learned the skill and art of risk assessment. No one can escape risk in life. The trick is to know which risks you can avoid, which you should prepare for, and which you simply don't have to worry about.

Estimating Probability

People who worry a lot consistently overestimate risk. Some think that there is a high chance of a traffic accident every time they start the car. Others worry excessively about making a mistake at work, even though they know their job well and have seldom or never made a big mistake.

Overestimation happens because of some combination of experience and belief: how much weight you give to your personal experience, and your beliefs about the function of worry.

1. **Experience** There are two ways that your own personal history can influence your worrying. First, you may be a person who ignores historical evidence. Nothing too bad has ever happened to you, but that doesn't stop you from worrying about forgetting something important or losing an important relationship. If you think this way, it seems that every day that passes without disaster increases the odds of bad things happening.

    The other way your personal history influences your worrying is if something bad *did* happen to you once. In this case, you give historical evidence too much weight. You figure that anything that happened once is likely to happen again—that lightning not only strikes twice, but actually likes to strike the same spot over and over.

2. **Belief** There are two ways that deeply held, unexamined beliefs can make worry worse. First, you might believe in the predictive power of worry. A woman who worried about her husband leaving her believed that he was likely to leave *because* she thought about it a lot. The second way belief can trap you is if you believe in the preventive power of worry. In this case, you unconsciously assume that bad things have not happened to you *because* you worry about them happening. You feel like a sentry on guard, ever vigilant, keeping trouble at bay.

The problem with these ways of overestimating risk is that they subtly increase your worry until it becomes a bigger problem than the dangers you worry about. The way out of this trap is to learn accurate risk assessment.

Predicting Outcomes

Even if your worries come to pass, will the outcome be as catastrophic as you fear? Most people who worry a lot consistently predict unreasonably catastrophic outcomes. This is "catastrophizing." For example, a man who worried about losing his job actually did lose his job. But instead of ending up homeless and poor, he got another job. It paid a little less, but he liked the work more. The catastrophic outcome he predicted did not come to pass.

When you worry, your anxiety makes you forget that people routinely cope with even the most serious disasters. You forget that you and your family and friends will probably find a way to cope with whatever happens.

You can use the Risk Assessment form on page 70 to make accurate risk assessments by lowering your anxiety, estimating accurate probabilities, and making reasonable outcome predictions. On the first line, record one of your worries in the form of a feared event. Write down the worst possible version of your worry you can think of. For example, if you worry about your teenager going out at night, imagine the worst: a head-on collision of drunk teens and a big truck, everybody dead on impact or dying in the emergency room after suffering horribly.

On the second line, write the automatic thoughts that typically come up: "She'll die . . . I'll die . . . bloody pain . . . Things will never be the same . . . awful . . . can't stand it . . ." Jot down whatever comes to mind, even if it is just an image or a fleeting word.

Next, rate your anxiety when considering this worst-case scenario. Use 0 for no anxiety and 100 for the worst fear you have ever experienced. Then rate the probability of this worst-case scenario coming to pass—from 0% for no likelihood at all to 100% for absolute inevitability.

The next four questions deal with catastrophic thinking. Assuming that the worst did happen, predict the consequences you most fear. Then spend some time figuring out what you would tell yourself and what you would do in order to cope with the catastrophe. When you have a clear picture of possible coping strategies, make a revised prediction of the consequences. After these predictions, re-rate your anxiety and see if it has diminished.

The next two questions address the issue of overestimation. List the evidence against the very worst outcome happening. Figure the odds as realistically as you can. Then list all the alternative outcomes you can think of. Finally, re-rate your anxiety and the probability of the event. You should find that both your anxiety and probability ratings have declined as the result of your making a full and objective risk assessment.

As an example, page 71 shows how Sally filled out her Risk Assessment form. She was afraid of failure in general, and specifically worried about her oral exam for her Marriage, Family, and Child Counselor license.

Fill out the Risk Assessment form each time you are confronted by a significant worry, or whenver you return to a worry more than once. It's important to do this exercise consistently. Each risk assessment helps you change old habits of catastrophic thinking.

When you've completed a risk assessment, keep the form. You may wish to refer to it again when confronting a similar worry.

Step 3. Worry Exposure

When practicing worry exposure, you expose yourself to minor worries first, experiencing them for thirty minutes at a time. When minor worries no longer cause you painful anxiety, you move on to more distressing worries. Gradually, you learn to take on your major worries with little or no anxiety.

Worry exposure is similar to flooding, a technique that "floods" your imagination with fearful images until you grow tired of them. Given enough time and focused attention, even the most upsetting material becomes overly familiar and boring, making it less upsetting the next time you encounter it. This effect doesn't happen when you simply worry on your own because you don't spend enough time dwelling on only the worst possible outcome. When you do "free form" worrying, without a structure, you try to distract yourself, argue with yourself, escape into another topic, perform ritual checking or avoiding behaviors, and so on, gaining none of the benefits of structured worry exposure.

Worry exposure also works well because it concentrates your worrying time. When you know that you will be worrying intensely during your daily exposure session, it's easier to clear your mind of worry during the rest of the day.

Risk Assessment

Feared event _____

_____

Automatic thoughts _____

_____

Rate anxiety from 0-100 _____

Rate probability of event from 0-100% _____

Assuming the worst happens:

    Predict the worst possible consequences _____

_____

    Possible coping thoughts _____

_____

    Possible coping actions _____

_____

    Revised prediction of consequences _____

_____

Re-rate anxiety from 0-100 _____

Evidence against the worst possible outcome _____

_____

Alternative outcomes _____

_____

Re-rate anxiety from 0-100 _____

Re-rate probability of event from 0-100% _____

Risk Assessment

Feared event *Flunking my orals*

Automatic thoughts *I can't do it. I'll choke up and sound stupid.*

Rate anxiety from 0-100 *95*

Rate probability of event from 0-100% *90*

Assuming the worst happens:

Predict the worst possible consequences *I'll be a failure. All my schooling will be wasted.*

Possible coping thoughts *Many people don't pass on the first try. I can take the test again.*

Possible coping actions *Study some more. Hire an orals exam coach to practice with. Try again.*

Revised prediction of consequences *I won't fail permanently. It will just take me a little longer.*

Re-rate anxiety from 0-100 *60*

Evidence against the worst possible outcome *I've studied hard and I got good grades on my course work.*

Alternative outcomes *I might do well and pass easily. I might stammer and choke, but squeak by and pass anyway. I might fail and have to take the orals over, and then pass. It might even take me three tries.*

Re-rate anxiety from 0-100 *40*

Re-rate probability of event from 0-100% *30*

Worry exposure consists of eight simple steps:

A. **List Your Worries.** Write a list of the things you worry about. Include worries about success and failure, holding relationships together, your performance at school or work, physical danger, health, making mistakes, rejection, shame over past events, and so on.

B. **Rank Your Worries.** Pick the least anxiety-provoking item on your list of worries and write it at the top of a new list. Then put down the next least distressing worry. Continue until you have reordered all of your worries, ranking them into a hierarchy that runs from the least to the most anxiety provoking. Here is an example of a hierarchy composed by Rachel:

- Forgetting to send my sister a birthday card
- Driving on the school field trip and losing my way
- Forgetting to pick up Cathy after school
- Missing a doctor's appointment
- Missing the property tax deadline
- Making a mistake on taxes at work and getting audited
- Screwing up the payroll and people don't get their paychecks

C. **Relax.** You are ready to work with the first worry on your list. Get into a comfortable position, breathe deeply, and begin cue-controlled relaxation. Let tension drain out of your body.

D. **Visualize a Worry.** Vividly imagine the item from your hierarchy of worries. See the worst coming to pass, over and over again. Stick with the worst possible outcome and focus on the sights, the sounds, the tastes, the smells, and the sensations as if it were really happening to you. Don't just see the scene from an outside vantage point, as if you were watching a movie. Rather, imagine that you are an active participant, in the middle of the action.

Try not to imagine any alternative scenarios. Stick with the worst alternative. Don't allow your mind to wander and escape into distraction. Do this for twenty-five minutes. Set a kitchen timer to keep track of the time. Don't stop early, even if your anxiety is high, even if you're bored.

Rachel imagined getting a phone call from her sister Mary. She heard the phone ring and saw the dark gray plastic of the cordless phone. She felt the cool, dry handset as she picked it up. She heard her sister's voice say, "Well hi, stranger," just as she realized with horror that Mary's birthday was last week, and she hadn't sent a card, bought a present, or even called her. She focused on the shame and embarrassment. She imagined Mary sarcastically saying, "So, you've been busy, or you just don't love me anymore?" Rachel imagined this for the full twenty-five minutes, going over and over the scene and adding enriching details. She resisted any alternative scenarios until the twenty-five minutes were up.

If you find that your anxiety level is low, nowhere near the anxiety you feel during a "real" worry session, you may be having trouble creating sufficiently vivid images. Try switching from the visual sense to another sense. Most people imagine with visual images. But some do better with sounds, textures, or smells. For example, John couldn't feel really anxious using visual images of being in a car wreck. Then he switched to other senses and imagined the screeching tires, the sound of metal smashing, breaking glass, and sirens. He imagined the texture of asphalt and broken glass, and the smell of leaking gasoline, blood, and smoke. These sensory images succeeded admirably and he rated his anxiety at 95 out of a 100.

E. **Rate Your Peak Anxiety from 0-100.** While you are visualizing, rate your highest anxiety level. You can jot down numbers on a piece of scrap paper without even opening your eyes. Use a rating of 0 for no anxiety, and a rating of 100 for the worst you've ever experienced.

   Rachel gave her scene a 70 after the first five minutes. But later in the scene she really frightened herself and raised the rating to a 90.

F. **Imagine Alternative Outcomes.** Allow yourself to visualize alternative, less stressful outcomes. Start this after a full twenty-five minutes of visualizing the worst possible outcome. Don't start it early. Spend just five minutes imagining an outcome that is not as bad as your worst scenario. For example, after a full twenty-five minutes of shame and horror, Rachel imagined that she had initiated the call just one day after her sister's birthday. She imagined calling to apologize and saying that a belated gift was in the mail.

G. **Re-rate Anxiety from 0-100.** After your five minutes of alternative outcomes, re-rate your anxiety. It will probably be notably lower than your previous rating. Rachel rated her final scene as a 30.

H. **Repeat.** Repeat steps D through G with the same worry until peak anxiety is 25 or less. Then go on and do the procedure with the next worry on your hierarchy. Do at least one session a day. If you have time and can tolerate it, you can do several sessions a day. By the time you have worked through your hierarchy, you should find that your worry is significantly reduced.

It took Rachel four weeks to work through her hierarchy, averaging one-and-a-half sessions a day. During that period, she worried a lot less. Whenever she started to worry, she told herself that she could postpone the worry until her next scheduled session. Even after she stopped doing regular worry exposure, Rachel found that her fear of making mistakes and forgetting things was significantly reduced. She would start to worry, remember her exposure sessions, and think, "I've worried this into the ground already." She was usually able to stop worrying soon or at least switch to a more balanced assessment of alternative outcomes.

Step 4. Worry Behavior Prevention

You may habitually perform or avoid certain behaviors to keep bad things from happening. For example, Pete never read the obituaries or drove past the cemetery, feeling that this would somehow keep loved ones from dying. His mother always "knocked on wood" whenever she made a positive prediction.

Close examination will show that these ritual or preventive behaviors are actually perpetuating your worry and have no power to prevent bad things from happening. For Pete, the active avoidance of the obituaries and the cemetery just made him worry about death more often, and he knew intellectually that such avoidance would not keep people from dying.

You can prevent worry behavior by following these simple steps:

A. Record Your Worry Behavior.

Write down the things you do to prevent the disasters you worry about from happening. For example, Carly was very worried about social disapproval. She couldn't stand the thought that others might think she was impolite, a bad hostess, or not doing her fair share. She identified three worry behaviors:

> Coming too early to appointments and parties, and driving around the block for twenty minutes until it's time to go in.

> Taking a main dish, a salad, *and* a dessert to potluck parties where you are only expected to bring one item.

> Making way too much food for parties at my house.

_____

_____

_____

_____

_____

_____

B. Pick the Easiest Behavior to Stop and Predict Consequences of Stopping It.

Pick the worry behavior that would be easiest to stop and write it here. Then write down the predicted consequences. Carly picked making too much food for her parties. She predicted simply: "We'd run out of food halfway through the party."

Behavior   **Consequences**

_____   _____

_____   _____

C. Stop the Easiest Behavior and/or Replace It With a New Behavior. This is the hard part. In order to find out if your prediction will come true, you have to be a good scientist and actually run the experiment. Resolve to refrain from the behavior the next time you start worrying. For example, Carly firmly decided that she would not make too much food for her husband's birthday party. Unfortunately, she couldn't just stop the worry behavior entirely—she had to make *some* food. First she considered just making half the amount of food she would normally make. But this was hard to judge. Finally, she carefully figured out how much food the average party guest ate at her house, and how many guests were really likely to come. She prepared just enough food. Every time she felt the temptation to add a "fudge factor," she stifled it.

If your worry behavior is a form of avoidance, such as not driving past the cemetery or never reading the obituaries, it's hard to stop doing it. You have to *start* doing what you have been avoiding. Resolve to drive past the cemetery every morning on the way to work, or read the obituaries with your morning coffee.

Sometimes even the "easiest" behavior to stop is not so easy. In that case, you need to create a hierarchy of replacement behaviors that allows you to taper off from your worry behavior. For example, Peggy was a perfectionistic legal secretary who worried about making mistakes on the senior partner's contracts and briefs. She would take an important brief home and spend hours of her own time proofing and reproofing it, agonizing over possible typos, changing type sizes and styles, far into the night. Every time she made the slightest alteration, she would run the entire document through the spell checker again.

The thought of spell checking and proofing just once and declaring a brief done was too alarming for Peggy to even consider. So she made up this hierarchy:

Take brief home and do three extra passes through it.

Take brief home and do two extra passes.

Take brief home and do one extra pass.

Stay up to one hour late and leave brief at work. No extra pass.

Leave brief at work and go home on time. No extra pass.

Deliberately leave one punctuation error in brief.

Deliberately leave one grammatical error.

Deliberately leave one spelling error.

Peggy worked her way through each step of her hierarchy. For each step, she predicted dire consequences and experienced high anxiety. At each step the consequences failed to appear and she gained confidence for the next step. You'll notice that the last three steps involve making deliberate mistakes. This is a good strategy to extinguish checking behaviors designed to prevent mistakes. In Peggy's case, she found that making small mistakes did not cause the firm to lose cases or get her fired. Nobody even noticed the errors. She was eventually able to eliminate other checking behaviors and reduce her perfectionism to what she called "high but not inflexible standards."

D. **Assess Your Anxiety Before and After.** When you felt like performing your old behavior and knew you were not going to do it, how anxious were you? Rate your anxiety from 0-100, with 0 standing for no anxiety. Now, after performing your new behavior or the cut-down version of the old behavior, how anxious are you? Rate your anxiety again from 0-100. Has your anxiety diminished?

Carly, the woman who habitually prepared too much food for guests, rated her anxiety a full 100 just before her husband's birthday party. She thankfully reduced the rating to a 25 by the end of the party, when there was still a little food left and everyone had had a fine time.

Also assess the consequences. What actually happened as a result of your reduced or new behavior? Did your dire predictions come true? In Carly's case, her prediction did not come true. They didn't run out of food halfway through the party. She felt an improved sense of confidence about her ability to enter into a social engagement without excessive worry and ritual preventive behavior.

E. **Repeat Steps B through D With the Next-Easiest Behavior.** From your initial list, pick the worry behavior that is the next easiest to stop, and repeat the steps: Predict the consequences of stopping the behavior; stop it and replace it with a new behavior if appropriate; then assess your anxiety level before and after the experiment.

Example

Rhonda's experience with worry control shows how all four steps fit together. She was chronically worried about rejection—being rejected by her boyfriend, her boss, her parents, and complete strangers. She avoided meeting new people for fear that they would reject her. She kept checking with her boyfriend, Josh, to make sure he still loved her. She would say "I love you" to him in such a way that he would have to respond, "I love you, too." Some evenings she'd do this five or six times—until it started to annoy Josh, who complained about her neediness.

Rhonda learned progressive muscle relaxation and did it every evening after dinner or just before she went to bed. She also mastered cue-controlled relaxation and set her watch alarm to go off every three hours so that she would remember to stop and relax and take a few deep breaths several times a day. This helped her reduce her ongoing arousal level so that the chronic worries in the back of her mind didn't build as much throughout the day.

She worked on her Risk Assessment form while she was learning relaxation skills. When she assessed the risk of Josh dumping her, she realized two things: first, that the odds were greatly against him dumping her; second, if he did dump her, she could survive the rejection and cope with the loneliness. It was very interesting and instructive to see how persistent overestimation and castrophizing had been feeding her worry.

Next Rhonda made a hierarchy of rejection experiences to use in worry exposure. She started with the mild rejection experience of being asked by a bus driver to step to the rear of the bus. That scene quickly became boring after two sessions. She went on to extinguish her reaction to scenes involving her boss asking her to redo some sloppy work, her mom rejecting her ideas for the family reunion, and finally, Josh saying that he thought they should break up.

She concluded her worry-control treatment with two kinds of worry-behavior prevention. She prevented her avoidance of strangers by forcing herself to say something each morning to whoever sat next to her on the bus. She learned that some people responded and some didn't—and she survived both types of responses. To change her checking behavior with Josh, she resolved to say "I love you" only twice a day. Then she cut it down to once a day. Then she said it every other day. She noticed that the less she said "I love you" to Josh, the more he said it to her without prompting.

Chapter 7

Thought Stopping

Thought stopping involves concentrating on an unwanted thought for a short time, then suddenly stopping it and emptying your mind. The internal command "Stop!" or snapping a rubber band on your wrist is generally used to interrupt the unpleasant thought.

One of the oldest cognitive techniques still commonly practiced, thought stopping was introduced by Bain in 1928 in his book *Thought Control in Everyday Life*. In the late 1950s it was adapted by Joseph Wolpe and other behavioral therapists for the treatment of obsessive and phobic thoughts.

Symptom Effectiveness

Thought stopping has proved effective with a wide variety of obsessive and phobic thought processes: color naming, sexual preoccupation, hypochondriasis, obsessive thoughts of failure, sexual inadequacy, obsessive memories, and frightening, recurring impulses leading to chronic tension and anxiety attacks. While thought stopping is only effective in approximately 20 percent of cases involving compulsive ritual behavior, it is more than 70 percent effective in controlling thoughts about simple phobias such as fear of snakes, driving, the dark, elevators, someone lurking in the house at night, fear of insanity, and so on. Thought stopping is recommended when the problem behavior is primarily cognitive rather than acted out. It is indicated when specific thoughts or images are repeatedly experienced as painful or leading to unpleasant emotional states.

Time for Mastery

This is a simple technique that you can master in three days to one week of conscientious practice, with three or four ten-minute sessions a day.

Instructions

Work through the following sections in order, using the Scene Logs to record the scenes and thoughts that you need to concentrate on.

Step 1. List Your Unwanted Thoughts.

On a piece of scratch paper, write down three or four topics that haunt you—things you can't stop worrying about. For example, you might list whether you remembered to turn off the stove, whether your loved ones are safe, how many germs might be around you, long lists of details to remember, obsessive sexual fantasies, and so on.

Now you can start you Scene Log. For each topic, include a brief description of a scene and a typical thought; for example, "See an attractive younger person . . . I'm getting old," or "Driving home from a trip . . . What if the house has burned down?"

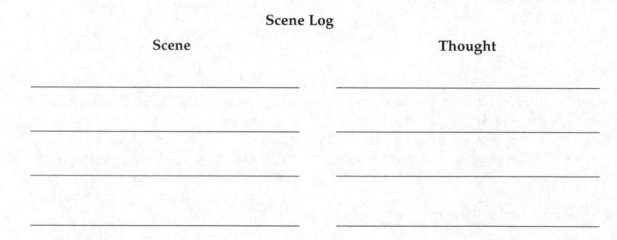

Scene Log

Scene	Thought
_____	_____
_____	_____
_____	_____
_____	_____

Step 2. List Your Pleasant Thoughts.

Now list three or four topics you like to think about. You can imagine playing your favorite sport, a sexual fantasy, a hobby, an upcoming vacation, an interesting project, a special achievement or award, a beautiful or peaceful place, or anything else that gives you pleasure. List things that have nothing to do with your unwanted thoughts. This is not a technique where you want to refute your painful thoughts or replace them with positive self-talk that is logically related. For thought stopping, you want to come up with very pleasant thoughts that have nothing to do with your unwanted thoughts.

Include a brief description of a scene and a typical thought; for example, "Skiing on fresh powder . . . I'm flying."

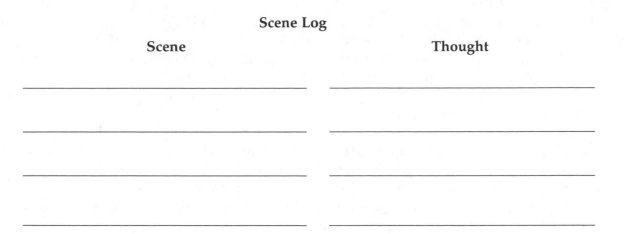

Step 3. Relax and Entertain Your Unwanted Thoughts.

Now you have all the tools you'll need to begin thought stopping. In the beginning, practice thought stopping when you're calm and stress free. Thought stopping can't be learned well in the heat of everyday life. Lie down or sit in a comfortable chair at a time when you have privacy and won't be disturbed. Make sure no one can hear you.

From your list of unwanted scenes and thoughts, pick the combination that bothers you least. Practice first on the one that interferes least in your life, and save the hardest thoughts for last. Close your eyes and concentrate on the thought and scene in detail. Really focus on any sights, sounds, tastes, or smells involved in the scene.

After the scene has become vivid, stay with it for a while. Dwell on it until you are really obsessing on the thoughts connected to it.

Step 4. Interrupt Your Unwanted Thoughts.

When the obsessive train of thoughts and images spawned by your scene is well underway, shout "Stop!" very loudly. Really belt it out. That's why you need privacy when you begin this technique. To accentuate the "Stop!" you can also clap your hands loudly or snap your fingers.

Step 5. Switch to Pleasant Thoughts.

Immediately empty your mind of the unpleasant thoughts and images and switch to your favorite pleasant scene. Enjoy all the pleasant sights, sounds, tastes, and smells for about thirty seconds. If unwanted thoughts or images return before the thirty seconds are up, shout "Stop!" again.

Step 6. Repeat with Variation.

Repeat the exercise. Focus on a troubling scene and its attendant thoughts, shout "Stop!", and switch to the pleasant scene. If one pleasant scene "wears out" and no longer holds your attention, use another one. You should practice until your shouted "Stop!" readily stops your unwanted thoughts and imagery, and your pleasant scene is vivid and enjoyable, without little wisps of obsessive thoughts sneaking back in.

When you have succeeded in interrupting your unwanted thoughts on several occasions with the shouted command, begin interrupting them with "Stop" said in a normal voice.

After succeeding in stopping your thoughts by using your normal speaking voice, start interrupting thoughts with "Stop" in a whisper.

When the whisper is sufficient, use the subvocal command "Stop." Imagine hearing "Stop!" shouted inside your mind. Tighten your vocal chords and move your tongue as if you were saying "Stop" out loud. Success at this stage means that you can stop thoughts alone or in public, without making a sound or calling attention to yourself.

Repeat the steps for each of the other obsessive thoughts that bother you, working your way up to the most disruptive topics.

Step 7. Use Thought Stopping in Real Life.

Once you have mastered thought stopping in a relaxed, private state, it's time to try it out in the real world. When you notice that you are entertaining obsessive thoughts, shout "Stop!" silently in your mind and think about one of your pleasant topics.

If the subvocalized "Stop!" is not successful for you, and you find it embarrassing to say it out loud in public, you can use a different interrupter. You can pinch yourself or "stab" yourself in the palm with your fingernails. Another popular and effective technique is to wear a rubber band around one wrist and snap it to interrupt thoughts.

Stopping obsessive thoughts takes time. They will return and you will have to interrupt them again and again. The main effort is to stifle each thought just as it begins, and to concentrate on something else that you enjoy thinking about. In time the unwanted thoughts will return less and less often.

Stop and Breathe Technique

This is a brief procedure that combines thought stopping and breath counting. It is effective because it supplies a calming, neutral focus of attention, and takes advantage of the naturally relaxing effect of deep breathing.

Whenever you notice disturbing or anxiety-provoking thoughts, internally shout "Stop!" to yourself, or snap a rubber band worn around your wrist. Shift your attention to your breathing. Begin taking slow, deep breaths into your belly. Place a hand over your abdomen to make sure it is expanding with each breath.

Now start counting your breaths. As you exhale, count one. As you exhale again, count two. Keep counting up to four. Each time you reach four, start over again at one. Try to keep your mind as empty as possible as you focus on the experience of breathing and counting. Continue the procedure until you feel relaxed; repeat it each time anxiety-provoking thoughts occur.

Example

A consultant who traveled extensively on business became afraid of sleeping in strange places. She developed this obsessive fear about the time of her divorce. When preparing to go to bed in a strange motel, she would worry about someone entering her room with a pass key while she slept. When she was planning her next trip, she became very tense anticipating the anxiety she would feel in the strange motel.

She decided to try thought stopping. She visualized unpacking in a strange motel, thinking about her presentation for the next day and what she would wear, anticipating going to bed. She imagined lying in the dark, thinking that she might have forgotten to double-bolt the door. She visualized the door swinging slightly ajar.

In the middle of these thoughts, when she could feel the familiar anxiety, she shouted "Stop!" and snapped her fingers. She immediately began to imagine that she was snorkeling in the Cayman Islands, watching huge shoals of tropical fish turn and flash as one over a coral reef. The thought of her impending trip returned before thirty seconds were up, so she shouted "Stop!" again.

She repeated the process until she could interrupt her obsessive thoughts successfully with one shout. Then she began saying "Stop" in a normal voice, and later in a whisper. Finally she was able to shout "Stop!" silently in her head. It took her five to ten repetitions to make each step between shouting out loud and subvocalizing.

During the next three days before her trip, she subvocalized or whispered "Stop!" every time phobic thoughts intruded. Occasionally she reinforced the command by snapping a rubber band that she kept around her wrist. To distract herself from and replace the unwanted thoughts, she used images of playing tennis, shopping for dollhouse furniture with her niece, and getting a massage. She also experimented with counting her breaths, and found this especially helpful just before sleep.

The thoughts gradually decreased in frequency and lasted only a few moments when they occurred. She had markedly less anxiety on her next trip. She wore her rubber band to bed and had to snap it only a couple of times before she fell asleep.

Special Considerations—Scheduling Worries

You can augment thought stopping by scheduling special times of the day to indulge your obsessive thoughts or phobic worrying. Actually set aside fifteen or twenty minutes during a coffee break, while driving, or in the shower. Plan to worry then and it will take the pressure off of other times of the day.

When an unwanted thought intrudes, shout "Stop!" internally and remind yourself that now is not the time to worry about this. Knowing that you will be able to worry later makes it easier to switch to a more positive and appropriate train of thought now.

Gradually schedule fewer and shorter worry periods as you gain control of your obsessive thoughts.

Sometimes you will obsessively worry about something that really does need thinking about. When that is the case, continue to schedule "worry periods," but spend them doing constructive planning and genuine problem solving (see chapter 14, "Problem Solving"). For example, a sculptor had her first one-woman show coming up and she couldn't stop worrying about it. She scheduled her second cup of coffee each morning as the official time to worry and plan for the show. She channeled her anxiety into making lists of all the pieces she needed to complete, compiling a mailing list, and planning what she would do each day to get ready for the show.

Chapter 8

Flooding

Flooding is a simple technique in which you intentionally imagine a feared situation or entertain an obsessive train of thought. You hold this situation or thought in your mind for a long time, at high intensity and without avoiding or neutralizing the images, until you finally grow bored and the images lose their power to upset you.

Flooding grew out of Thomas Stampfl's Implosion Therapy. Stampfl found that the fears of phobic patients would disappear, or "implode," after the patients were bombarded with six to nine hours of continuous verbal descriptions of their feared situations (1967). Most therapists and clients found this technique too time-consuming and exhausting until Zev Wanderer (1991) devised Physiologically Monitored Implosion Therapy in the early 1980s. He used blood pressure biofeedback to pinpoint the most disturbing phrases and images in a client's hierarchy of fears. By intensifying the imagery, he reduced the average time needed for an initial flooding session to two hours. Subsequent sessions could be as short as thirty minutes.

Still, this took up quite a few office hours and didn't fit into neat, fifty-minute modules. So Wanderer took advantage of another technological aid, the loop tape. He asked clients to record their fearful imagery on a three-minute constant-loop cassette tape while hooked up to a blood pressure monitor. When the monitor indicated that a client had reached a sustained maximum arousal, Wanderer would stop the tape recorder. The client would take the loop tape home and do the actual flooding session as homework. Wanderer later found that many clients could self-monitor their arousal and make their own loop tapes at home.

Paul Salkovskis and Joan Kirk (1989) use a thirty-second loop tape to treat obsessional thinking. They instruct clients to stay away from thoughts that avoid or neutralize the obsession while they listen to the tape. Chapter 8 is based on the Wanderer, as well as the Salkovskis and Kirk, methods for self-monitored loop-tape flooding.

Symptom Effectiveness

Flooding is often the treatment of last resort because it is upsetting and because of a lingering false impression that it is too time-consuming. This is unfortunate, because flooding is quite effective for treating simple phobias, such as fear of snakes, heights, small spaces, freeways, and so on. It is also very effective for reducing obsessional thinking that is not accompanied by compulsive behavior, such as fear of losing control, being hurt, or going crazy.

Because flooding will elevate your blood pressure for an extended period, you should not attempt the technique if you have high blood pressure or a family history of heart attack or stroke. Flooding is also contraindicated if there is any chance at all that you might perform a feared action such as suicide or harming others (McMullin 1986).

Time for Mastery

Flooding is intense, but it's relatively simple and fast. For each phobia or obsession, it will take you about an hour to make a loop tape, and three to ten sessions of at least one hour's duration to reduce your anxiety level to near zero.

Instructions

Before you begin the procedure, read all of the instructions, and photocopy the Discomfort Rating Chart from step 4.

Step 1. Obtain a Loop Cassette Tape.

This is the type of tape used for message machines, available at most office-supply and electronics stores. A thirty-second tape is sufficient for most obsessional thoughts. For phobias, you might need a longer tape, up to three minutes. If you have trouble finding the longer loop tapes, you can order a three-minute loop from

New Harbinger Publications
5674 Shattuck Ave.
Oakland, CA 94609
(800) 748-6273

Loop tapes are more expensive and delicate than standard cassette tapes. Don't fast-forward or rewind your loop tape. Don't put it in your car stereo or any auto-reverse player.

Step 2. Record Intense Fear Images.

Sit in a comfortable chair with your tape recorder handy. You might also need a pencil and paper to make a list of your frightening images.

Put on earphones if you want to use them. Put your loop tape in the machine and press the record button. The loop tape will record endlessly. When it gets full, it will continuously record over the oldest material.

Close your eyes and tune into your body for a moment to take a "base line" reading: How do you feel? How fast and deeply are you breathing? Can you feel your heart beating?

How cold or warm are various parts of your body? Do you have any aches or pains, hunger pangs, nausea, or other internal sensations? Notice how you feel now so that you'll know more clearly when conditions change in your body later.

You can open your eyes or leave them closed as you ask yourself these questions:

What is the most important thing I wish to overcome?

What am I avoiding that I want to approach?

What do I want to do that I'm afraid of?

What is holding me back?

What am I afraid will happen to me in this situation?

What thoughts continually prey on my mind?

What worries can't I put out of my mind?

When you have a clear idea of the phobia or obsession you want to work on, start talking about it. If you have a hard time just starting to talk, you may have to use your pencil and paper to jot down some frightening situations or phrases to get you started. Try reading each scene or thought out loud. Elaborate on it and see how scary it feels.

Describe what you fear in the most vivid detail possible, as if it were actually happening to you. For example, don't describe your fear of heights in an abstract way, as you might relate them to a therapist:

I sometimes get nervous when I'm in a high place. I'm afraid I might fall out the window or over the railing.

Instead, describe what you fear as if it were happening in a movie you're watching:

I walk out onto the observation platform of the Sears Tower. I trip and fall against the railing; it breaks and I plunge over the edge, flailing in the air and screaming my guts out.

Likewise, if you're recording a train of obsessional thoughts, don't be dry and analytical about it:

I can't stop thinking about my baby getting sick.

Instead, describe your worst nightmare as if it were happening right now:

Suddenly I realize I haven't fed or changed Sally all day. I rush into her room to find her convulsing in the crib, covered with shit and vomit. I pick up her thrashing body, and it goes limp in my arms. I know she's dead dead dead, and it's all my fault.

Do not include any descriptions of avoidance of your fear, such as "I turn away so I won't have to see.... I try not to think about it.... I run from the room," and so on.

Likewise, don't describe any "neutralizing" thoughts. Neutralizing can take several forms. In the case of obsessions, neutralizing can be compulsive mental rituals like counting, repeating nonsense syllables, magical thinking, reciting prayers or affirmations—anything you typically do in your mind to neutralize the obsessive thoughts.

In the case of phobias, neutralizing might be reminding yourself that your fears are out of proportion—that you really know the bridge won't collapse. Or you may use phrases such as "Whatever happens, happens," or "Forget it, and let go." Such thoughts may have a coping value in other applications of cognitive therapy, but for flooding you need to wallow in the worst, craziest, most unrelieved and unmitigated fear images you can muster. Leave yourself no escape and no respite from your fear.

Include sights, sounds, smells, tastes, and physical sensations of pain, textures, and temperatures. Using all five senses makes your tape much more vivid. See chapter 16, "Changing Core Beliefs with Visualization," for more help with vivid imagery.

Keep talking and adding details until you start to get scared. Keep track of your physical reactions. Your breathing should speed up and become more shallow. You might notice that you're breathing from the middle of your chest instead of deeply from your belly. You might start sweating. Your hands may feel clammy and your stomach queasy. You might start to cry or feel like crying. You might tremble or get a headache.

Don't stop talking, even if you're shaking and crying. Keep asking yourself, "What could be worse than what I'm describing?" Use your physical reactions to get yourself just as scared and upset as you can be.

When you have reached what feels like the peak of your arousal and you can't get any more upset, stop the tape. Depending on the length of your loop tape, you will have thirty seconds to three minutes of the thoughts and images that scare you the most.

Some people have stage fright when it comes to talking into a tape recorder, even though there is no audience beyond themselves. If this is the case for you, you may have to practice a long time before you get a usable tape. You may have to write out a script for your tape and read it.

Step 3. Listen to Your Loop Tape.

Get comfortable in your chair. Have your pencil and photocopies of the rating chart from step 4 handy. Put your earphones on if you want. Hit the play button and turn up the volume until it's nice and loud, filling your consciousness and really affecting you.

Listen attentively for at least an hour. Try to stay with it and avoid your usual magical thinking, mental rituals of counting or nonsense syllables, favorite prayers or sayings and the like. If you are flooding yourself with phobic images, stay with them. Don't argue against them with positive counterstatements like, "This could never happen. . . . It will be over soon. . . . It really wouldn't be this bad," and so on.

Step 4. Rate Your Discomfort Every Five Minutes.

Use the chart on the following page to rate your discomfort from one to ten, with one representing no discomfort and ten representing the worst you've ever felt. Put a check mark or an X next to the appropriate discomfort level at each five-minute interval.

Flooding is so unpleasant that you will probably be peeking at your watch frequently enough to know when each five-minute interval is up. If you have trouble keeping track of the time, use an egg timer and keep resetting it for five minutes after each rating.

You'll notice that your discomfort rating often increases during the first ten to twenty minutes. Don't be discouraged by that—it's normal.

Step 5. Stop When Peak Discomfort is Halved.

You can stop the tape when your discomfort has declined to 50 percent of the highest level you reached during the session. Keep listening until you reach 50 percent improvement, and never quit prematurely. Stopping early is a form of avoidance, and successful avoidance will act like a reward, reinforcing your fear or obsession. It could make it more intense next time.

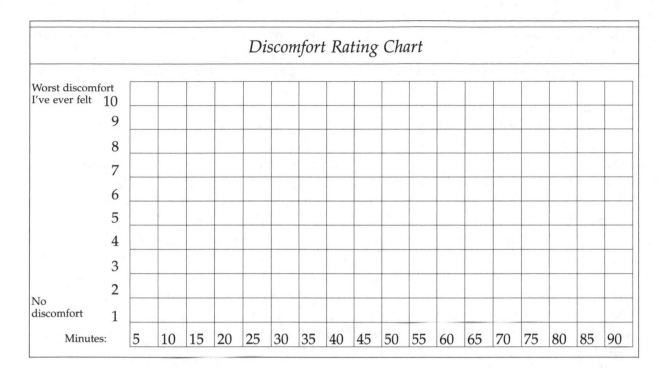

Step 6. Repeat Steps 3 through 5.

Give yourself a few hours or a day to recover, then listen to your tape again, following the directions for Steps 3, 4, and 5. The next time you listen to your tape, you will probably find that your discomfort level is greater at the start than it was at the end of your previous session, but not as high as the peak of the previous session. This is a normal discomfort "rebound."

Schedule flooding sessions every day and keep working with the same loop tape until you can start a session at a minimal level of discomfort that drops quickly to near zero. It will take from three to ten sessions to get to near zero discomfort for each phobia or obsession.

Examples

Robert's Dog Phobia

Robert was a mail carrier who had experienced several close calls with large dogs. Recently a large rottweiler attacked him on a front porch. The dog came up the stairs, blocking Robert's exit, and gave him multiple bites. He was trapped by the dog for more than ten minutes before the owner called off his animal.

Robert now had a serious phobia of dogs, especially large dogs. He went on leave from the post office and, contrary to his lawyer's advice, decided to work on the phobia himself.

He found a one-minute loop tape at a local Radio Shack store and attempted to record details of his most feared situation. But his mind went blank, and he had difficulty making the scene very horrible or vivid.

To improve the imagery for his tape, Robert made a list of the worst angry dog images he could think of. Then he closed his eyes and one by one visualized them, noticing which triggered the largest fear reactions. The worst scene involved being attacked and dragged down by two German shepherds.

The list of images proved useful when he attempted his next loop-tape recording. Now he had something to work with. As the tape ran, he elaborated on the scene until he could feel a strong anxiety reaction in his body.

Robert was careful to include no images in the tape that involved escape, relief of fear, coping, or any other neutralizing thought. For example, one rendition of his tape included an attempt to bolt past the dogs to freedom. He re-recorded, making sure that every image maintained the same trapped, terrified experience. Here's the final script that Robert taped:

The shepherds are lunging, their mouths foaming. Their teeth are red with my blood. One of them has my arm, his teeth deep in my flesh. I try to throw him off, but he's hanging on my arm, biting deeper. I can feel the teeth crunching the bone. I feel a searing pain in my leg—the other dog's got my calf, trying to pull me down. I feel the dog's hot breath and razor fangs. I hear ferocious growls. They're lunging, growling, blocking my way. They want to kill me, rip my throat; they want to pull me down and rip my neck open. My clothes are red, my wounds are gushing blood. Their claws are scratching as they rip at me. They want me down where they can finish me, their jaws crunching my throat, ripping my jugular. Searing pain racks my body; I'm stumbling, ready to fall, knowing I'm going to die. . . .

Robert's tape worked well because the end looped nicely back to the beginning. There was no awkward sequence of events to repeat over and over. He didn't have to imagine himself on the ground having his throat crunched, then suddenly being on his feet again at the tape's beginning. Robert cleverly got the throat-crunching in as a future fantasy on the tape.

The recording completed, Robert sat in a comfortable chair with ear phones. He closed his eyes and listened to the gruesome scene for an hour. He worked hard to keep his mind focused. Whenever his thoughts started to drift away from the scene on the tape, he forced himself to concentrate again. If he had a neutralizing image or thought—for example batting the dog away or the hope that a passerby might help—he quickly shut it out.

Robert charted his anxiety level every five minutes. Below is the graph of his first flooding session. Notice that he had to go longer than an hour to reduce his anxiety to 50 percent of its highest point.

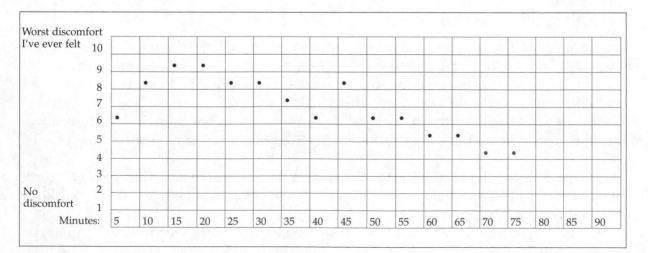

The following three sessions over the next three days were gradually easier. Robert's fifth and last session is recorded here. Notice that after brief initial anxiety, Robert experienced no discomfort for the remainder of the session.

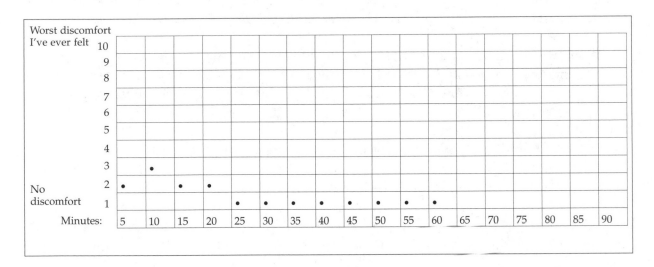

Salina's Cancer Obsession

Salina was just finishing a med school rotation in an oncology unit when a friend asked her about a dark mole on Salina's arm. She had it checked and was surprised when her internist seemed alarmed and ordered a biopsy. The mole turned out to be a melanoma, a fast-growing and dangerous kind of skin cancer.

The mole was surgically removed, and her surgeon declared the melanoma to be "small, contained, and completely gone." An examination of Salina's lymph nodes revealed no reason to suspect that the cancer had spread to any other part of her body.

Despite the excellent outcome, Salina remained in shock. She began to obsess about the melanoma spreading, about the pain of advanced metastatic cancer she'd witnessed in other patients in the hospital. She focused on sites of unusual tenderness or vague discomfort in her body. Her concentration and memory began to worsen as the obsession grew in power.

Out of desperation, and hoping for a quick fix, Salina recorded the worst of her worries on an old answering-machine tape. It wasn't hard to identify her most disturbing thoughts because they were rolling around inside her head continuously. She just kept the tape running and kept talking until she felt that the obsessional worries had been stated clearly.

Salina was careful to stay away from any thoughts that avoided or neutralized her fear. For example, at one point in the recording she described the doctor shaking his head and saying, "We may have a problem here." She realized that she had seized on the word *may* as indicating that things might still be all right. At another point, while imagining a test report showing full metastatic cancer, she said, "Here we go, here we go, here we go." On reflection, Salina recognized this phrase as avoidance because its repetition had the effect of switching off her mind for a second and helping her numb the fear.

Here's the script that Salina finally settled on:

The doctor's shaking his head, "We have a problem." I see the words "metastatic cancer" at the top of the report. I'm going to die. I know it. I imagine myself with tubes down my nose, weak and nauseous, the monitor beeping. Pain—pain everywhere as the cancer eats me, consuming and destroying my organs. I'm going to die, weak and helplessly slipping away. The report says it's growing, claiming me for early death. Everything is shutting down, pain and weakness overwhelming me.

What she had taped was so frightening that Salina waited a day before attempting her first flooding session. As she imagined, her reaction to the tape at first was extreme. In less than ten minutes, her anxiety had already reached 10 on the scale. Her heart was racing, she was sweating, and waves of fear swept through her body. Her shoulders and chest seemed clenched, as if she were preparing for a blow.

It was extraordinarily hard to stay in the scene. Her mind wanted to run, to fasten on anything that didn't relate to cancer. Images of her mother, the comfort of her childhood, rose up unbidden. She had to push them away to stay with the flooding.

She'd catch herself thinking, "This is just a tape; it isn't real," or "This is about somebody else," or "I'm still well." But these were neutralizing thoughts and she cut them off.

A graph of the progress of Salina's first session appears below.

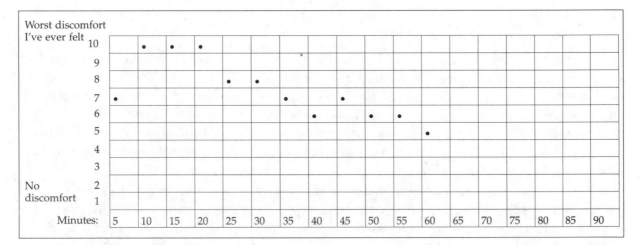

As with most flooding sessions, the anxiety quickly escalated to a plateau, then gradually diminished. Salina was exhausted, but impressed that she'd been able to lower her distress from a score of 10 to 5.

During the following day's session, Salina was discouraged because her anxiety again surged quite high—up to a 9. But the drop-off was steeper, and she was able to get down to a score of 2 after an hour. By the third session she achieved a breakthrough of zero anxiety toward the end of practice.

Salina waited three days before her next session. Her anxiety was elevated to a score of 6 near the beginning. But at the forty-minute point she reached 1 and stayed there. By session seven, Salina listened to the tape for almost the whole practice without anxiety. Her cancer concerns were also greatly reduced in real life.

Two months later, just prior to her checkup at the dermatologist, Salina had a resurgence of her obsession. Three sessions of flooding, plus a good report from the dermatologist, were sufficient to greatly diminish her worry.

Chapter 9

Coping with Panic

Panic disorder has been likened to standing on a trap door many stories in the air—never knowing when or if it will open. When a panic strikes, there's an overwhelming feeling of terror that you could die or completely lose control. Your body reacts with a host of stress symptoms that may include a racing heart, shortness of breath, a flushed feeling, weakness, dizziness, and feeling faint, as well as feelings of detachment, spaciness, and unreality. For many people struggling with panic disorder, the feelings of unreality and depersonalization are the most frightening of all because they interpret them as harbingers of insanity.

Panics often come unpredictably, and as a result, panic-prone individuals are burdened with anticipatory dread. They try to avoid any situation where they feel at all vulnerable to panic. This explains why untreated panic disorder often evolves into agoraphobia—the fear of leaving the confines of your safe place.

Fortunately, in recent years there have been important breakthroughs in the treatment of panic disorder by several research teams (Barlow & Craske 1989; Clark 1989). The result is a treatment program that includes four main components:

1. Education about the nature of panic—what causes it and how it can be controlled.

2. Breath control training—a simple technique to simultaneously relax your diaphragm and slow down your breath rate.

3. Cognitive restructuring to help you reinterpret frightening physical symptoms while learning to control catastrophic thinking.

4. Interoceptive desensitization—a technique that exposes you to your most feared physical sensations in a safe, controlled way, while teaching you how to cope.

Symptom Effectiveness

A variation of the treatment program described in this chapter was found by Barlow and Craske to free 87 percent of panic disorder subjects from symptoms of panic. This treatment response was maintained at a two-year follow-up. Many other researchers have reported 80 to 90 percent effectiveness with similar protocols.

Hackmann and his associates (1992) showed that panic disorder treatments can be effective with minimal therapist contact—his subjects used self-help manuals during a four-week program.

Time for Mastery

Some people can use this program to master panic symptoms in as little as six to eight weeks. However, if you are now struggling with significant problems of avoidance or agoraphobia, you will need additional treatment steps to expose you to situations where you fear having a panic attack.

Instructions

Step 1: Understanding Panic

Panic differs from most forms of anxiety in that the primary focus is not external dangers and events. Panic disorder centers on events going on inside your body—physical sensations that scare you and make you afraid of losing control.

If you are prone to panic, you may become hyperalert to physical symptoms that you associate with anxiety. You're vigilant for the first sign of a racing heart, shortness of breath, or feelings of detachment and unreality. You monitor your body for sensations of weakness, dizziness, flushing, or light-headedness. This vigilance has one purpose—to brace yourself for a rush of panic. By watching and worrying about bodily sensations, you are trying somehow to prepare for that awful moment when the panic swells, screaming that you are going to die or go insane.

The Panic Sequence

Ironically, it is this vigilance and fear of the body's symptoms that actually causes your panics. The diagram on the next page shows how it works.

Panic starts with an *event* that can be internal or external. External events include upcoming stresses and challenges, or situations where you've experienced panic before. Internal events are the physical symptoms you've begun to recognize as the precursors of panic.

The *event* triggers *worry*. Typical worry thoughts include:

- Oh no, the meeting room is crowded and stuffy. I could start feeling weird. I might lose control.

- I hope the plane doesn't sit too long on the runway. I'll feel trapped and freak out.

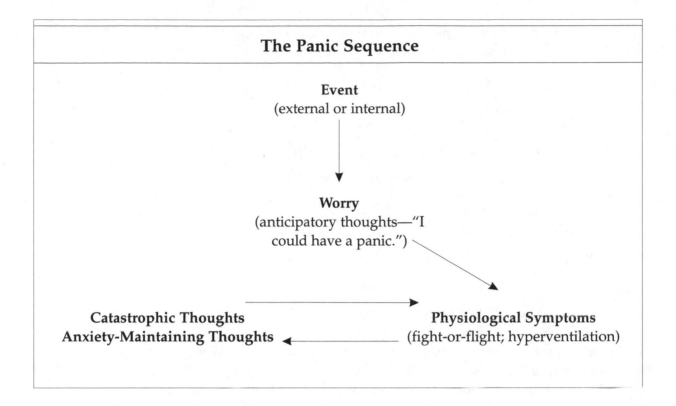

The Panic Sequence

Event
(external or internal)

↓

Worry
(anticipatory thoughts—"I could have a panic.")

Catastrophic Thoughts
Anxiety-Maintaining Thoughts ← → **Physiological Symptoms**
(fight-or-flight; hyperventilation)

- I hope I can sell the marketing plan to our new account. All eyes will be on me. I could get all spacy and panic in front of everybody.

- My heart's going kind of fast. What's that about? And I'm getting hot—am I losing it?

- Dizzy . . . Oh, God, here we go—another panic.

- I feel funny, unreal, out of it . . . not myself. . . . Stop it. . . . Oh no—it's happening again.

Your worry thoughts anticipate danger. They interpret external stressors and key bodily sensations as signals to get ready for catastrophe. This step in the panic sequence can be lightning fast. The worry thoughts often appear in a shorthand that's so compressed, you may not notice it. But while this step may be all but invisible, it sets the panic cycle into motion.

The next step is an intensification of *physiological symptoms* called the *fight-or-flight response*. Your body starts to get ready to confront danger. Heart rate increases to provide blood to the large muscles needed to run or do battle. As blood pools in your legs, they often feel weak and shaky—despite the fact that the extra blood makes them stronger than ever. Your rate of breathing increases to provide more oxygen for sudden, strenuous movement. But a common, harmless side effect is the feeling that you can't get enough air, accompanied by pain or tightness in the chest.

The blood supply to your brain decreases, producing feelings of dizziness, confusion, and unreality. The blood flow also diminishes to skin, fingers, and toes to reduce bleeding if you are injured. This makes your extremities cold while, simultaneously, you may feel flushed.

The fight-or-flight response triggers sweating, so your skin will be slippery and hard for a predator to grasp. It also slows digestion, often triggering cramping, nausea, and so on.

While fight-or-flight symptoms are harmless, they are quite noticeable and even at times dramatic. That's how you get to the next step in the panic sequence—you begin to have *catastrophic thoughts* about your fight-or-flight sensations, thought like:

- I'm going to have a heart attack.

- I'll stop breathing. . . . I'm going to suffocate.

- I'll pass out while I'm driving or on the street.

- I'll get too weak to walk. I'll fall down and humiliate myself.

- I'm going to lose my balance—I can't stand up.

- I'm too spacy to think or work.

These catastrophic thoughts signal your body, through the release of adrenaline, to intensify preparations for danger. All the fight-or-flight symptoms start cranking up. Your heart rate and respiration increase, you may start to hyperventilate, your legs feel shakier and weaker, you find yourself even dizzier, hotter, and more depersonalized.

Observing these symptoms, your catastrophic thinking becomes more dire:

- I'm going to die.

- I'm losing control—I'm going to run and jump and scream and go crazy.

- I'll never recover from this.

The cycle gathers momentum: Catastrophic thoughts trigger adrenaline and more fight-or-flight symptoms, which generate more catastrophic thoughts, spiraling upward until you pass the panic threshold.

This cycle, once triggered, does *not* have to continue. The key is changing how you interpret and react to normal stress symptoms. When you can recognize the hot flush, the dizziness, and the spacy, depersonalized feelings as harmless symptoms of fight-or-flight, you'll have taken a crucial step toward controlling panic.

Maintaining Thoughts

How long panic and the subsequent anxiety last is something you control. Maintaining thoughts can keep the fight-or-flight reaction going for hours.

Maintaining Thoughts Chart

Anxiety-Maintaining Thoughts	Medical Reality
• I'm falling apart. • This is going to go on till I can't function. • I won't be able to work. • I'll end up on the street. • I won't be able to take care of my kids. • My kids will be in a foster home. • I won't be able to think or concentrate. • My life is over.	A panic, once initiated, will last no more than two or three minutes if you stop all catastrophic and anxiety-maintaining thoughts. Because adrenaline from your fight-or-flight reaction takes three minutes or less to be metabolized, your panic must end unless new anxious thoughts cause the release of more adrenaline. This is the most important fact to remember about panic—it can't last more than three minutes if you stop scaring yourself with anxious thoughts. To control your panic, you will learn to control your thoughts.

What Your Symptoms Mean

The chart on the next page provides medical explanations for the symptoms of panic. Put an asterisk by the symptoms that most disturb you. On a file card that you can carry with you, write the medical explanation for each symptom you have marked.

Symptom Explanation Chart		
Physical Symptoms	**Catastrophic Thought**	**Medical Reality**
Increased heart rate; palpitations	"I'll have a heart attack."	According to panic specialist Dr. Claire Weekes, a healthy heart can pump 200 beats per minute for days, even weeks, without damage. Your heart was made to handle stress. An hour of panic is nothing compared to what the heart was designed to deal with.
Feeling faint and light-headed	"I'll pass out while driving or walking."	The light-headed feeling is caused by reduced blood and oxygen supply to the brain, but it almost never results in fainting. Panic triggers higher blood pressure, quite the opposite of low blood pressure problems associated with fainting.
Feeling you can't get your breath; pain or pressure in your chest	"I'll stop breathing; here comes a heart attack."	Fight-or-flight causes chest and abdominal muscles to tighten. This can create pressure and muscular pain in your chest, as well as reduced lung capacity. To compensate, you may start to hyperventilate, which just makes the feeling worse. No one has ever stopped breathing from panic. No matter how uncomfortable the feeling, you will always get enough air.
Feeling dizzy	"I'll fall if I stand up."	The dizzy feeling is caused by hyper-ventilation and reduced blood and oxygen flow to the brain—a brief and harmless reaction. It's very rare, even during the worst panic, for anyone to lose balance.
"Jelly legs"—weak, shaky feeling in legs	"I'm too weak to walk; I'll fall down."	The fight-or-flight reaction causes temporary dilation of the blood vessels in your legs, allowing blood to accumulate in the large muscles. Your legs are as strong and able to carry you as ever.
Hot flush	"Here comes the panic."	The hot flush comes from increased oxygen and brief changes in your circulatory system. They're harmless and will *not* cause panic unless you interpret the symptom as a cause for alarm.
Feeling spacy, unreal, depersonalized	"I'm going crazy; I'm losing hold of myself; I won't make it back this time."	These, too, are harmless fight-or-flight reactions associated with hyperventilation and reduced blood and oxygen flow to the brain. They are temporary and *never* result in insanity or losing your control of your actions. There are *no* reported incidents of schizophrenia, paralysis, or "running amuck" following a panic attack.

Step 2: Breath Control Training

This exercise, which has been adapted from Nick Masi's audiocassette, *Breath of Life* (1993), is designed specifically for individuals with panic disorder. When most people feel panic, they have a tendency to gasp, take in a breath, and hold onto it. Then they take short, shallow breaths that fail to empty their lungs. This creates a sensation of fullness and a feeling that you can't get enough air. The feeling that you're not getting enough air is an illusion, a simple consequence of not emptying your lungs. Even though you are, in fact, getting plenty of air, your breath comes faster and faster. Eventually, you may cross the threshold into hyperventilation, which will likely trigger a panic attack. Here are the five simple steps of breath control training:

A. **Exhale first.** At the first sign of nervousness or panic, at the first worry thought about a physical symptom, completely empty your lungs. It's important that you exhale first so that you feel like there's plenty of room to take a full, deep breath.

B. **Inhale and exhale through your nose.** Inhaling through your nose will automatically slow down your breathing and prevent hyperventilation.

C. **Breathe deeply into your abdomen.** Put one hand on your stomach, the other on your chest. Breathe so that the hand on your stomach moves, while the one on your chest is nearly still. By directing the breath deep into your abdomen you stretch your diaphragm and relax tight muscles that make it seem hard to breathe.

D. **Count while you breathe.** Exhale first, and then breathe in through your nose, counting, "One . . . two . . . three." Pause a second, then breathe out through your mouth, counting, "One . . . two . . . three . . . four." The counting protects you from rapid, panic breathing. Make certain that your exhalation is always one beat longer than your inhalation. This will ensure that you empty your lungs between breaths.

E. **Slow your breathing by one beat.** Breathe in and count, "One . . . two . . . three . . . four"; pause and breathe out, counting, "One . . . two . . . three . . . four . . . five." As always, you breathe out one beat longer than you breathe in.

Breath control training is an extraordinarily effective way to slow your breathing and prevent the hyperventilation so often associated with panic. If you can slow your breathing at the first sign of anxiety, you can very often protect yourself from the worst of the fight-or-flight symptoms.

The key is practice. Your first efforts at breath control training should occur only in safe and relaxing environments. Don't try at the beginning to use this technique when you're panicked, or even anxious. Get comfortable and competent at slowing your breaths where you won't be disturbed. After several weeks of daily practice the technique will become "overlearned." When you can easily initiate deep breaths while counting, begin using breath control in situations where you are mildly nervous. Then try breath control as you approach situations where you are worried about panic or when you first notice disturbing physical symptoms.

Don't try breath control training during a full-blown panic yet. Wait until you've mastered interoceptive desensitization, a technique you will learn later in this chapter. That will give you the practice you need so that you can slow your breathing even during the most disturbing anxiety symptoms.

Step 3: Cognitive Restructuring

Human beings are constantly trying to make sense of their experience. They try to label events and predict what those events will mean for the future. When you are anxious and on guard to the possibility of a panic, you tend to make two crucial errors of thinking. The first is *overestimation*—exaggerating the odds that a negative event is likely to occur. The second is *catastrophizing*—assuming events will be far more painful and unmanageable than you can endure.

Overestimation and catastrophizing are likely contributors to your anxiety. But there's a way to overcome these patterns of thinking while you diminish your anxiety in the process. It involves exploring hard evidence about your fears, as well as identifying alternative coping strategies. The key is a special kind of thought record called the Probability Form. A blank Probability Form appears on the next page. Make fifty copies of the form and use it to respond to catastrophic or maintaining thoughts whenever they occur.

Here's how to use the Probability Form. In the first column write down the event that's triggering anxiety. Remember, it can be external (you're meeting friends at a theater) or internal (you're feeling dizzy and spacy). Now, under Automatic Thoughts, write your interpretations and beliefs about the event. Try to include your worst and most catastrophic thoughts.

As you focus on your automatic thoughts, you need to rate (1) the percent probability that what you fear will come true and (2) the intensity of your anxiety. A probability rating of 100 percent means there's no possibility the catastrophe *won't* happen. Note that many probabilities are less than 1 percent (1 in 100 chances of occurring) and can be expressed as a decimal (1 in 200 equals .5 percent; 1 in 1,000 equals .1 percent; 1 in 100,000 equals .001 percent). Anxiety is rated on a 0–100 scale, where 100 is the worst anxiety you've ever experienced.

These ratings of probability and anxiety are very important because you can watch them change. After you fill in the Evidence and Coping Alternatives columns, you may see significant reductions in your scores.

It's time now to examine your automatic thoughts. Under Evidence, write down any facts or experiences that either support or contradict your automatic thoughts. Ask yourself these key questions:

1. Out of all the times you've done or felt this in the past, how many times did the catastrophe occur?

2. What has *usually* happened during similar circumstances in the past?

3. Is there anything in your past that leads you to expect a better outcome than you fear?

4. What are the objective (medical) facts? It's important to list here the relevant medical realities you've read in this chapter.

5. How long is this experience likely to last? Can you cope with it for that period?

Probability Form

Event (External or Internal)	Automatic Thoughts	Rate % Probability (0–100%) Anxiety (0–100)	Evidence	Coping Alternatives	Re-Rate % Probability (0–100%) Anxiety (0–100)

After you've listed all the evidence you can think of, move on to Coping Alternatives. This is your action plan if the worst case should happen—how you'd cope with the crisis. Even though it's uncomfortable, it helps to face what you fear most. Nearly every outcome, no matter how difficult, can be gotten through if you have a plan to cope. Include

1. Any relaxation or breathing skills that might be helpful.

2. Any resources you have for coping (friends, family, financial resources, problem-solving skills).

3. Successful coping strategies you've used in the past.

4. Strategies others might use in this situation.

Be sure to take your time with the coping column. Brainstorm until you've developed at least three believable coping alternatives. If an alternative doesn't seem realistic *for you*, leave it out. But if there's a chance it might work, include it and evaluate the outcome later.

The last step in completing your Probability Form is to re-rate percent probability and anxiety. Most people discover that the probability of catastrophe seems lower after weighing the evidence and developing a coping plan. They also report reduction in anxiety intensity.

Practicing with Probabilities

Use your Probability Form whenever you feel anxious. Try to fill in the columns as soon after the event as possible (the evening following an anxiety experience at the very latest).

Even events that are only physical sensations require a Probability Form. That's because catastrophic interpretation of bodily sensations is the prime cause for panic. If you use the form consistently over the course of three to four weeks, you'll find new confidence in your ability to handle fear.

Example.

Sandra, a thirty-two-year-old single mother, had been experiencing panic attacks for about three months. She was terrified of the physical symptoms, but also worried about losing her ability to function as a mother and a hard-working investment analyst. On the next two pages is the probability form Sandra completed on her first day of record keeping.

Sandra's Probability Form

Event (External or Internal)	Automatic Thoughts	Rate % Probability (0–100%) Anxiety (0–100)	Evidence	Coping Alternatives	Re-Rate % Probability (0–100%) Anxiety (0–100)
Drank coffee, feel jittery.	I'm going to slide into a panic.	80% 80	I've drunk coffee thousands of times and only on two occasions had a panic. The odds are pretty low, particularly if I start coping right away.	I can do my breath control and shut off all scary thoughts. It'll be over in three minutes.	30% 35
Anxious feelings getting ready for work.	I'm ruining my reputation at work. I may lose my job if I stay like this.	65% 70	I felt anxious a lot at work over the past few months, but I always get things done. My performance evaluation was good in spite of being anxious.	If I get negative feedback, I'll find out exactly what I need to change in my behavior and make a plan. If I lose my job, I'll look for something part-time, something less stressful. My dad would help with money if I was earning less. I could also work at home and have more time for my son.	35% 15
"Jelly legs"	I'm going to fall and humiliate myself.	85% 90	I've felt this way at least fifty times and I've never fallen. It's just blood pooling in my muscles from fight or flight—no real weakness.	If I fell, I'd have someone help me to a place I could sit till the feeling passed. It would be embarrassing, but I'd get over it.	20% 35

Continued on the following page

Sandra's Probability Form—Continued

Heart racing/anxious	I can't stand this. I might have a heart attack.	90% 100	I *can* stand my heart beating; my heart beats at least this hard when I exercise. The doctor says I have a healthy heart. A healthy heart can go 200 beats a minute for weeks. Mine's at 140 bpm—and it's been less than five minutes. My heart's built to handle this.	If I had a heart problem, I'd get treatment, change my diet, get more exercise and try to really take care of myself. I'd cope because I had to.	45% 55
Spacy, unreal feeling while talking to my boss.	I can't think, I'm not myself. This is a sign that I'm losing my mind and I'll be spacy all the time.	80% 95	The spacy feeling usually passes after I relax. I've felt this way dozens of times. It always passes with no lasting effects. It's just the fight-or-flight reaction—a temporary reduction in blood flow to my head.	If I lost my ability to concentrate and felt out of it, I'd be very sad. But I'd try to get an undemanding job. Even if I was spacy, I'd still love my son and be a mom to him.	45% 60
Need to call ex-husband regarding late child-support payment.	I won't be able to deal with him. I'll be upset by his anger. I might feel panicky.	50% 60	Usually when I call to remind him he's cold and cutting, but not raging. I'm okay when he's cold. He's just his usual jerk self.	I'll remind myself that it's his problem, nothing really bad is happening. He always pays even if he's late. I'll use controlled breathing and just repeat my request over and over.	5% 20
Mowed the lawn after dinner, feel hot.	Oh no, I might panic. This is going to ruin my night.	90% 90	I'm hot from exercising, not anxiety. I've worked hard and I'm perspiring. From past experience, this feeling can be over very soon—I can still enjoy my evening.	I'll do controlled breathing, cut the fear thoughts, and wait it out for a few minutes.	15% 20

Step 4: Interoceptive Desensitization

Interoceptive desensitization is among the most effective—and challenging—components of the treatment program for panic disorder. What you're about to do is re-create, in a safe way, bodily sensations similar to those you associate with panic. You can learn to experience these sensations as something uncomfortable, but not frightening. Dizziness, rapid heart beat, even feelings of unreality can become no more than annoying effects of fight-or-flight. And when these feelings are no longer associated with panic, you'll find yourself less vigilant toward and less focused on the sensations inside your body.

Desensitizing to frightening bodily sensations is accomplished in three stages. In stage 1 you briefly expose yourself to ten specific sensations and then rate your reactions. Most of the following exposure exercises were developed and tested by Michelle Craske and David Barlow (1993). They induce feelings similar to those many people report prior to or during a panic.

1. Shaking your head from side to side

2. Lowering your head between your legs, then lifting it

3. Running in place (Check with your doctor first)

4. Running in place with a heavy jacket

5. Holding your breath

6. Tensing the major muscles—particularly in your abdomen

7. Spinning while you sit in a swivel chair (not to be done standing up)

8. Very rapid breathing

9. Breathing through a single, narrow straw

10. Staring at yourself in a mirror

As you review this list, you can probably already tell that some of these sensations will be quite uncomfortable. But it is precisely the feelings you most fear that you must desensitize in order to recover from panic disorder. If exposing yourself to these interoceptive (physically arousing) experiences feels too frightening to do alone, enlist a support person to be present throughout the exercise. Later you can discontinue support as you get more comfortable with the sensations.

When you expose yourself to each of the ten sensations, you'll need to keep records to identify which ones create the most anxiety and have the greatest similarity to your panic feelings. Fill in the Interoceptive Assessment Chart on page 104 as you sequentially expose yourself to each interoceptive experience.

Interoceptive Assessment Chart			
Exercise	**Duration**	**Anxiety (0-100)**	**Similarity to Panic Sensations (0-100%)**
1. Shaking head from side to side	30 seconds		
2. Lowering your head between your legs, then lifting it (Keep repeating)	30 seconds		
3. Running in place	60 seconds		
4. Running in place with a heavy jacket	60 seconds		
5. Holding your breath	30 seconds (or as long as you can)		
6. Tensing the major muscles—particularly in your abdomen	60 seconds (or as long as you can)		
7. Spinning while you sit in a swivel chair	60 seconds		
8. Very rapid breathing	Up to 60 seconds		
9. Breathing through a single narrow straw	120 seconds		
10. Staring at yourself in a mirror	90 seconds		

When rating your anxiety intensity, the scale ranges from 0 to 100, where 100 is the worst anxiety you've ever felt. The column where you rate each exercise's similarity to panic sensations is very important. The range is from 0 percent similarity to 100 percent—absolutely identical feelings.

Stage 2 of interoceptive desensitization involves making a hierarchy of frightening sensations from the Assessment Chart. Here's what you do: Put a check by each exercise that you rated 40 percent or above in similarity to actual panic sensations. Now, on the Interoceptive Hierarchy/Anxiety Intensity Chart, rank the *checked* exercises from the least to the greatest anxiety-intensity rating. Fill in the anxiety rating from your first exposure under Trial 1.

Interoceptive Hierarchy/Anxiety-Intensity Chart								
Exercise	**Trial 1**	**Trial 2**	**Trial 3**	**Trial 4**	**Trial 5**	**Trial 6**	**Trial 7**	**Trial 8**
1.								
2.								
3.								
4.								
5.								
6.								
7.								
8.								
9.								
10.								

Example

Sandra, the single mother described earlier, filled in the following interoceptive assessment.

Sandra's Interoceptive Assessment Chart			
Exercise	**Duration**	**Anxiety (0-100)**	**Similarity to Panic Sensations (0-100%)**
1. Shaking head from side to side	30 seconds	10	20%
2. Lowering your head between your legs, then lifting it (Keep repeating)	30 seconds	0	0%
3. Running in place	60 seconds	60	80%
4. Running in place with a heavy jacket	60 seconds	70	95%
5. Holding your breath	30 seconds (or as long as you can)	45	50%
6. Tensing the major muscles—particularly in your abdomen	60 seconds (or as long as you can)	15	10%
7. Spinning while you sit in a swivel chair	60 seconds	25	30%
8. Very rapid breathing	Up to 60 seconds	80	95%
9. Breathing through a single narrow straw	120 seconds	50	60%
10. Staring at yourself in a mirror	90 seconds	40	45%

The assessment was scary for Sandra. To help her get through, she asked her best friend to be present during the exercises. It took her two sessions to finish, but she found the results interesting. Exercises that created dizzy or light-headed sensations felt dissimilar to actual panic feelings and didn't much bother her. But exercises that made her heart race or overheated her were both anxiety evoking and very similar to panic. Rapid breathing induced sensations the most similar to her panic feelings—and the most frightening of all the sensations. Sandra's hierarchy chart appears on the next page.

Sandra was careful to include in her hierarchy only items rated 40 percent or greater in similarity to actual panic feelings. They were then ranked from the exercise with the lowest anxiety intensity (stare in the mirror: 40) to the highest (rapid breathing: 80).

Once you've developed your hierarchy, it's time to begin stage 3—the actual desensitization process. Start with the item lowest in anxiety on your hierarchy chart. If you need to have a support person present during initial exposure, that's fine. Here's the actual desensitization sequence:

1. Begin the exercise and note the point where you first experience uncomfortable sensations. Stick with the exercise at least thirty seconds *after* the onset of uncomfortable sensations—the longer the better.

2. As soon as you stop the exercise, rate your anxiety in the box for each exposure trial (on your Interoceptive Hierarchy Chart).

3. Immediately following each exercise, begin controlled breathing.

4. Following each exercise, remind yourself of the medical realities relevant to the bodily sensations you're experiencing. For example, if you feel light-headed or dizzy after rapid breathing, remind yourself that this is a temporary and harmless sensation caused by reduced oxygen to the brain. Or, if you have a rapid heart rate after running in place, you could remind yourself that a healthy heart can beat 200 times a minute for weeks without damage, and it's certainly built to handle this little bit of exercise.

5. Continue trials of desensitization with each exercise until your anxiety rating is no more than 25.

Sandra's Interoceptive Hierarchy/Anxiety-Intensity Chart								
Exercise	**Trial 1**	**Trial 2**	**Trial 3**	**Trial 4**	**Trial 5**	**Trial 6**	**Trial 7**	**Trial 8**
1. Stare in the mirror	40							
2. Holding breath	45							
3. Breathing through straw	50							
4. Running in place	60							
5. Running with jacket	70							
6. Rapid breathing	80							
7.								
8.								
9.								
10.								

Example

Sandra began desensitization with her best friend present. She started with the exercise of staring in the mirror. It took fifty seconds to set off some of her familiar feelings of unreality, and she stuck with the exercise for another minute. By trial 3, Sandra's anxiety intensity was down to 20. Now she needed to face the feeling alone. Trial 4 (alone) saw her anxiety jump to 40 again, but trial 5 found it quickly reduced to 20.

After each trial, Sandra immediately initiated breath control. She reminded herself that feelings of unreality were harmless fight-or-flight reactions triggered by reduced oxygen to the brain.

Sandra's next exercise, holding her breath, seemed easier than she had expected. After one trial in the presence of her friend, she continued alone till her anxiety dipped below 25. Breath control helped her relax quickly after each trial. She reminded herself that the out-of-breath feeling could easily be fixed when she inhaled deeply.

Sandra's greatest challenge during interoceptive desensitization was rapid breathing. The spacy, unreal feelings deeply frightened her. On the second trial, even with her friend holding her hand, her anxiety intensity was 90. It took eight trials before it went down to 25, then she continued the exercise alone for four more trials. She learned to remind herself during the exercise that her scary feelings were just brief effects from hyperventilation and the fight-or-flight response. With a few minutes of controlled breathing they'd be over.

As Sandra developed more trust in her ability to calm herself after rapid breathing, the feelings became far less scary. Instead of fearing that she might lose control, she saw hyperventilation as something uncomfortable but manageable.

During the exercises, Sandra found that her greatest problem was a tendency to catastrophize. She was aware of saying to herself, "I can't stand this," and, "This is too much." But she'd learned from her Probability Form to talk back to these thoughts. During trials she now said to herself, "I can stand anything for a few minutes. It can't really harm me."

Interoceptive Desensitization in Natural Settings

When you've worked through your hierarchy to the point where each exercise triggers an anxiety-intensity rating of no more than 25, you can begin desensitization in real-life settings. With medical clearance, you can begin exposure to activities and experiences you've avoided because you feared a panic. Make a list of these activities and arrange them on a Hierarchy/Anxiety-Intensity chart. Rank them from least anxiety-evoking to most.

Sandra's desensitization hierarchy for natural settings appears on the following page.

Sandra immediately began desensitization to item 1 (a man at work asked her to lunch), and employed both controlled breathing and helpful items from her Probability Form to cope. Since her main fear in the restaurant was feeling spacy and unreal, Sandra reminded herself that it was a harmless feeling and wouldn't be noticed by her companion. Using similar strategies, Sandra worked through the necessary trials for each of her items. When an item fell below 25 on her anxiety scale, she tackled the next one.

As Sandra reached the end of her hierarchy, she felt far less afraid of panic. In part it was because she'd now gone several weeks without having a panic attack. But it was also because she no longer watched for and feared sensations she'd always associated with panic. Now her heart could beat fast without scaring her. Now she could feel hot or spacy without the clutching anxiety that a panic was near.

Anxiety-Intensity Chart								
Exercise	**Trial 1**	**Trial 2**	**Trial 3**	**Trial 4**	**Trial 5**	**Trial 6**	**Trial 7**	**Trial 8**
1. Going to restaurants	35	30	20					
2. Drinking coffee	50	30	35	25				
3. Brisk one-mile walk on a cool day	55	40	15					
4. Brisk one-mile walk on a hot day (while wearing jacket)	65	60	50	35	25			
5. Running uphill to my house	80	55	25	30	20			

Special Considerations

1. If you have difficulty counting during breath control exercises, you can make a tape to help you learn the proper pacing.

   To make a twelve-breaths-per-minute tape:
   a) Say the word "in" for two seconds.
   b) Say the word "out" for two seconds.
   c) Pause one second.
   d) Continue repeating "in" for two seconds and "out" for two seconds, followed by a one-second pause.
   e) The tape should last about five minutes.

   To make an eight-breaths-per-minute tape, do everything the same except say "in" and "out" for three seconds each.

2. If you have difficulty desensitizing and lowering anxiety during interoceptive exposure, it may be because you have catastrophic thoughts that haven't been addressed. As you begin an exposure exercise, monitor your thoughts about the bodily sensations that come up. What are you telling yourself? What terrible thing do you fear might happen? What is the worst possible outcome?

Once you've identified one or more catastrophic beliefs, complete a Probability Form on those thoughts. Then, from the Evidence and Coping Alternatives columns, choose some realistic responses that you can use during exposure.

Chapter 10

Coping Imagery

Coping imagery (Freeman et al. 1990) is a blend of stress inoculation (chapter 11) and covert modeling (chapter 18). It combines the best features of both to enhance performance in problematic situations while simultaneously lowering your anxiety. You begin by identifying the detailed sequence of events that make up a problem situation—everything you do from beginning to end in the situation. Then you note which elements of the sequence are the most anxiety evoking. Finally, you rehearse performing the entire sequence while using specific relaxation techniques and coping thoughts to lower anxiety at crucial junctures in the sequence.

Coping imagery helps you

- see yourself handling an anxiety-arousing situation successfully, perhaps one you have long avoided.

- prepare relaxation and cognitive coping strategies specifically tailored for this situation.

- rehearse and refine your coping strategies at crucial anxiety-arousing points as the situation unfolds. This builds your confidence that you can reduce your anxiety response *in vivo* (in real life).

- prepare for each step in the sequence that you will soon perform in real life.

Coping imagery is outlined here in six simple steps that can be mastered with regular practice:

1. Learning to relax.

2. Writing the sequence of events that make up a problematic situation.

3. Identifying the stress points in the sequence.

4. Planning specific coping strategies for each stress point.

5. Rehearsing the sequence in your mind using newly developed coping strategies.

6. Applying coping imagery to real-life events.

Symptom Effectiveness

Coping imagery is most effective at reducing anxiety and avoidance symptoms associated with an existing problematic situation. It can be used to reduce avoidance behavior due to phobias and test anxiety, and to increase assertiveness. Coping imagery can also be helpful in reducing procrastination, resentment, and depression that often result when you don't cope successfully with specific anxiety-provoking situations.

Coping imagery relies on your ability to conceive clear and detailed images. If it is difficult for you to achieve clear visual images, the alternative is to create a detailed image using auditory or physical impressions. If either approach enables you to clearly imagine the scene, this technique may be used successfully.

Time for Mastery

You may get results after as few as six to eight fifteen-minute sessions.

Instructions

Step 1: Learn to Relax.

The relaxation skills that you will need to master—progressive relaxation, relaxation without tension, and cue-controlled relaxation—can be found in chapter 5, "Relaxation." Don't proceed past step 4 until you have learned and practiced each of these procedures. We suggest that you "overlearn" cue-controlled relaxation to the point that you can do it automatically. Eventually, you should be able to attain deep muscle relaxation in two minutes or less. The more you practice, the quicker and deeper your relaxation will be.

Step 2: Write a Narrative.

Even while learning your relaxation skills, you can still take additional steps to prepare for using coping imagery. Right now, choose a real-life situation that makes you anxious. Something you want or need to do, but tend also to avoid or struggle with. It can be anything from job interviews to visiting your critical in-laws, from making a date to explaining your needs to an angry friend.

One of the first steps towards mobilizing yourself to cope with a difficult situation is to understand how and why it makes you anxious. What particular aspects of the situation are most difficult for you to deal with? What are your worst fears about what might happen? At which points do you feel most out of control of your emotions? The answers to these questions are not always clear, particularly if you are facing a complex situation. However, the more you understand about the situation you are facing, the easier it will be to cope.

Begin by writing out the sequence of events that make up the problematic situation. Write it in the form of a narrative, using as much detail as possible. The sequence should start with your anticipation of the situation, then move on to describe the opening of the scene, and continue until the situation is resolved. The most important details to include are those aspects of the situation that make you anxious. Also include how you are specifically affected by the anxiety: What are your physical as well as your emotional responses? How and why are these responses intensified by the scene?

Step 3: Identify the Stress Points.

You can use your narrative to identify the particular parts of the sequence that are acutely stressful to you. An effective way to do this is through visualization. Tape-record yourself reading the narrative slowly. Later, when you play it back, you can sit in a relaxed state, eyes closed, with all of your attention focused on building the scene in your mind. If it isn't possible to tape yourself, you might have a friend slowly read the sequence to you while you visualize the scene.

The object is to experience the scene with as much vividness and detail as possible. Where are you? Who is present there? Is it warm? Cool? What sounds can you hear in the distance? What smells surround you? Engage as many senses as you can to create the scene in your mind. Continue through the sequence. Pay close attention to the physical and emotional reactions that you experience. Tense muscles with increased heart rate and quickened respiration are some common signs of anxiety.

When you come to a segment of the sequence where you experience elevated anxiety, make a mental note of it. After you are finished, you should mark each of these points with an asterisk on your narrative. The places you marked with an asterisk are *stress points*. Later, as you visualize the sequence, these will be points where you pause to do special relaxation and coping exercises.

Example

Dave was asked by his supervisor to give a presentation before a small group in his firm. Though he felt confident in his interactions with individuals, the thought of standing before a group was frightening. In order to prepare for the presentation, Dave wrote out the sequence of events as he imagined it would go.

> *I'm on my way to the presentation, hoping it goes well but imagining embarrassing faux pas and mistakes.* In my mind, I picture people whispering in the audience during my presentation. I arrive in the parking lot and experience another wave of worry as I see the building where the presentation will take place.* I'm going through the front door, greeting the receptionist. As I wait for the elevator, I check my briefcase to see if all the papers are in order. I have another wave of anxiety as I look at the file folder containing the outline of my presentation.* I ride the elevator up to the third floor, and begin walking towards the room. I recognize several people in the hall; I'm trying not to appear nervous as I greet them. Now I'm standing outside the meeting*

room, saying "Hello," as people arrive. I'm setting up the mike, adjusting the tabletop podium. Most of the people have arrived now and are looking at me expectantly.* I glance down at my outline and have a wave of concern about the coherence and usefulness of the material.* I clear my throat, which quiets the room substantially, and I greet them: "Glad you could make it." *I'm aware of the sound of my voice as everyone becomes silent. All eyes are on me. *I begin with my introduction, trying to stay focused on what I'm saying. At one point during the presentation, I lose my place in the outline and have to stop for a moment to reorient myself. The silence is heavy in the room, and I imagine that people are doubting my competence.* My face feels flushed, and I worry that my nervousness is apparent. I continue my presentation, aware of people shifting in their chairs, and mumbling in the back of the room. As I continue, I begin to feel anxious about the question-and-answer period that grows closer as I near the end of my presentation.* I wrap it up as best I can, and invite everyone's feedback.

Possible Conclusion 1: I have just opened the floor for comments or questions, but people seem hesitant to respond. *There is a long silence, during which I feel at a loss for what to say next. Someone finally offers feedback by questioning the usefulness of the information. I feel embarrassed and hurt but struggle not to respond defensively.* The next question is about something only mildly related to the subject matter, and I am unable to answer it. There is another long silence before I finally thank the group and begin to put my papers away. I am eager to get back to my car and hope that I can put the whole experience behind me.

Possible Conclusion 2: People seem pleased with the presentation, and several people offer feedback. Their questions are pertinent, allowing me to explain aspects that needed clarification. I feel very relieved that it's over and that I made it through successfully. I congratulate myself for managing my fear and anxiety.

In this example, Dave chose to use two possible endings, one negative and one positive. This format allowed him to prepare for either possibility so he could minimize surprises. After he completed the narrative, he taped himself reading the sequence out loud. He then used the tape to visualize the situation from beginning to end. He placed an asterisk by each point in the visualization that elevated his anxiety.

Step 4: Plan Coping Strategies.

Most anxiety-provoking situations are made up of several combined stresses. In Dave's case, the pressure of an audience, Dave's own doubts about the content of his presentation, and his discomfort with appearing uneasy and scared were all stresses that contributed to his anxiety.

One of the main goals in writing out a narrative and identifying the stress points is to demystify the sources of anxiety. If you can see the situation as a combination of smaller stresses, your anxiety will be much easier to understand and manage.

Anxiety reactions have two basic components: a physiological stress response, and thoughts that interpret a situation as dangerous. Coping imagery, therefore, must include a method for physical relaxation, as well as a set of statements that are calming and reassuring to you.

Relaxation

As you visualize the sequence, you will use cue-controlled relaxation with deep breathing at each stress point.

Cognitive Coping Statements

You will also need to develop cognitive coping statements for each stress point in your sequence. Effective coping statements remind you that you have the ability to handle the situation and may offer specific strategies to deal with problems. Some examples of effective statements are: "There's no need to panic. . . . I can get through this. . . . It doesn't need to be perfect—my best is good enough"; "It'll be over in a few minutes"; "I have a plan if there's a problem"; "I know how to do this." You'll find that each stress point carries its own set of worries. Try to find statements for each that really address and relieve the worry in that moment.

The following are some important functions that cognitive coping statements can serve:

- Emphasize that you have a plan to cope, and specify what the plan is in that situation.

- Reassure that there's no need to panic, that you have the skills to cope with the situation.

- Remind yourself just to relax away stress.

- Assert that a catastrophic fear isn't true, and that the worst that could happen is _____.

- Lower unreasonably high expectations—i.e, "I'll get through this; it doesn't have to be great."

- Instruct yourself to stop the crazy, catastrophic thoughts and get down to meeting the challenge.

Here are a few examples of coping statements that Dave developed for the stress points in his narrative:

- *I'm . . . imagining embarrassing faux pas and mistakes.*
  "Relax, breathe deeply. It's OK to make some mistakes. I will be satisfied with my best effort."

- *. . . another wave of worry as I see the building where the presentation will take place.*
  "I can do this. It's OK to feel scared. Just keep breathing."

- *The silence is heavy in the room, and I imagine that people are doubting my competence.*
  "Take a deep breath, relax. I know my stuff. I'll just pick up where I left off."

- *I begin to feel anxious about the question-and-answer period that grows closer . . .*
  "Relax. The hard part is over. I made it this far, just hang in there until the end."

- *I feel embarrassed and hurt but struggle not to respond defensively.*
  "My best is good enough. I can accept criticism. I know I'm OK."

See chapter 11, "Stress Inoculation," for more examples of coping statements and how to develop them.

Re-record your narrative so that it now includes instruction for cue-controlled relaxation and specific coping thoughts at each stress point. On the tape, give yourself time at the stress points to relax and let your coping thoughts sink in.

Step 5: Rehearse Your Sequence.

Now it's time to listen to your taped narrative while using your coping strategies.

The goal of this step is to keep practicing the sequence until your anxiety is below 4 on a 10-point scale. The scale should range from 0, no anxiety at all, to 10, the highest level of anxiety you've ever experienced. It's not necessary to bring your anxiety level down to 0, but you should reduce it. Keep in mind that some stress points in your narrative may be more difficult to cope with than others. The key word here is *practice*. As you hone your coping skills and get more familiar with the procedure, your coping strategies will become more and more effective.

If after a few repetitions you don't feel any reduction in anxiety, you may need to revise your coping strategy:

A. **Practice more deep breathing.** Relaxation is critical to the effectiveness of your coping efforts. Make sure that the cue-controlled relaxation is, in fact, helping you to relax. If not, you may need to practice it alone for a period of time.

B. **Review coping statements.** Sometimes it's hard to pinpoint what the real source of anxiety is at each stress point. It's possible that some of your coping statements are not addressing the main elements that are making you anxious. Practicing the sequence will help you identify which statements need to be rewritten, and what needs to be added to make them more effective.

Step 6: Cope in Real Life.

The final step in mastering coping imagery is applying it to real-life situations. When you can visualize the entire sequence while successfully reducing your level of anxiety at each stress point, you are ready to approach the situation *in vivo*. Of course, you will have less control over your environment in real situations than you had during your visualizations, but you need not feel out of control. One of the most important skills you've learned from this technique is how to stay in control of your emotional and physical reactions. Feelings and tension that used to trigger fear can now be seen as cues to relax and encourage yourself.

If possible, use your new coping strategies with a mildly to moderately stressful situation at first. Because real-life situations are usually more difficult to cope with than visualizations, one of your priorities should be to avoid feeling overwhelmed. Allow yourself time for practice, and expect a few setbacks before your coping strategies feel totally comfortable and effective.

As with each of the prior steps in this technique, practice is the key to success. As you become more adept at using coping imagery, it may become a significant resource for you in dealing with many different sources of stress.

Example

For as long as Susan can remember, she has dreaded dentist visits. The fear that she experiences every time she is due for an appointment often results in her avoiding needed dental work for months. The longer she avoids seeing the dentist, the more she dreads it, and the harder it becomes to face the inevitable. In an attempt to break that downward spiral, she set out to overcome some of her fear about visiting the dentist. While she was learning cue-controlled relaxation, she wrote a narrative describing what she expected to happen when she finally got there.

When Susan had finished writing her narrative, she taped herself reading it slowly. Choosing a moment when she had plenty of time and no distractions, she used the tape to visualize the entire sequence. She made note in her mind of each part of the narrative that elevated her anxiety. When she had located all of the stress points, she put an asterisk next to each one. Here is her narrative:

> *I'm in my car, on the way to the dentist. My teeth are freshly brushed and flossed. My tongue feels around for the swollen parts of my gums that were bleeding slightly when I brushed this morning. I think about the weeks I neglected to floss and imagine the dentist will know immediately how irresponsible I've been.* I know that whatever problems I have are worse now that I'm two months late for an appointment. I scold myself for being the kind of person who cannot handle basic adult responsibilities. As I near the office building, I become irritable with the traffic around me* and feel my stress level start to increase. As I park the car and approach the building, *I am already rehearsing excuses for the dentist as to why I waited so long to come in. I decide not to take the crowded elevator because I'm afraid the waiting will make me more anxious and irritable. The empty staircase gives me a moment to myself. I'm listening to my footsteps echo in the staircase, trying to disconnect myself from what I'm doing. The receptionist recognizes me as I enter the office and instructs me to sit down. I am acutely aware of the smell,* disinfectant and nitrous, which gives me a slight feeling of nausea. I attempt to read a magazine, but it is not enough to draw my attention from the sound of the drill coming from down the hall. The longer I sit waiting, the more anxious I become. In my mind I can hear the dentist's voice as he peers into my mouth: "Oh no, we've got some problems."**

> *I can see the receptionist joking around with another woman behind the desk. I'm irritated with her lack of empathy, and I feel more isolated in my fear and anxiety. The assistant calls my name* in a happy, singsongy voice. I try not to look resentful as she leads me to a room. I lie back in the chair. The sound of the chair moving is cold and electric.* I hope that I lessen the impact by describing the condition of my mouth before she looks at it.*

> *Now I am in the chair, head back and mouth open, feeling robbed of all my power and dignity. I can feel the assistant's pointed instrument moving across my teeth and gums. I know when she's getting close to a sore spot,* and I tighten my whole body in anticipation of the pain. When she hits it, I jump. *I imagine that makes her angry. After scribbling some notes, she explains to me regretfully that I have a lot of plaque that should have been removed sooner. Some of my pockets are deeper, and there's been*

some bone loss.* Now she's prepping to clean my teeth. I can see out of the corner of my eye the metal tray containing all of the instruments. My whole body is tense, and my jaw is starting to ache from holding it open. *I can feel her rubber gloves, and hear the scraping of metal on my teeth.

Possible Conclusion 1. She's finished, and she's calling in the dentist. I'm listening as she describes everything she found wrong with my teeth and gums. He's nodding and glancing at me occasionally. My mouth is inspected again.* He, too, expresses his regret that I didn't come in sooner. They both explain to me the importance of flossing. *I feel humiliated, as though I'm being treated like a child. I can't wait to get out of there so I can be a real person again. She finally hands me some free floss and a toothbrush, and leads me to the receptionist to discuss a good time for my next appointment. I leave with a sense of relief that it's over.

Possible Conclusion 2. When she is finished, the dentist is called in. He reviews the notes she made, and carefully checks my mouth for himself. He is explaining to me that, with a little more flossing and regular use of a Water Pic, I can reverse a lot of the damage that now exists. He suggests that I buy a Water Pic and gives me some special mouthwash that will help get things under control again. He tells me to have a nice day, and I show myself out to the receptionist to make an appointment. I feel relieved upon leaving, and I'm filled with hope that next time may not be as bad.

Next, Susan wrote out a set of coping statements that addressed the particular fears and worries that intensified her anxiety at each stress point. Here are some examples of her statements:

- *I . . . imagine the dentist will know immediately how irresponsible I've been.*
  "I forgive myself. I do the best I can. He will be a good source of information."

- *I am acutely aware of the smell . . . which gives me a slight feeling of nausea.*
  "I made it all the way here. I can get through this. I'll relax my stomach."

- *I tighten my whole body in anticipation of the pain.*
  "Breathe deeply. Relax. It's almost over. It's worth a little pain to get my teeth really clean."

- *I feel humiliated, as though I'm being treated like a child.*
  "I forgive myself. They say the same thing to everyone. I made it through. I'm glad it's finally over."

With her coping statements completed, Susan was ready to continue with her visualizations. She re-recorded her narrative to include a reminder to use cue-controlled relaxation and specific coping thoughts for *each* stress point. After four repetitions, Susan had successfully reduced her anxiety at most stress points to about 5 on a 10-point scale. However, two of the stress points remained at about 9. The next time she visualized the sequence, she paid extra attention to the feelings she was experiencing at each of those two stress points. She experimented with different coping statements and found alternatives that were more effective in reducing her anxiety. She continued this exercise for one and a half weeks before she felt confident enough to call the dentist and schedule an appointment.

Chapter 11

Stress Inoculation

Two pioneering techniques have made a huge impact on the treatment of anxiety and phobia: systematic desensitization and stress inoculation. Systematic desensitization was developed by behavior therapist Joseph Wolpe in 1958. Wolpe assisted anxious people in developing a hierarchy of stressful scenes related to their phobia. The hierarchy stretched from scenes that produced almost no anxiety all the way to images that were terrifying. With a hierarchy in place, Wolpe provided training in progressive muscle relaxation and helped people desensitize to the frightening scenes by pairing these scenes with deep relaxation.

Systematic desensitization is a simple process: first you relax, then you imagine a stressful scene until it produces anxiety. The scene is immediately erased and the process repeated until the scene no longer evokes any anxiety. Because each new scene is only slightly more anxiety evoking than the one before, you progress in *gradual* increments all the way to the most frightening items in the hierarchy.

Systematic desensitization teaches you to master your anxiety. The expectation is that you'll feel little or no anxiety in situations you have desensitized yourself to. This is simultaneously the strength and the weakness of the technique. You feel a tremendous sense of accomplishment and freedom when you're relaxed in situations that formerly provoked anxiety. But what if anxiety begins to creep back in? What if you're suddenly hit with a wave of the old panic? Systematic desensitization offers nothing to help you cope with this situation. You're supposed to be anxiety free—but you're not.

To solve this problem, Donald Meichenbaum developed stress inoculation. He taught people how to *cope* with their anxiety—whenever and wherever it occurs. Meichenbaum argued in his book *Cognitive Behavior Modification* (1977) that a fear response can be conceived of as an interaction of two main elements: (1) heightened physiological arousal (increased heart and respiration rates, sweating, muscle tension, chills, the "lump in the throat") and (2) thoughts that interpret your situation as dangerous or threatening and attribute your physiological arousal to the emotion of fear. The actual stressful situation has very little to do with your emotional response. Your appraisal of the danger and how you interpret your own body's response are the real forces that create your anxiety.

Stress inoculation training involves learning to relax, reducing stress by using deep breathing and muscle relaxation. But there's more to coping with fear than merely relaxing your body. You also learn to create a private arsenal of coping thoughts. These are used to counteract habitual thoughts of danger and catastrophe that arise in your phobic situation.

As with systematic desensitization, you develop a hierarchy and use deep relaxation prior to imagining each scene. But that's where the similarity to Wolpe's technique ends. You don't cut off the scene when you feel anxious. Instead you continue to imagine the scene for up to a minute while using relaxation techniques and coping thoughts. Instead of trying to master anxiety so it never comes back, you learn effective coping strategies so you develop confidence in your ability to handle *any* situation, no matter how frightening it may feel.

There is one problem with stress inoculation as a technique to treat phobia. Staying in the stressful scene and coping, if you experience high levels of anxiety, can be unpleasant to the point where you are discouraged from further practice. Research indicates that extensive exposure to high-anxiety situations results in a much greater drop-out rate from treatment than gradual exposure where you're permitted to escape (Jannoun et al. 1980; Mathews et al. 1977). Conversely, if you are allowed to escape a scene when anxiety reaches a critical threshold, it gives you a greater feeling of control and reduced overall anxiety (Rackman et al. 1986) while losing none of the treatment's effectiveness (Emmelkamp 1982).

Edmund Bourne, author of *The Anxiety and Phobia Workbook* (1995), recognized this issue and modified the stress inoculation technique to make it a more user-friendly treatment. Bourne follows the same approach as Meichenbaum—deep relaxation and coping thoughts applied to a hierarchy of phobic scenes—but he gives people a way out if they get too anxious. You continue to cope in the scene unless you reach a threshold of marked anxiety. Then you shut the scene off and return to deep relaxation, exactly as Wolpe recommends in systematic desensitization.

In the opinion of the authors, Bourne's modification of stress inoculation is the best available imagery technique for treating phobias.

Symptom Effectiveness

Stress inoculation and systematic desensitization have been proven effective with a wide variety of phobias in dozens of outcome studies. However, it appears that their effectiveness depends on additional *in vivo* (real life) exposure. In other words, you actually have to *do* the things you've avoided to successfully complete a phobia treatment program.

Neither stress inoculation nor systematic desensitization is indicated for panic disorder without phobia, generalized anxiety, or interpersonal situations that require assertive behavior.

Time for Mastery

Learning the relaxation techniques necessary for stress inoculation will take a minimum of two to three weeks. You can construct your hierarchy at the same time you are learning to relax. The systematic visualization of scenes can be done daily. Results will usually be noticed in the first several days, but the average phobia will take a week or more to treat effectively with the imagined scenes.

Complete recovery from a phobia requires you to expose yourself in real life to the situations you're imagining in stress inoculation. Only when you learn to enter situations *in vivo* that you used to avoid will you be certain that you can learn to cope with your fear.

Instructions

Step 1: Relaxation Training

Following the instructions in chapter 5, "Relaxation," start with the exercise to learn deep, diaphragmatic breathing. When you've learned to breathe deeply into your abdominal area and can reliably create feelings of relaxation, move on to progressive muscle relaxation (PMR). This exercise will teach you what it feels like when your muscles have released all tension.

When you have mastered PMR and can relax the major muscle groups in your body, it's time to practice relaxation without tension. Here you'll follow the same sequence of muscle groups as with PMR, but you'll no longer tighten and release your muscles. Instead you'll will them to relax and let go.

The next technique you'll learn is cue-controlled relaxation. This will allow you to relax your whole body by taking a series of deep breaths and using a cue word or phrase to trigger relaxed and peaceful feelings.

The final technique to master is learning to visualize your special place. Here you'll use visual, auditory, and physical images to create in your mind a place where you feel calm, safe, and deeply relaxed.

While you're learning these skills in the relaxation chapter, you can continue preparation for stress inoculation by choosing a fear to work on and building a hierarchy. By the time your relaxation training is complete, you'll be ready to begin visualizing and desensitizing the stressful scenes of your hierarchy.

Step 2: Choosing a Fear to Work On

Almost everyone has something they really fear. And many people have more than one significant phobia.

If you have only one fear and are ready to work on it, skip this section. But if you have several phobias and are uncertain which to work on first, or whether to work on them at all, do the following simple assessment exercise for each of your fears.

Fear Assessment Exercise

Fear #1:

How distressing is your fear?

1	2	3	4	5	6	7	8	9
Slightly								Extremely

How frequently do you encounter your fear?

1	2	3	4	5	6	7	8	9
Almost never								Constantly

How much does your fear limit you?

1	2	3	4	5	6	7	8	9
Not at all								Extremely

Fear #2:

How distressing is your fear?

1	2	3	4	5	6	7	8	9
Slightly								Extremely

How frequently do you encounter your fear?

1	2	3	4	5	6	7	8	9
Almost never								Constantly

How much does your fear limit you?

1	2	3	4	5	6	7	8	9
Not at all								Extremely

Fear #3:

How distressing is your fear?

1	2	3	4	5	6	7	8	9
Slightly								Extremely

How frequently do you encounter your fear?

1	2	3	4	5	6	7	8	9
Almost never								Constantly

How much does your fear limit you?

1	2	3	4	5	6	7	8	9
Not at all								Extremely

Now you have a short profile of how each of your fears affects you. Notice which fear has the highest total score. You might wish to work on this one. However, you might decide that one of these factors is more important than the others, and the highest-scoring fear on that factor should be your choice for stress inoculation. Many people, for example, are concerned less with how distressing or frequent a phobia is than with how much their lives may be limited by it. It's your decision. Once you've made it, move on to the next section.

Step 3: Building a Hierarchy

Hierarchies should comprise from eight to twenty scenes. In constructing your hierarchy of threatening scenes, you will manipulate four variables:

1. Spatial proximity—how physically close you are to the feared object or situation. If you were afraid of snowstorms, for example, you'd probably feel more fearful as you got closer to the mountains on the annual ski trip. You could create hierarchy scenes in which you imagine the car reaching the first prolonged grade to the mountains, or you're high enough to see the first drifts by the side of the road, and so on.

2. Temporal proximity or duration—how close you are in time to the feared object or situation, or how much time you spend exposed to it. A hierarchy on the fear of subways might have scenes in which you're getting closer and closer in time to the subway ride. Or it might list rides of progressively longer duration.

3. Degree of threat—how difficult and scary the scene is. With the fear of elevators, for example, you can manipulate the degree of threat by altering the number of floors you'll ascend or descend.

4. Degree of support—how close you are to a support person during a threatening scene. With freeway fears, for example, your support person could be in the seat next to you, behind you, behind you and out of sight, driving one car length behind you, five car lengths behind you, or just be on call in case you need help.

In many cases you will use all four of these variables to think of scenes for your hierarchy. Right now, take a look at the sample hierarchies. The scenes are all marked SP for spatial proximity, TP for temporal proximity, T for degree of threat, and S for degree of support. As you examine how these hierarchies are built, you're likely to get a better idea of how to use the variables to create many different scenes.

Three Sample Hierarchies

		Phobia about Driving on Freeways
Variable	**Rank**	**Scene**
TP	1	Thinking about freeway driving the day before a practice session
SP	2	Parked on a side street watching an on-ramp
T	3	Riding on a freeway with someone else driving
S	4	Driving one exit with a support person next to you—light traffic
T	5	Driving one exit with a support person next to you—heavier traffic
S	6	Driving one exit alone—light traffic
T	7	Driving one exit alone—heavier traffic
T	8	Two exits with support person—heavy traffic
S	9	Two exits with support person in back seat—heavy traffic
S	10	Two exits alone—heavy traffic
T, S	11	Four exits with support person next to you—light traffic
T, S	12	Four exits with support person in the back seat—heavier traffic
S	13	Four exits alone—light traffic
T	14	Four exits alone—heavy traffic
T, S	15	Six exits with support person next to you—heavy traffic
S	16	Six exits alone—lighter traffic
T	17	Six exits alone—heavier traffic
T	18	Eight exits alone—heavier traffic

		Phobia about Getting Injections
Variable	**Rank**	**Scene**
T	1	Watching a movie in which a minor character gets a shot
T	2	Talking to a friend about her flu shot
T	3	Pricking finger with pin
T	4	Making doctor's appointment for a nonmedicinal saline injection
SP	5	Driving to medical center
SP	6	Parking car in medical-center parking lot
T, SP	7	Thinking about shots in doctor's waiting room
SP	8	Entering treatment room
TP	9	Nurse entering room with injection materials
TP	10	Nurse filling syringe
T	11	Smelling alcohol on cotton ball
TP	12	Seeing hypodermic poised in nurse's hand

T	13	Receiving small saline shot in right arm
T	14	Receiving larger saline shot in left arm
T	15	Receiving flu shot in arm
T	16	Having a blood sample taken

Phobia about Being Near Bees

Variable	Rank	Scene
T	1	Seeing a picture of a bee
TP	2	Planning to practice in back yard later in the day
SP	3	Standing at door, looking out at back yard
SP, TP	4	Standing outside, near back door, for one minute
TP	5	Standing outside, near back door, for three minutes
SP	6	Standing halfway to dahlias (where there are lots of bees) for one minute
TP	7	Standing halfway to dahlias for three minutes
SP	8	Standing close enough to hear buzzing—one minute
TP	9	Standing close enough to hear buzzing—three minutes
SP	10	Standing next to dahlias (bees all around)—thirty seconds
TP	11	Standing next to dahlias—two minutes
TP	12	Standing next to dahlias—five minutes

Preparing for Real-Life Exposure

Where at all possible, make each scene something you could intentionally do in real life. Consider the fear of snakes, for example. Hierarchy scenes in which you're walking in the woods and see a snake are hard to set up when you want to test your coping skills *in vivo*. It's better to have scenes in a store that sells snakes, where you get closer and closer to the glass terrariums, finally touching a snake, picking it up, and so on.

Getting Started

The first step is to imagine dealing with your feared object or situation in a way that creates almost no anxiety. You can imagine yourself at a distance in space or time, having a support person by your side, or dealing with only mildly threatening aspects of the situation.

Now imagine the worst possible exposure you could have to your feared object or situation. For example, if you're afraid of public speaking, you might imagine giving a long presentation before a large audience. Or, if you are afraid of crowded theaters or classrooms where you're far from the exit, you could create a very claustrophobic scene where the room is stuffy and you would have to step across many people in their seats to get to the exit. Think about the four variables that you can manipulate to make the scene the worst imaginable.

But remember, with both the lowest- and highest-anxiety scenes, make them something you can replicate in real life for later practice.

Fill In the Middle Scenes

Now it's time to imagine from six to eighteen scenes of graduated intensity that are connected to your phobia. At first just brainstorm, thinking of as many scenes as you can. Think of temporal and spatial proximity. Try to increase the degree of threat. If you plan to use a support person in later real-life exposure, build varying levels of support into your hierarchy as well.

Once you have a good number of scenes, try to rank them from least threatening (number 1) to most threatening (the highest number).

Now go through the scenes in your hierarchy, and see if the increments of anxiety are approximately equal throughout. If some increments are larger than others, you'll need to fill in these "holes" with additional scenes. Keep working on it until the steps are close to even.

You may find that some of your scenes have equal ranking. If that's so, either throw one or more of them out or manipulate the variables to give each a unique place in the hierarchy.

Finalizing Your Hierarchy

Once you've ranked your hierarchy scenes, photocopy the form on the next page and fill in the items you've developed.

Step 4: Developing Coping Thoughts

You should develop one or two coping thoughts as you get ready to visualize each new scene in your hierarchy. Here's how you do it. Briefly visualize the scene, making it as real as possible. Notice what you see, what you hear, and even what you feel physically. Now listen to your thoughts. What are you saying to yourself about potential dangers or catastrophes that might occur in the scene? If you notice your anxiety rising as you listen to these thoughts, you'll need to find a way to answer back with coping thoughts.

Here are some key questions to ask yourself when developing your coping thoughts:

A. Do I have a plan to handle this situation? What would I do if the problem I fear occurred?

B. How likely are the frightening outcomes that I imagine? Can I estimate the odds against these happening?

C. How long would I have to endure this if I were really in this situation? (Sometimes it's enough just to remind yourself, "I can do this; it's only a short time.")

D. What coping skills do I have to handle this? What relaxation skills, ways to reassure myself, things I can remind myself to do?

The answers to these questions may give you one or two ideas for coping thoughts to manage anxiety in this scene. You can also consult the list of "generic" coping thoughts on page 128. It may give you some other good ideas.

	Hierarchy Worksheet	
	Hierarchy for _____	
	(your phobia)	
Rank	**Scene**	**Coping Thoughts**
1.		
2.		
3.		
4.		
5.		
6.		
7.		
8.		
9.		
10.		
11.		
12.		
13.		
14.		
15.		
16.		
17.		
18.		
19.		
20.		

Note: Make copies of this sheet to use with other phobias.

Coping Statements

- This feeling isn't comfortable or pleasant, but I can accept it.

- I can be anxious and still deal with this situation.

- I can handle these symptoms or sensations.

- This is an opportunity for me to learn to cope with my fears.

- This will pass.

- I'll ride this through—I don't need to let this get to me.

- I deserve to feel okay right now.

- I can take all the time I need to let go and relax.

- I've survived this before and I'll survive this time, too.

- I can do what I have to do in spite of anxiety.

- This anxiety won't hurt me—it just doesn't feel good.

- These are fight-or-flight reactions—they won't hurt me.

- This is just anxiety—I'm not going to let it get to me.

- Nothing serious is going to happen to me.

- Fighting and resisting this isn't going to help—so I'll just let it pass.

- These are just thoughts—not reality.

- I don't need these thoughts—I can choose to think differently.

- This is not dangerous.

- So what.

Now it's time to distill the one or two best coping thoughts for the first scene in your hierarchy. Record them in the space provided on the Hierarchy Worksheet. You'll do the identical process for each succeeding scene you come to.

Example

On the following page are examples of coping thoughts from Linda's hierarchy about her fear of talking to strangers.

Notice in Linda's example that she always reminds herself to "breathe and relax." This helps her let go of physical tension before moving on to the other coping thoughts. You might experiment and see if this works for you.

If a coping thought proves ineffective while you visualize a scene, drop it and try another one.

Now go back to your Hierarchy Worksheet and use it to gradually fill in your coping thoughts as you work down your hierarchy.

	Linda's Coping Thoughts	
Rank	**Scene**	**Coping Thoughts**
4	Driving to a small gathering at a friend's house.	• Breathe and relax. • I'll talk mostly to friends—I can handle strangers if they're with a group of my friends.
7	Standing at the snack table with a stranger.	• Breathe and relax. • I'll ask them who they're friends with at the party. (Didn't work) • I can do this in spite of anxiety.
9	Walking into a party where I know only a few people.	• Breathe and relax. • This is an opportunity to learn to cope. • I can ask the standard questions when I meet somebody.
14	Some motor mouth traps me in a boring conversation. I want to escape.	• Breathe and relax. • I can ride this through—it doesn't have to get to me. (Didn't work) • I'll excuse myself to go to the bathroom.

Step 5: Stress Inoculation Procedure

The stress inoculation sequence goes as follows:

A. **Set ten to fifteen minutes aside to get relaxed.** Go through progressive muscle relaxation, cue-controlled relaxation (which includes deep breathing), and a special-place visualization of somewhere you feel calm and safe.

  Now briefly review your coping statements for the first (or next) scene.

B. **Visualize the first (or next) scene in your hierarchy.** Try to bring it to life. See the situation, hear what's going on, feel any physical sensations. What objects or people are in the scene? What colors? What's the quality of light? Do you smell anything, notice the temperature, feel anything against your skin? Do you hear voices, wind, a ticking clock?

  Be careful not to picture yourself as anxious in the scene. If you're in the scene at all, see yourself as comfortable and confident.

C. **Start to cope.** Once the visualized scene is clear in your mind, immediately begin relaxing and using coping thoughts. It's recommended that you use cue-controlled relaxation during hierarchy scenes. It's the quickest stress reduction strategy because it involves just a few deep breaths and your cue word or phrase.

  As you cope physically using cued relaxation, recall one or more of your coping thoughts. Keep visualizing the scene while coping for thirty to sixty seconds—unless your anxiety becomes *marked* (see D).

D. **Rate your anxiety.** Use the Bourne Anxiety Scale as a reference during stress inoculation.

Bourne Anxiety Scale

7-10	*Major Panic Attack*	All of the symptoms in Level 6 exaggerated; terror; fear of going crazy or dying; compulsion to escape.
6	*Moderate Panic Attack*	Palpitations; difficulty breathing; feeling disoriented or detached (feeling of unreality); panic in response to perceived loss of control.
5	*Early Panic*	Heart pounding or beating irregularly; constricted breathing; spaciness or dizziness; definite fear of losing control; compulsion to escape.
4	*Marked Anxiety*	Feeling uncomfortable or "spacy"; heart beating fast; muscles tight; beginning to wonder about maintaining control.
3	*Moderate Anxiety*	Feeling uncomfortable but still in control; heart starting to beat faster; more rapid breathing; sweaty palms.
2	*Mild Anxiety*	Butterflies in stomach; muscle tension; definitely nervous.

If at any time while visualizing a scene you reach Level 4—*marked anxiety*—immediately discontinue the scene and return to your relaxation exercises. Be sure you get clear what constitutes Level 4 for you in advance of visualizing any hierarchy item. According to Bourne, "This is the point at which—whatever symptoms you're experiencing—*you feel your control over your reaction beginning to diminish*" (1995). You start feeling the danger of a full panic.

Marked anxiety is the cutoff point for good reason. Staying in the scene while fearing that you'll lose control can resensitize you and make you more, rather than less, anxious when the scene is over.

After you've coped for thirty to sixty seconds, or cut a scene because of marked anxiety, immediately rate your anxiety on the Bourne Scale. Write the number down on your Hierarchy Worksheet. If your anxiety is Level 0 or 1, you can move on to visualize the next scene. If it's 2 or above, relax and revisit the same scene.

Also spend a moment evaluating your coping thoughts. Stop using any that proved ineffective. If none of them worked, it's time to look at the generic list and experiment with one or two others.

E. **Always do deep relaxation between scenes.** Typically, you might use cue-controlled relaxation and spend time calming yourself with your special place.

If you reached marked anxiety or above during a scene, spend some additional time doing progressive muscle relaxation or relaxation without tension. These powerful techniques can help you achieve a deeper level of calm.

F. **Keep alternating between hierarchy items and relaxation.** Immediately cut scenes that reach Level 4. Cope for up to a minute in scenes where your anxiety is Level 3 or below. Move to the next item on your hierarchy whenever you achieve an anxiety level of 1 or 0 while coping in a scene. It usually takes at least two exposures to a scene to fully desensitize to it. The lowest-ranked scenes, where your anxiety is quite low from the outset, may be exceptions.

Practice daily. Your first practice session should be fifteen to twenty minutes. Later you can extend stress inoculation sessions to as much as thirty minutes. The main limiting factor is fatigue. Always stop a session if you begin to feel tired or bored.

Expect to master from one to three hierarchy items during each practice session. When starting a new practice session, always go back to the last scene you successfully completed. This helps you consolidate your gains before facing more anxiety-evoking items.

Step 6: Real-Life Exposure

In most cases you can use your same hierarchy to practice *in vivo* exposure to feared situations. If some of your items can't be easily manipulated in a real-life situation, modify them so they can. Consider the item "Elevator stuck between floors." This is clearly something you can't create on demand. But you can modify it to "Standing in the elevator at the Barclay Building—where the door closes and it waits a *long* time before starting to rise." This isn't the same as being stuck between floors, but it evokes some of the same feelings.

As with imagery desensitization, you need to retreat from an exposure session if your anxiety reaches Level 4. Retreat doesn't mean going home and giving up. It's not having a drink at your favorite bar. Retreat means going somewhere relatively safe where you can refocus on your relaxation exercises, returning to your exposure practice once your anxiety has been reduced. See chapter 12, "Coping During Exposure," for guidelines to use during exposure practice.

Example

Jennifer was a product manager for a major apparel firm. She had become extremely phobic in meetings where she was expected to speak before the group, particularly when she had to make quarterly product presentations. Her anxiety increased greatly after the most recent product presentation, where she was criticized for giving a sloppy, disorganized description of her product line and manufacturing plans.

It took Jennifer about three weeks to learn progressive muscle relaxation, relaxation without tension, and cue-controlled relaxation, and to develop an effective special-place visualization. During that time she built the following hierarchy and began developing coping thoughts. All of Jennifer's coping thoughts are provided by way of example, even though she developed them one scene at a time as she progressed through her hierarchy.

Jennifer developed her coping thoughts by imagining the scene first and listening to the scary things she was saying to herself. When she was able to identify the thoughts she was using to frighten herself, she used the list of four key questions to either develop a coping plan or remind herself of some of her coping skills. She also found a number of helpful coping thoughts on the generic list.

	Jennifer's Hierarchy Worksheet	

Hierarchy for: <u>**Meetings where I'm expected to speak before the group**</u>

Rank	Scene	Coping Thoughts
1	Product-planning meeting scheduled in two weeks.	• Let go and relax. • I've time to prepare.
2	Trying to assemble the material I'll need to present—one week before meeting.	• Let go and relax. • Everything will be ready, I know what I need to do.
3	Bring presentation home—night before meeting.	• Let go and relax. • I'll read it if I get nervous and don't trust my memory.
4	Arrive at work on the morning of the ten o'clock meeting.	• Let go and relax. • This is just anxiety, it won't hurt me (ineffective). • I've survived this before; I'll get through it this time.
5	Walking into meeting, greeting people, stacking papers on desk in front of me.	• Let go and relax. • I'll ride this through; I'm prepared.
6	Listening to other, very well-prepared product presentations.	• Let go and relax. • I can do what I have to do in spite of anxiety (ineffective). • I've done my best, I accept whatever happens.
7	My product line is introduced.	• Let go and relax. • I've done my best, I accept whatever happens. • I've survived this before.
8	Begin speaking, looking around at all the faces turned expectantly to me.	• Let go and relax. • I can do this, I've done it before. • I'm doing my best.
9	It just goes on and on, it seems like the end is still a long way off. They're all looking intently at me. Don't know what they're thinking.	• Let go and relax. • It's all prepared, just keep going; you'll get there eventually.
10	Moment of silence at the end, before there's any reaction. Don't know what they think.	• Let go and relax. • Smile at them. • I did my best.

Jennifer used the "let go and relax" coping suggestion in each scene because it reminded her to release the tension in her body. On occasion, a coping thought proved ineffective, and Jennifer replaced it with something new.

Jennifer followed the stress inoculation procedure carefully, finding that the low-ranked items were easy and evoked very little anxiety. She was feeling moderate anxiety while visualizing Scene 3, and had her first experience of marked anxiety with Scene 4. She immediately erased the scene, did some progressive muscle relaxation, and spent extra time relaxing in her special place. It took three attempts with Scene 4 until Jennifer was able to cope in the scene without reaching marked anxiety. Six visualizations of the scene were required altogether before Jennifer's anxiety fell to Level 1.

She proceeded through the scenes, alternating between visualizing and relaxing, until she got to Scene 9. Here she experienced marked anxiety six times in a row. Jennifer decided to break the scene down into smaller units, making two scenes out of one. The first scene was: "It just goes on and on, it seems like the end is still a long way off." She found herself able to cope without marked anxiety and completed desensitization after three more visualizations. The second scene—"They're all looking intently at me. Don't know what they're thinking"—was more difficult. Twice more she reached marked anxiety, but on the third visualization she stayed at Level 3, and was able to cope for the full sixty seconds. With four more visualizations, Jennifer was able to reach Anxiety Level 0.

Jennifer used the same hierarchy and coping thoughts in real life as she prepared for her next product presentation. The stress inoculation paid off. She was able to get through the actual presentation with only mild to moderate anxiety. While Jennifer didn't eradicate all anxiety, she achieved something vitally important—the ability to cope with and control feelings of fear so she could continue to meet the challenges of her job.

Special Considerations

If you experience difficulties in practicing stress inoculation, they are likely to be in one of the three common problem areas:

1. **Incomplete Relaxation.** If you can't relax at the beginning of a session, try to imagine lying on a soft lawn on a calm summer day, watching clouds slowly floating by. Or imagine watching leaves float by on a broad, slow river. Each cloud or leaf takes some of your muscular tension away with it.

    You may also want to record your relaxation routine on tape and play it at the beginning of each session or scene.

2. **Visualization Difficulty.** If you find that your scenes seem flat, unreal, and unevocative of the distress you would feel in real-life scenes, you probably have trouble visualizing things clearly. To strengthen your powers of imagination, ask questions of all your senses to make your scenes real:

    Sight: What colors are there in the scene? What colors are the walls, the landscape, people's clothes, cars, furnishings? Is the light bright or dim? What details are there—books on the table, pets, chairs, rugs? What pictures are on the walls? What words can you read on signs?

    Sound: What are the tones of voices? Are there plane or traffic noises, dogs barking or music playing in the background? Is there wind in the trees? Can you hear your own voice?

    Touch: Reach out and feel things—are they rough or smooth? hard or soft? rounded or flat? What's the weather like? Are you hot or cold? Do you itch, sweat, have to sneeze? What are you wearing? How does it feel against your skin?

Smell: Can you smell dinner cooking? flowers? tobacco smoke? sewage? perfume or aftershave? chemicals? decay? pine trees?

Taste: Are you eating food or drinking water? Are the tastes sweet? sour? salty? bitter?

It also helps to go to the real setting of one of your scenes. Then you can gather images and impressions, and practice remembering details. Close your eyes and try to see the scene, then open your eyes and notice what you missed. Close your eyes and try again. Describe the scene out loud to yourself. Open your eyes and see what you missed this time, and what you changed in your mind. Close your eyes and describe the scene again, adding the sounds and textures and smells and temperatures. Keep this up until you have a vivid sense picture of the scene.

3. **Misconstructed Hierarchies.** If you find no reduction in anxiety with repetitions of a particular scene, your hierarchy probably needs to be reconstructed with a more gradual gradient.

If you can visualize your scenes clearly and experience little or no anxiety, your hierarchy probably needs to be reconstructed with a steeper gradient between scenes, or with a greater variety of content in the scenes.

If you can visualize your scenes clearly, and experience erratic levels of tension, either the scenes in your hierarchy aren't evenly spaced with regard to intensity, or you have scenes depicting different kinds of items mixed together. In either case, reconstruct the hierarchy and try again.

Chapter 12

Coping During Exposure

Full recovery from any phobia depends on successfully exposing yourself in real life to core elements of your fear. In chapter 11 you learned how to develop a hierarchy of feared situations and to imagine scenes from that hierarchy while relaxing your body and using helpful coping thoughts. Now you'll continue work on your phobia through *in vivo* exposure to the actual scenes and situations you previously only imagined. To handle the inevitable anxiety that will come up during exposure, you'll need a coping script to help you respond effectively to anxious arousal.

The use of self-instructional coping statements was first introduced by Donald Meichenbaum (1974) when he proposed a method for people to talk themselves through stressful events. In his research with children, Meichenbaum observed that kids use self-instruction while undertaking new or difficult tasks. They softly talk themselves through the process, reminding themselves of steps in the sequence. While adults have forgotten how to do this, Meichenbaum found that he could train them to do what had once been natural—to use subvocal reminders of coping techniques.

The authors have adapted Meichenbaum's ideas into a coping script that you can use while learning to face feared situations. You will develop specific self-instructions to (1) help you physically relax, (2) remind yourself of your action plan should you encounter problems during exposure, (3) cope with anxious arousal and fight-or-flight symptoms, (4) cope with catastrophic thoughts, (5) accept anxious feelings as temporary and learn to float past them and, finally, (6) distract yourself, if necessary, from frightening thoughts.

There are two options for how to use your coping script. The first is to memorize key elements of the script and use them as needed during exposure. The second is to record the script on tape and then listen to it on a portable casette player while entering a feared situation. The one advantage of a portable cassette player is that it will remind you of your coping strategies even if anxiety is making it hard to think and remember what you want to do.

Symptom Effectiveness

The use of coping scripts has been studied as a part of stress inoculation training (Meichenbaum 1977). Coping scripts used in imagery desensitization have been shown effective in the treatment of phobias.

Time for Mastery

You can develop your own individualized coping script in one to three hours. Once you've written it on a file card or recorded it, it can be used immediately to help you cope during exposure.

Instructions

Step 1: Relaxing Your Body

The key element in your coping script is reminding yourself to use your relaxation skills. The most effective stress control techniques during exposure are deep breathing and cue-controlled relaxation in combination.

Deep-breathing skills should be overlearned so that you can take a deep, diaphragmatic breath without a lot of thought or effort. See page 58–59 for instructions on deep breathing if you have not fully mastered this skill. Instructions for cue-controlled relaxation are on page 62. Be sure that you have selected your cue word or phrase, and that you have learned how to relax your whole body while taking deep breaths and repeating your cue.

With mastery of deep breathing and cue-controlled relaxation, you should be able to relax the major areas of tension in your body in less than a minute. The speed with which you achieve cue-controlled relaxation is important because real-life stressful situations require a rapid response. The longer you feel tense, the more likely you are to experience anxiety.

Now you can write the first component of your coping script. This is a sentence or phrase that will remind you to use deep breathing and cue-controlled relaxation. Here are some examples:

- Take a deep breath and relax.

- Relax the hot spots.

- Relax and let go.

- Breathe away stress.

- Breathe and let go.

If none of these reminders feels right, write your own. Another option is simply to use your cue word or phrase as the instruction to relax.

Step 2: Your Action Plan

Now it's time for some contingency planning—planning things you'll do if you have problems during exposure practice. The first problem you need to prepare for is too high a level of anxiety. The Bourne Anxiety Scale allows you to gauge whether your anxiety is too high during imagery or *in vivo* exposure. If your anxiety is at Level 4—marked anxiety—or above, you'll need a way to retreat from the situation. Remember that marked anxiety means "feeling uncomfortable or spacy; heart beating fast; muscles tight; beginning to wonder about maintaining control." When your anxiety symptoms reach this point during exposure, you need a place to go where you're out of the immediate stressful situation and you have the freedom to do relaxation exercises.

If you were practicing exposure to freeway driving, your action plan for retreat might involve exiting to a side road where you can park your car and thoroughly relax. If you are practicing exposure to elevators, your action plan for retreat might involve sitting in a coffee shop, a nearby park, or your car while you focus on relaxation. If you are exposing yourself to supermarkets or crowded places, your action plan for retreat might be going home, walking for a while in the parking lot, or chatting with a support person who has come with you.

The key element of the action plan for retreat is to identify a safe zone that you can easily reach. Once in the safe zone, you can focus on muscle relaxation, breathing, and peaceful visualizations to bring your anxiety back down to moderate or mild levels. When you have reduced your anxiety to Levels 2 or 3 on the Bourne Scale, you should return to *in vivo* exposure. Letting anxiety stop your exposure work altogether only reinforces phobia. Your action plan for retreat allows you to relax in a safe place, but then you must return to finish your practice. It's not at all unusual to retreat two, three, or even more times before you are successful with a certain step in your exposure work. Don't be discouraged. Retreating is a necessary part of recovery.

A second element in your action plan is developing strategies for handling typical problems that may arise in exposure settings. For example, what do you do if you're attempting exposure practice in a restaurant, but you have to wait a long time to give your order and service seems extremely slow? You might plan that you'll continue your exposure work at a short-order coffee shop, or order just a single course. Suppose your exposure work involves conversing with strangers in a social situation? You might need a plan for dealing with someone who is a bit rejecting or irritated. If in your exposure work on the freeway you encounter traffic heavier than usual, your action plan might involve exiting and returning in the opposite, more lightly traveled direction. Or you might have an alternative freeway in mind to continue your practice.

By anticipating typical problems and having a pre-established strategy for coping, you'll feel more confidence when approaching your exposure work. Now you can include in your coping script a reminder that your action plan is in place. You might use phrases such as

- I have a plan to cope.

- I know what to do when problems occur.

- I can handle problems; I have a plan.

Step 3: Coping with Arousal

If you have physiological symptoms of anxiety that worry you during exposure practice, you'll need to include in your coping script reminders of how harmless these symptoms truly are. Right now review the chapter on coping with panic to get specific medical information on the cause of your anxiety symptoms. Armed with clear medical information, you can reinterpret these symptoms as harmless fight-or-flight reactions. Here are some recommended coping thoughts for specific anxiety symptoms:

- **Racing heart:** A healthy heart can go more than 200 beats a minute for weeks without damage. A few minutes, or even a few hours, of rapid heartbeat can't hurt me.

- **Light-headedness/feeling faint:** This is due to simple hyperventilation or the normal temporary narrowing of the blood vessels triggered by stress hormones. It can't hurt me and will pass as soon as the fight-or-flight reaction eases. Fainting comes from low blood pressure; I'm not going to faint because anxiety tends to make my blood pressure higher.

- **Dizziness:** This is just a temporary effect of hyperventilation. When I relax, it'll all go away.

- **Feeling depersonalized/not yourself:** This is just a symptom of hyperventilation and blood-vessel constriction that comes from the stress hormones. It feels strange, but it can't hurt me. It will pass as soon as I begin to relax.

- **Weakness in legs:** This is just the stress hormones making the blood pool in my big leg muscles. The blood is there to give me strength to fight or run. I feel shaky and weak, but that's because I'm not running. I'm actually stronger than usual right now.

- **Shortness of breath:** Anxiety makes my diaphragm tighten so it's harder to take a deep breath. My body will always make sure I get enough air. As I relax my diaphragm with slow, deep breaths, the feeling will go away.

- **Fear of acting crazy:** I may feel scared and overwhelmed, but I've never acted crazy. Anxious feelings *never* turn into crazy behavior.

- **Feeling hot or cold:** Stress hormones are playing havoc with my thermostat. This is normal, it can't hurt me, and it will pass as I relax.

Part of coping with arousal is remembering that stress hormones such as adrenaline are released in your body when you anticipate danger. But they are quickly metabolized (in two or three minutes), and the physical symptoms they trigger will pass quickly if you don't start worrying about them. In other words, your elevated heart rate, dizziness, weakness, or shortness of breath is a harmless by-product of stress hormones and the fight-or-flight reaction. These symptoms cannot hurt you. And they will pass quickly if you focus on relaxation rather than scary thoughts about what they mean and what they might do to you. An important coping thought you might use is: In a few minutes this will all start to pass; the stress hormones and their symptoms will all fade away.

Other coping thoughts shown to be helpful include

- There's an end to these feelings.

- Relax and these feelings will gradually pass.

- I've handled this before; I can get through it.

- When I stop the worry, these feelings will slowly pass.

- These are normal fight-or-flight reactions that can't hurt me. I'll ride them out.

- This is just adrenaline; it'll pass.

- This is just my body's way of coping. My body does what it needs to do.

Right now put an asterisk by the key coping statements that seem relevant for you. You can also tailor or rewrite any of the coping thoughts to make them better fit your situation.

Step 4: Coping with Catastrophic Thoughts

Some of the worst anxiety is associated with "what if's": "What if I'm so anxious, I lose control of the car?" "What if the elevator stops between floors?" "What if there's an earthquake when I'm doing exposure work in a high rise?" "What if everyone sees how screwed up I am?" Catastrophic thinking can greatly increase your anxiety during exposure. That's why your coping script needs to include alternative, balanced thoughts in response to the "what if's."

On the following page, write down any catastrophic, "what if" thoughts pertaining to the exposure practice that you're planning. Don't include thoughts about your physical symptoms—you've already worked with them in the previous section.

The best way to identify catastrophic thoughts is to visualize yourself actually doing the exposure work. Try to experience what the scene looks like, what it sounds like, and what it feels like physically. Give yourself time for the anxiety to begin building. Now listen to your automatic thoughts. What are you saying to yourself? What's the worst thing you can imagine happening? How might things really go wrong? What kind of danger are you in? When you've identified the key catastrophic thoughts, it's time to rate them. Rate each thought from 0 to 100 on a scale of anxiety where 0 is feeling completely relaxed and 100 is the worst anxiety you can imagine. Circle the thought with the highest rating—this is the hot thought you'll examine first. From now on everything on the worksheet will relate to this thought only.

Move to the Evidence For column, and write down anything that would support the possibility that the catastrophe might come true. This column might include things you've read in the newspaper, things others have told you, statistics, and any other information that seems to support the feared outcome.

Now move over to the Evidence Against column. Here you list things that tend to weigh against the likelihood of catastrophe. To fill in this column on your worksheet, ask yourself the following key questions:

1. What would the *likely* outcome be if the problem I worry about occurred? Is it as bad as I imagine?

2. What are the realistic odds that the problem I worry about will occur? How many people in the country have done in the last month what I plan to expose myself to? In how many of these cases did the thing I worry about happen?

Catastrophic Thoughts Worksheet

Catastrophic Thoughts (Rate 0–100)	Evidence For	Evidence Against	Alternative or Balanced Thoughts

3. Are there things that make the problem I worry about unlikely to happen?

4. What past experience do I have that suggests the problem is unlikely to occur?

5. What is most *likely* to happen while I'm in the exposure situation? What could I realistically expect?

6. How could I cope if the problem I worry about occurred? Have I ever coped with this before or known anyone who successfully coped with this problem? How did I or they handle it?

7. Could others help me if the problem I worry about occurred?

8. Are there other resources I have or could bring to the situation that would make me feel safer?

9. Is there anything about the situation that might, if I thought about it, increase my feelings of confidence or safety?

As you read through these questions, if you have answers that might be helpful in the Evidence Against column, write them down and underline the ones that seem especially helpful to you.

Now, having filled in the Evidence For and Evidence Against columns, it's time to develop your Alternative or Balanced Thoughts. Read through the evidence both for and against your fear. Make a balanced summary statement that accurately reflects the evidence you've gathered on both sides of the question. Write your alternative thoughts in the fourth column. This is the coping statement you'll use whenever the hot thought comes up during exposure.

Rona was planning exposure work to overcome her fear of crowded public places. Her fear hierarchy ranged from Scene 1 (spend thirty seconds in the bus station during off hours) to Scene 16 (attend a major rock concert). On the next page you can see how she filled out her worksheet to respond to catastrophic thoughts about being in the bus station.

When you look at Rona's catastrophic thoughts, you'll see that number 4 has an asterisk, indicating that this is Rona's hottest thought. Number 3 also contributes significantly to Rona's anxiety. The rest of Rona's worksheet was focused entirely on thought number 4, but she filled out a second worksheet later about her other intense hot thought.

Step 5: Accepting and Floating Past Anxiety

You can control your thoughts, and you can control your breathing, but you can't control adrenaline. Once adrenaline gets released in your bloodstream, you're going to feel anxious and physically uncomfortable for a few minutes. It's critical that you learn to accept this feeling and not try to fight it. Remember, in three minutes or less the adrenaline will be metabolized and your body will begin to calm down. If you don't fight the feeling and don't struggle to stop it, it will soon pass.

There are two key mantras (repeated calming phrases) to use during an adrenaline rush to keep yourself from thrashing, struggling, and scaring yourself further. The first is:
Float past, do not listen in.

The first part means detach from the feeling, try to experience it as an observer. Notice but don't fight the sensations in your body. The second part of the mantra is equally im-

Rona's Catastrophic Thoughts Worksheet			
Catastrophic Thoughts Rate 0–100	**Evidence For**	**Evidence Against**	**Alternative or Balanced Thoughts**
1. People will stare at me because I look freaked out. **40** 2. People will think I'm crazy. **55** 3. There'll be such a crush of people, I won't be able to escape. **85** *4. I'll be assaulted, pushed around or have my purse stolen. **95**	1. There were more than fifty rapes in this city last year. 2. My mother had her purse snatched. 3. A seven-year-old was kidnapped from a bus station recently. 4. Purse snatchers often find victims in crowded places.	1. With all the people going in and out of the bus station each day, the odds are low of being physically assaulted. 1 in 10,000, maybe. 2. There's no way to rape or kidnap an adult in a crowded bus station. 3. I'll keep my police whistle in my hand in case there's trouble. 4. The worst that can happen—still unlikely—is my purse might be snatched, and I'd have to replace my credit cards. A bummer, but no real damage done. 5. The most likely problem is just getting pan-handled. 6. If someone really bothered me, I'd run to the ticket window and ask for help.	While rapes and purse snatchings occur, the odds of physical assault are 1 in 10,000, and I could probably get help before anything really bad happened. Losing my purse would be a bummer, but I could cope.

portant: *Do not listen in.* You need to stop listening to the catastrophic voice inside that tries to scare you with all the awful things that could happen. If you can turn your attention away from that voice, you will likely prevent a second rush of adrenaline and your anxiety will gradually calm down.

A second mantra is:

Accept, do not fight.

Here again, the emphasis is on accepting the feelings inside your body, letting them happen. The feeling will pass soon enough if you don't scare yourself with more catastrophic thoughts. Fighting the feeling won't help; it only makes you feel more helpless and panicked.

One or both of these "acceptance" mantras (developed by Claire Weekes, 1978) should be integrated into your coping script.

Step 6: Distraction

This is an optional component. Some people find distraction more useful than others. You can distract yourself from anxious thoughts during exposure sessions by focusing your attention on a mental task. Such tasks might include counting backwards by seven from a hundred (100, 93, 86, 79, etc.), counting the number of Buicks, Toyotas, or any other auto brand you see on the street, estimating people's heights, counting the number of suits you've owned in your lifetime, and so on. You can also distract yourself with a special-place visualization (see chapter 5, "Relaxation"), sexual fantasies, memories of beautiful places you have been, even fantasies of future successes or triumphs.

Making Your Script

Now it's time to assemble the components of your coping plan into a powerful resource you can use during exposure. Remember your two basic choices: You can condense your script into a file card that you carry with you, or record it to play on a portable cassette player or in your car during exposure sessions. If you're using a file card, here's what you'll need to put on it:

1. A sentence or a phrase to remind you to use deep breathing and cue-controlled relaxation whenever you feel tense.

2. A sentence to remind you of your action plan in case problems occur.

3. One or more coping thoughts to help you respond to typical symptoms of arousal (rapid heartbeat, dizziness, shortness of breath, etc.).

4. The alternative balanced thoughts from your worksheet.

5. Your acceptance mantra(s).

6. Specific distraction techniques you want to try (if you plan to use distraction).

If you would like to record your coping script for use during exposure sessions, simply read your coping statements into the tape recorder in a calm, slow voice. Start with a reminder to relax (cue-controlled relaxation) and your action plan. Go on to one of your coping thoughts for dealing with physiological arousal, then go back to a relaxation reminder. Move on to the alternative balanced thought you developed in response to one of your hot thoughts. Use an acceptance mantra. Then do a relaxation reminder again. Try a different coping thought for physiological arousal. An acceptance mantra. A reminder to relax. And so on. Make sure you leave lots of blank space on the tape between each of your coping suggestions so you'll have time to let them sink in during exposure. Keep coming back to your relaxation reminder and acceptance mantras. You can mix in the other coping thoughts almost randomly.

Make the tape long enough to last the length of one exposure session. By leaving blank spaces between coping thoughts and repeating them as necessary, you can make a tape of virtually any length. You'll also need to experiment with the tape to see how it works for you. See if there's enough space between coping thoughts to let them sink in. Also notice which coping thoughts seem believable and effective, and which ones aren't helping. Be aware of which coping thoughts may need to be repeated more often, and which you'll need to hear only once or not at all. You may go through several versions of your taped coping script before you feel confident in its effectiveness.

Example

Charles was doing exposure work to overcome his fear of heights. The first item on his hierarchy was to look out of a first-floor window for thirty seconds. The last item was to stand at a tenth-floor window, looking straight and then down. Getting through the hierarchy was going to require courage and a good coping script.

Charles started with a relaxation step. To remind himself to use deep breathing and cue-controlled relaxation, he developed the phrase "Breathe and relax."

The action plan step took more thought. Charles was afraid of looking foolish as he inched toward a high-rise window to peer down. He decided that if people entered the area where he was practicing, he'd stand reading a newspaper till they moved on. He also decided that if his anxiety reached Level 4 on the Bourne Scale, he'd temporarily retreat to a little park across from the building and do relaxation exercises there. To remind himself of these strategies, he chose the statement "I'm OK, I've got a plan."

The main anxiety symptoms that disturbed Charles were dizziness and leg weakness. He wrote a coping thought to remind himself that they were harmless: "Adrenaline does this—it's normal. I won't faint or fall down."

The fourth step, coping with catastrophic thoughts, took some time. Charles started by imagining himself looking out from a high window, and writing down his thoughts. He had two concerns: (1) that he might somehow accidentally break through the glass and fall out, and (2) that he might have a crazy impulse to jump through the sealed window. When he tried to determine which was the hotter thought, he realized he was far more frightened by a scenario of the glass accidentally breaking. On the following page is Charles's worksheet regarding his thought about accidentally breaking the glass and falling out.

For his acceptance mantra, Charles felt drawn to "Float past, do not listen in." He wanted to remind himself that the feeling of anxiety would end soon if he didn't listen to his scary thoughts.

Charles's Catastrophic Thought Worksheet		
Evidence For	**Evidence Against**	**Alternative or Balanced Thought**
1. Glass can break if you hit it hard enough. 2. A person can lose his balance or faint into the glass. (Charles couldn't think of any further real evidence.)	1. High-rises have safety glass that's very strong. 2. There's no way I could fall through safety glass if I was just standing next to it. 3. Feeling dizzy and full of adrenaline won't make me faint. 4. No one has ever accidentally fallen through a sealed high-rise window. The odds are a million to one. 5. The worst that can happen is tripping, leaning for a second against the window, then getting my balance. 6. When I tap on the glass, I can tell it's really thick.	Safety glass is too strong to be accidentally broken by someone standing next to it.

Charles decided to try putting his coping script on tape to play on his portable cassette player. He spoke slowly and calmly, leaving six to ten seconds between coping thoughts. Here's what he recorded:

> *Breathe and relax. . . . You're OK, you've got a plan. . . . Breathe and relax. . . . If you feel dizzy, remember adrenaline does that. It's normal. You won't faint or fall down. . . . Safety glass is too strong to accidentally break. . . . Breathe and relax. . . . Float past, do not listen in. . . . Breathe and relax. . . . It's just adrenaline. It's normal. You can't really faint. . . . Breathe and relax. . . . Safety glass is too strong to accidentally break. . . . Float past, don't listen in. . . . Breathe and relax. . . . Float past. . . . Adrenaline is normal, it can't hurt you. . . . Breathe and relax. . . . Float past, you can do it, you're OK. . . . Breathe and relax.*

Charles experimented with his tape, re-recording it several times, until the pacing, sequence of coping thoughts, and frequency of repetition felt really effective.

Chapter 13

Getting Mobilized

One of the effects of depression is feeling immobilized. It's hard to push yourself to do normal self-care activities, and pleasure seems all but absent from your life.

Feeling immobilized is not only a symptom of depression—it is a cause. The less you do, the more depressed you feel; and the more depressed you feel, the less you do. It's a negative spiral that maintains withdrawal—and prolongs depression.

The solution is to push yourself to higher levels of activity—even though you don't feel like it. Aaron Beck (Beck et al. 1979), Arthur Freeman (Freeman et al. 1990), Christine Padesky (Greenberger and Padesky 1995), and others have shown that a technique called activity scheduling can re-energize you and offer significant help in overcoming depression. The initial steps of the technique involve monitoring and recording your daily activities and rating them for levels of pleasure and mastery. The later steps encourage you to schedule in advance increasing numbers of pleasurable and mastery activities.

Symptom Effectiveness

Several studies by the National Institute of Mental Health have demonstrated the effectiveness of activity scheduling as one component in the cognitive behavioral treatment protocol for depression. Numerous studies have shown that increasing your activity level alone, without any other intervention, can significantly reduce depression.

Time for Mastery

The initial assessment period during which you monitor and record your activities lasts for one week. It will take four to eight weeks thereafter to schedule the gradual increase of pleasure and mastery activities.

Instructions

Step 1: Monitoring and Recording Your Weekly Activities

Make at least eight photocopies of the Weekly Activity Schedule that appears on the next page. Each box on the schedule represents an hour of your time. Throughout the next week record your main activity or activities during each hour. Whatever you're doing, just write it down. If you don't have time during the day to keep a record of your activities, be sure to record them each evening.

The reason you're keeping detailed accounts of your activities is to establish an activity baseline that will help you recognize progress in the weeks ahead. This is the foundation on which you will build a plan to both mobilize yourself and help yourself feel less depressed.

Step 2: Identifying and Rating Pleasure and Mastery Activities

While you are recording your first week's activities, you need to pay attention to two variables: pleasure and mastery. First, has the activity you've written down provided you *any* pleasure? If so, write a *P* in that box and rate the pleasurable activity on a scale from 1 (minimal pleasure) to 10 (extreme pleasure).

You also need to identify mastery activities, in which you take care of yourself or others. A list of example mastery activities is provided under step 3. If a box contains a mastery activity, write an *M*. Then rate your sense of achievement, *given how tired or depressed you may have felt at the time*. The scale goes from 1 (minimal sense of achievement) to 10 (great sense of achievement). Remember that the scale doesn't measure how much you objectively achieved, nor does it reflect what you would have achieved before you were depressed. Instead it measures a *sense of achievement* that takes into account how hard this activity was, considering how you were feeling.

Identifying and rating pleasure and mastery activities is very important. It may help you recognize how life has gotten out of balance; many things you formerly enjoyed are no longer part of your week. What you are now doing provides very little emotional nourishment. Pleasure ratings also give you information about the activities you still enjoy, and which ones offer the best boost to your mood. Noticing and rating your mastery activities may help you recognize that, despite everything, you're still trying hard. You're still doing things to cope. And even though you're not as efficient or effective as you were before becoming depressed, the things you do are real achievements, given how you feel.

Alicia's first Weekly Activity Schedule appears on page 151. Notice that every box is filled in, even if she is only sleeping. Also notice which activities she labels as pleasure or mastery.

Weekly Activity Schedule							
	M	**T**	**W**	**TH**	**F**	**S**	**S**
6-7							
7-8							
8-9							
9-10							
10-11							
11-12							
12-1							
1-2							
2-3							
3-4							
4-5							
5-6							
6-7							
7-8							
8-9							
9-10							
10-11							
11-12							
12-6							

When Alicia reviewed her activity schedule at the end of the week, she made some interesting discoveries. First of all, she was watching a lot of TV and not enjoying it. Most of her pleasure came from interacting with people and sometimes reading. Sitting around the house or lying in bed late in the morning seemed associated with increased depression.

Alicia had higher mastery ratings in school when she had studied the night before. And while she had some consistent sense of mastery at work, she felt higher levels of achievement when doing a special project. She also felt more mastery when she made her own dinner and paid some attention to her appearance before going out.

Step 3: Scheduling Activities

It's time to increase both pleasure and mastery activities during your week. Identify at least ten hours on your activity schedule when you're engaged in an optional activity that provides neither pleasure nor a sense of mastery. See if you can find one or two of these hours each day. Soon you will schedule new pleasure or mastery activities for these hours to replace the old, unprofitable activities.

Pleasure Activities

Examine the following list of pleasure activities:

- Visiting friends/family
- Phone calls to friends/family
- Movies/plays
- Videos/TV
- Exercise
- Sports activities
- Games
- Computer activities
- Internet surfing
- Internet chat room
- Listening to music
- Going away for a weekend
- Planning vacation
- Hobby activities
- Collecting
- Crafts
- Enjoying the sun
- Relaxing with a hot drink
- Listening to educational tapes, relaxation tapes, or audio books

- Walking/hiking
- Shopping
- Hot bath
- Reading
- Gardening
- Writing
- Going out to eat
- Eating favorite treat
- Being held/touched
- Massage
- Sexual activities
- Going for a drive
- Picnic
- Going to a favorite beautiful place
- Sitting in a peaceful place
- Writing letters
- Artistic activities
- Watching/reading the news

Alicia's Weekly Activity Schedule

	M	T	W	TH	F	S	S
6-7	Sleep	Sleep	Sleep	Coffee/read paper P3	Sleep	Sleep	Sleep
7-8	Sleep	Sleep	Sleep	Shower/dress M2	Sleep	Sleep	Sleep
8-9	Shower/dress M2	Dress/no makeup	Dress/worry	Dress/no makeup	Shower/dress M2	Sleep	Sleep
9-10	Class M1	Sit around house, thinking	Class M1	Sit around; crossword puzzles	Class M3	Lay in bed	Sleep
10-11	Class M1	Sit around house, thinking	Class M1	Sit around; crossword puzzles	Class M3	Lay in bed	Lay in bed
11-12	Class M2	Call Bill P2	Class M1	Reading	Class M3	Make breakfast M2	Read in bed: novel
12-1	Lunch Ice cream sandwich P1	Sandwich at home	Buy school supplies M3	Sandwich at home	Sleep in car	Sit around house, thinking	Eat out: lunch P1
1-2	Taking orders M3	Taking orders M2	Taking orders M3	Taking orders M3	Taking orders M2	Sit around house, thinking	TV
2-3	Taking orders M3	Taking orders M3	Taking orders M3	Taking orders M3	Taking orders M2	Bill comes back—talk P2	TV
3-4	Taking orders M3	Writing new phone script P3 M7	Taking orders M3	Taking orders M3	Research project at work M6	Make love P5	TV
4-5	Talking to Rita at work P3	Ice cream with Rita P4	Taking orders M2	Talking to Rita P3	Research project at work M6	TV	TV
5-6	Work till 5:45, drive home	Sit in car reading	Sit around at home	Study M3	Clean desk M3	TV	Nap
6-7	Make/eat dinner M3	Eat out P3	Make/eat dinner M2	Make/eat dinner M2	No food in house: order pizza	Dinner out: fight with Bill	Study, can't focus M1
7-8	TV P1	Study, can't focus M2	TV	Brother calls P3	Kissing/talking with Bill P5	TV	TV while eating
8-9	TV	Give up, watch TV	TV	TV	Eat out P3	TV	TV
9-10	TV	TV	Call Susan, Lori P4	TV	Movie P4	TV P2	TV
10-11	TV: good program	TV	TV	TV P1	Movie P4	TV	TV
11-12	Make love with Bill (rushed) P3	Worry about school	Reading P2	Study M3	Talking with Bill P4	TV	Lying in bed; thinking
12-6	Reading till 2:30; can't sleep P1	Sleep	Sleep	Watch TV 2-4:30; can't sleep	Reading till 1:00 P2	Sleep	Reading; TV till 2; can't sleep P1

This is a short list, and there are many other possibilities for activities that would bring you pleasure. In the blanks below, write some of your own ideas about pleasurable activities. Think back over the years to the things you've enjoyed. Attempt to remember everything you've ever tried that was fun. Review the list above and try to turn some of the generic categories into specific things that give you pleasure. For instance, under games, you might enjoy playing pool or cards. Under crafts, you might have enjoyed needlepoint or building miniature models. Under artistic activities, you might enjoy going to galleries or writing haiku. Under calling or visiting friends, there may be certain people you'd enjoy spending more time with. Right now fill in *all* the blanks below with specific pleasures that you have enjoyed or can imagine enjoying in the future.

Some of My Pleasure Activities

_____   _____

_____   _____

_____   _____

_____   _____

_____   _____

_____   _____

_____   _____

_____   _____

Don't be surprised if many of the things you've enjoyed in the past seem totally without interest now. Or if things you once looked forward to seem more of a hassle or a burden. This is the effect of depression. When you begin to schedule pleasurable activities into your week, you will feel better, even if the activities seem uninteresting at the moment.

Right now, select five to seven pleasurable activities to schedule on the next week's activity chart. At this time you should also try to add one new mastery activity each day.

Often these are self-care efforts that you may have neglected. You may need to grocery shop, run errands, clean or straighten something, write letters, or make important calls. When you're depressed and immobilized, even normal self-maintenance can seem impossibly hard. The following is a list of mastery activities you might schedule into your week.

Mastery Activities

- Shopping
- Going to bank
- Helping child with homework
- Supervising children's bedtime activities
- Bathing
- Preparing a hot meal
- Paying bills
- Getting up before 9:00
- Walking dog
- Fixing something
- Cleaning something
- Doing dishes
- Exercising/stretching
- Resolving a conflict
- Doing laundry/going to cleaners
- Gardening
- Doing an errand
- Going to work
- Tackling challenging tasks at work

- Folding and putting away clothes
- Watering garden
- Solving a problem
- Straightening/putting things in order
- Improving environment/decorating
- Changing oil in car
- Making a business call
- Calling back friends
- Writing in journal
- Self-help exercise
- Spiritual/religious activities
- Grooming
- Getting hair cut
- Deciding which clothes to wear
- Dressing up
- Writing letters
- Transporting your children
- Artistic activities
- Arranging activities for your children

After reviewing the above items, it's time to make your own list of mastery activities that might give you a feeling of accomplishment. Fill in *all* the blanks with possible activities that you eventually might schedule into your week.

Some of My Mastery Activities

_____   _____

_____   _____

_____   _____

_____   _____

_____   _____

_____   _____

_____   _____

From the list you've made of possible mastery activities, select from five to seven to sprinkle through your coming week. Try not to do more than one *extra* mastery activity a day—that may be pushing too hard. Notice the hours in your Weekly Activity Schedule where you have typically been unproductive and depressed. These are prime opportunities for you to substitute a mastery activity that can give you a sense of achievement.

Note that some mastery activities may be too involved to accomplish in an hour, or simply too overwhelming when tackled all at once. It may help to break a mastery activity into smaller steps that you can accomplish in no more than five to fifteen minutes. For example, a plan to improve the appearance of your living room might involve many steps, starting with a decision to buy and hang a new poster. Some mastery activities may stretch over two or more weeks as you work through each step in the process.

Example

On the following page are the new activities that Alicia scheduled for the second week of her program to get mobilized.

In the past, Alicia had struggled to do any studying at all and usually did all her studying on the day before she went to class. Now for the eve of each class day she was actually scheduling two hours of study time—often with an hour of relaxation in between.

Alicia's mastery list included items such as ordering new checks, doing her laundry, and food shopping. She integrated these items into her week during times when she would otherwise have been watching television or brooding.

From Alicia's pleasure list she selected items such as listening to her new CDs, calling friends, reading in the tub, backboard tennis, hiking, dinner out, and a movie. These were all activities she had enjoyed in the past and felt willing to try in the coming week.

When Alicia wrote an item into her Weekly Activity Schedule, she considered it to be a commitment to herself. She tried to think of it as an appointment she was making with someone she respected and didn't wish to disappoint.

Weeks 3 through X

Set a goal that you will add a combination of seven mastery and pleasure items to each new Weekly Activity Schedule. Try to keep as many of the old items as were pleasurable or practical to repeat. But don't hesitate to drop anything that simply didn't work.

Be particularly aware of things you've been avoiding as a good source of mastery items. If you've been putting off doing the dishes, make an appointment with yourself on

Alicia's Newly Scheduled Activities

	M	T	W	TH	F	S	S
6-7							
7-8							
8-9							
9-10		Call to order new checks (M2)		Backboard tennis (P1)			
10-11						Food shop (M1)	Study (M2)
11-12							Study (M2)
12-1						Hike in Muir Woods (P2)	
1-2							
2-3							Walk—Lake Merced (P3)
3-4							
4-5							
5-6	Shop for some CDs (P2)						
6-7					Dinner out at Solernos (P3)		
7-8	Listen to new CDs (P3)	Study (M2)	Laundry I've put off (M1)	Study (M2)	Dinner out at Solernos (P3)		
8-9		Listen to CDs (P2)	Call Sandi or Gail (P2)	Read novel in tub (P3)	Movie (P3)		
9-10		Study (M2)		Study (M2)	Movie (P3)		
10-11			Folding clothes (M1)	Watch video (P2)			
11-12				Watch video (P2)			
12-6							

the Weekly Activity Schedule to get it done. If you've been putting off renewing your driver's license, write in a definite time when you'll accomplish this task.

Make your commitment to pleasure items as important as the mastery activities. Right now your life is out of balance—there isn't enough that you genuinely enjoy. Increasing the number of nourishing experiences in your week is an absolutely essential step to overcoming depression.

Step 4: Prediction Ratings

You may have noticed on Alicia's Weekly Activity Schedule that each new mastery or pleasure item had already been rated on a 1–10 scale. That's because Alicia was predicting how great her sense of achievement or pleasure would be when later in the week she undertook the activity. Alicia's "P1" prediction for playing some backboard tennis indicates that she expected very little enjoyment from this activity. Her "P3" prediction for dinner out and a movie suggests that she expected a modestly good time.

A very important part of planning your activities is trying to anticipate how they will make you feel. Most depressed people make very conservative predictions about the amount of pleasure or achievement they will feel during a planned activity. It's OK not to feel hopeful. You may anticipate very little in the way of good feelings from your planned activities. But do them anyway and evaluate what happens.

Right now use a blank Weekly Activity Schedule to plan the new mastery and pleasure activities for your coming week. Use the 1–10 scale to predict how much pleasure or achievement you will feel, and circle that number on your schedule.

During the week you should write the *actual* mastery or pleasure rating for your new activity. This can go right next to your circled prediction. One of the things you're likely to notice is that actual pleasure or achievement experiences often feel better than you expected. As noted earlier, depression tends to make you pessimistic. Comparing your prediction to the actual pleasure or mastery levels you experience may help you recognize how depression distorts your view of things. The fact that your new activities may feel better than you anticipated could help you resist the discouraging inner voice that tells you, "Don't bother with anything new; it's a lot of work and you'll still feel lousy."

Alicia was surprised to learn that she enjoyed things more than she had thought she would. Note the difference between her circled predictions and her actual pleasure or mastery ratings as they appear on the following page.

In particular, Alicia felt significantly more achievement and pleasure than she'd predicted in her new evening activities. She realized that television was numbing and depressing her. The new activities were a way to get her off the couch and doing something that offered a chance of feeling better.

During week 3, Alicia began to focus on replacing some of her TV time on the weekend. She chose additional items from her mastery and pleasure lists and used successes from the previous week (listening to CDs, calling friends, reading in the tub, and tennis) to replace the endless hours of weekend TV. While this was an effort, Alicia found that she felt much better when her weekend was dotted with scheduled activities. It kept her moving, and although she sometimes longed for the couch, she found she was less depressed as she did more.

Alicia's Newly Scheduled Activities for Week 2							
	M	**T**	**W**	**TH**	**F**	**S**	**S**
6-7							
7-8							
8-9							
9-10		Call to order new checks ⓂM2 M3		Back-board tennis ⓅP1 P4			
10-11						Food shop ⓂM1 M4	Study ⓂM2 M3
11-12							Study ⓂM2 M3
12-1					Hike in Muir Woods ⓅP2 Didn't go		
1-2							
2-3							Walked—Lake Merced ⓅP3 P4
3-4							
4-5							
5-6	Shop for some CDs ⓅP2 P4						
6-7					Dinner out at Solernos ⓅP3 P3		
7-8	Listen to new CDs ⓅP3 P4	Study ⓂM2 M3	Laundry I've put off ⓂM1 M4	Study ⓂM2 M2	Dinner out at Solernos ⓅP3 P3		
8-9		Listen to CDs ⓅP2 P4	Call Sandi or Gail ⓅP2 P5	Read novel in tub ⓅP3 P4	Movie ⓅP3 P4		
9-10		Study ⓂM2 M3		Study ⓂM2 M2	Movie ⓅP3 P4		
10-11			Folding clothes ⓂM1 M3	Watch video ⓅP2 P3			
11-12				Watch video ⓅP2 P3			
12-6							

Special Considerations

Some people feel that they don't have time in their week for anything new. Since the weekly activity schedule is a crucial intervention for overcoming depression, you may need to limit or suspend some of the activities that you typically do in order to increase the ratio of pleasure and mastery experiences. Go through your first Weekly Activity Schedule and cross out any box where the activity isn't *absolutely essential*. These are the hours where you may now substitute new mastery and pleasure activities.

After four or five weeks of adding new activities, nearly everyone will find their days becoming rather full. At this point a certain amount of pruning may be in order—eliminating some of the new activities that offer little nourishment.

Despite the fact that you'll be adding fewer new activities after weeks 4 or 5, you should still continue to make plans on your Weekly Activity Schedule. Writing something down increases the chance that you will do it. Keep filling in planned mastery and pleasure activities in your weekly schedule until you feel a real improvement in your level of depression.

Chapter 14

Problem Solving

Problems that elude solution result in chronic emotional pain. When your usual coping strategies fail, a growing sense of helplessness makes the search for novel solutions more difficult. The possibility of relief seems to recede, the problem begins to appear insoluble, and anxiety or despair can increase to crippling levels.

In 1971, Thomas D'Zurilla and Marvin Goldfried devised a five-step problem-solving strategy for generating novel solutions to any kind of problem. They defined a problem as "failure to find an effective response." For example, the fact that a person can't find one of his shoes in the morning is not in itself a problem. It becomes a problem only if he neglects to look under the bed where the shoe is most likely to be found. If he looks in the sink, the medicine cabinet, and the garbage disposal, he is beginning to create a problem—his response is not effective in finding the missing shoe and, therefore, the situation becomes "problematic."

A convenient acronym for the five steps of problem solving is *SOLVE*, which stands for

State your problem.
Outline your goals.
List your alternatives.
View the consequences.
Evaluate your results.

Symptom Effectiveness

Problem solving is effective for reducing anxiety associated with procrastination and the inability to make decisions. It is useful for relieving the feelings of powerlessness or anger associated with chronic problems for which no alternative solution has been found. Problem solving is not recommended for the treatment of phobias or conditions of global, free-floating anxiety.

Time for Mastery

Problem-solving techniques can be put into effect the same day they are learned. After several weeks of practice, applying the steps becomes largely automatic.

Instructions

Step 1: State Your Problem

The first step in problem solving is to identify the problem situations in your life. People normally experience problems in areas such as finances, work, social relationships, and family life. The checklist on the following pages will help you identify the area in which you operate least effectively and have the most problems. This is the area you will concentrate on as you develop problem-solving skills.

After each situation listed, check the box that best describes how much of a problem it is for you. If you have trouble determining whether a situation is a significant problem for you, imagine yourself in that situation. Include lots of sights and sounds and actions to make it seem real. In that situation, do you feel angry? depressed? anxious? confused? These are "red flag" emotions. When you experience anger, depression, anxiety, or confusion, you are probably in a situation that is a problem for you—something about the way you are responding to the situation isn't working for you. Mark the appropriate box:

No interference—This doesn't apply to me or doesn't bother me.

Interferes a little—This mildly affects my life and is a small drain on my energy.

Interferes moderately—This has a significant impact on my life.

Interferes a great deal—This greatly disrupts my day-to-day existence and strongly affects my sense of well-being.

Problem Checklist

Health

	Interference			
	None	Little	Moderate	Great Deal
Difficulty sleeping				
Weight problems				
Feeling physically tired and run-down				
Stomach trouble				
Chronic physical problems				
Difficulty getting up in the morning				
Poor diet and nutrition				

Finances

Difficulty making ends meet				
Insufficient money for basic necessities				
Increasing amounts of debt				
Unexpected expenses				
Too little money for hobbies and recreation				
No steady source of income				
Too many financial dependents				

Work

Monotonous and boring work				
Poor relations with boss or supervisor				
Being rushed and under stress				
Wanting a different job or career				
Needing more education or experience				
Fear of losing job				
Not getting along with coworkers				
Unemployment				
Unpleasant working conditions				
Needing more freedom at work				

Living Situation

	Interference			
	None	**Little**	**Moderate**	**Great Deal**
Bad neighborhood				
Too far from work or school				
Too small				
Unpleasant conditions				
Things in need of repair				
Poor relationship with landlord				

Social Relationships

Timidity or shyness around the opposite sex				
Not having many friends				
Too little contact with the opposite sex				
Feeling lonely				
Not getting along well with certain people				
A failed or failing love affair				
Feeling left out				
Lack of love and affection				
Vulnerablity to criticism				
Wanting more closeness to people				
Not being understood by others				
Not really knowing how to converse				
Not finding the right mate				

Recreation

Not having enough fun				
Ineptitude at sports or games				
Too little leisure time				
Wanting more chance to enjoy art or self-expression				
Little chance to enjoy nature				
Wanting to travel				
Needing a vacation				
Inability to think of anything fun to do				

Family	Interference			
	None	Little	Moderate	Great Deal
Feeling rejected by family				
Discord at home with mate				
Not getting along with one or more of the children				
Feeling trapped in painful family situation				
Insecurity—fear of losing mate				
Inability to be open and honest with family members				
Desire for sexual contact with someone other than mate				
Conflict with parents				
Having interests different from those of mate				
Interference by relatives				
Marriage breaking up				
Children having problems at school				
Sick family member				
Excessive quarreling at home				
Anger, resentment toward mate				
Irritation with habits of a family member				
Worry about family member				

Psychological

Having a particular bad habit				
Religious problems				
Problems with authority				
Competing goals or demands				
Obsession with distant or unobtainable goals				
Lack of motivation				
Feeling very depressed at times				
Feeling nervous at certain times				
Feeling blocked from attaining goals				
Feeling angry a lot				
Worrying				

Other

(If particular situations not listed above significantly interfere with your life, write them here and rate them.)

_____

_____

_____

_____

Using the problem checklist you have just completed, determine the general category that causes the most interference in your life. From that area, pick one of the situations that you have ranked as interfering moderately or a great deal.

Using the situation you have chosen, fill out the Problem Analysis on the next page. Try to put at least one word in each blank. When a blank isn't large enough for all you have to write, use a separate sheet of paper.

By describing the situation in terms of who, what, where, when, how, and why, you will get your problem clearer in your mind. You'll also uncover many more details than you usually have available for consideration. Take your time. The details of your behavior, feelings, and wants are also important because they will provide clues for generating solutions later.

Step 2: Outline Your Goals

Having completed your Problem Analysis, it's time to set one or more goals for change. Examine your response to the problem—what you do, how you feel, and what you want. These statements, in particular, are helpful for developing specific goals.

Jane was struck by how many ineffective methods she used to get her son, Jim, to obey. And how she kept using them even though she was largely ignored. But the problem was greater than Jim's resistance. Jane was concerned about how angry and stressed she felt during her interactions with her son. She needed to calm down. And she was aware that much of her upset stemmed from a growing sense that Jim didn't care about her. This feeling needed to change as well.

Jane developed the following three goals to address her concerns:

Goal A: Develop an effective strategy to get Jim to cooperate.

Goal B: Feel calmer.

Goal C: Feel more cared for by Jim.

Problem Analysis

Situation (from problem checklist or briefly in your own words):

_____

_____

Who else is involved?

_____

What happens? (What is done or not done that bothers you?)

_____

Where does it happen?

_____

When does it happen? (What time of day? How often? How long does it last?)

_____

How does it happen? (What rules does it seem to follow? What moods are involved)?

_____

Why does it happen? (What reasons do you or others give for the problem at the time?)

_____

What do you do? (What is your actual response to the problem situation?)

_____

How do you feel? (Angry? Depressed? Confused?)

_____

What do you want (What things do you want to change?)

_____

Example

This is the Problem Analysis completed by Jane, the mother of a rebellious twelve-year-old son:

Problem Analysis

Situation (from problem checklist or briefly in your own words):

Not getting along with child.

Who else is involved?

Twelve-year-old son, Jim.

What happens? (What is done or not done that bothers you?)

He won't do chores—take out garbage, water garden, set table.

Where does it happen?

At home—especially in family room, in front of TV.

When does it happen? (What time of day? How often? How long does it last?)

Afternoon and evening, for about two hours, nearly every day.

How does it happen? (What rules does it seem to follow? What moods are involved)?

The more I remind him of chores, the more sullen he gets. Just sits there while I get madder.

Does chores resentfully after I threaten no TV.

Why does it happen? (What reasons do you or others give for the problem at the time?)

He's going through a stage. I expect too much. He doesn't care how I feel.

What do you do? (What is your actual response to the problem situation?)

Suffer in silence, then remind, then nag, then yell and threaten.

How do you feel? (Angry? Depressed? Confused?)

Angry at Jim; feel he doesn't care about me; feel stressed and upset.

What do you want (What things do you want to change?)

I want Jim to obey me.

Step 3: List Your Alternatives

In this phase of problem solving, you "brainstorm" to create strategies that will help you achieve your newly formulated goals. The brainstorming technique set forth by Osborn in 1963 has four basic rules:

A. **Criticism is ruled out.** This means that you write down any new idea or possible solution without judging it as good or bad. Evaluation is deferred to a later decision-making phase.

B. **Freewheeling is welcomed.** The crazier and wilder your idea is, the better. Following this rule can help lift you out of mental ruts. You may suddenly break free of your old, limited view of the problem and see it in an entirely different light.

C. **Quantity is best.** The more ideas you generate, the better your chances are of having a few good ones. Just write them down, one after another, without thinking a lot about each idea. Don't stop until you have a good, long list.

D. **Combination and improvement are sought.** Go back over your list to see how some ideas might be combined or improved. Sometimes two pretty good ideas can be joined into an even better idea.

Brainstorming during this phase should be limited to *general strategies* for achievement of goals. Leave the nuts and bolts of specific actions for later. You need a good overall strategy first. Particular behavioral steps come in the next phase.

Use this form to list at least ten alternative strategies for accomplishing each of your goals:

Alternative Strategies Lists

Goal A.

1. _____

2. _____

3. _____

4. _____

5. _____

6. _____

7. _____

8. _____

9. _____

10. _____

Goal B.

1. _____
2. _____
3. _____
4. _____
5. _____
6. _____
7. _____
8. _____
9. _____
10. _____

Goal C.

1. _____
2. _____
3. _____
4. _____
5. _____
6. _____
7. _____
8. _____
9. _____
10. _____

Jane used brainstorming techniques to generate the following strategies for achieving her three goals:

Goal A: Develop an effective strategy to get Jim to cooperate.

- No TV until the chores are done.
- Give Jim a larger allowance and tie it to the chores.
- Blow up Jim's CD player.
- Let him keep his room any way he wants. Limit chores to common areas.
- Explain expectations for chores in the morning before school.
- Keep a chore chart.
- Give a reward each week for completed chores (credits toward a CD?).
- If chores aren't done by a specific time, he loses his phone.
- If he doesn't do chores, he has to make his own lunch.
- Computer privileges depend on finishing chores.

Goal B: Feel calmer.

- No matter what, stop yelling.
- Rest whenever I start feeling upset or angry.
- Blow up the TV—the noise drives me crazy.
- Husband does disciplining.
- Take a week off and go to the mountains.
- Get a massage vibrator.
- Take a course in relaxation.
- Exchange massages with husband after the kids are in bed.
- Take Valium.
- Start to swim again.

Goal C: Feel more cared for by Jim.

- No matter what he does or doesn't do, stop yelling at him.
- Talk to him instead of blasting him.
- Let my husband do the disciplining.
- "Spontaneously" hug him two or three times a day.
- Reward him with a hug when he actually does his chore.
- Praise him a lot.
- Ask him about school and "check in" with him at least once a day.
- If he doesn't obey, take a few minutes with him and find out if anything's wrong.

- It's more important to me to share good feelings with my son than to have him do his chores every day—put a sign on my mirror to remind me.

- Explain my problems to him and ask for his help.

It is important not to give up the search for alternative strategies too quickly. Your tenth idea may be the best one. Jane went over her list and combined some of the ideas. For example, she combined three items under Goal A: No computer, phone, or TV until chores are done. And under goal C she combined checking in with her son once a day with explaining her problems and asking for his help.

Step 4: View the Consequences

By now you should have several goals, each with at least ten strategies for its accomplishment. The next step is to select the most promising strategies and view the consequences of putting them into action. For some people this process of figuring and weighing consequences happens automatically as soon as they think of a possible strategy for getting what they want. Others are likely to ponder the consequences more slowly. Whichever category better describes you, it will be helpful to do this step thoroughly and conscientiously.

Pick the goal that is most attractive to you. Go over its strategies and cross out any obviously bad ideas. Whenever possible, combine several strategies into one. Try to reduce your list to three strategies representing your best ideas.

List these three strategies in the spaces provided on the following Evaluating Consequences form. Under each strategy, list any negative and positive consequences you can think of. How would putting that strategy into action affect what you feel, need, or want? How would it affect the people in your life? How would it change their reaction to you? How would it affect your life right now, next month, or next year? Take some time to get *both* positive and negative consequences for each possible strategy.

When you have the major consequences listed, go over each one and ask yourself how likely it is to come about. If the consequence is very unlikely, cross it out—you're telling yourself horror stories or being falsely optimistic.

Then score the remaining consequences as follows:

- If the consequence is predominantly personal, give it two points.

- If the consequence predominantly affects others, give it one point.

- If the consequence is predominantly long range, give it two points.

- If the consequence is predominantly short range, give it one point.

Note that consequences can be both personal and long range at the same time (total score of 4), affect others long range (total score of 3), and so on.

Add up the scores for each strategy to see whether the positive consequences outweigh the negative. Then select the strategy whose positive consequences most greatly outweigh the negative consequences.

Evaluating Consequences

Strategy: _____

Positive Consequences	Score	Negative Consequences	Score
_____	_____	_____	_____
_____	_____	_____	_____
_____	_____	_____	_____
_____	_____	_____	_____
_____	_____	_____	_____
total:	_____	total:	_____

Strategy: _____

Positive Consequences	Score	Negative Consequences	Score
_____	_____	_____	_____
_____	_____	_____	_____
_____	_____	_____	_____
_____	_____	_____	_____
_____	_____	_____	_____
total:	_____	total:	_____

Strategy: _____

Positive Consequences	Score	Negative Consequences	Score
_____	_____	_____	_____
_____	_____	_____	_____
_____	_____	_____	_____
_____	_____	_____	_____
_____	_____	_____	_____
total:	_____	total:	_____

Steps to Action

Now you need to decide on the steps you will have to take to put your strategy into action. Jane thought of four steps to put "Husband does the disciplining" into action:

1. Discuss the subject with husband after Jim goes to bed on Tuesday.

2. Take five minutes each day after work to discuss with husband how well chores are being done.

3. Have husband spend time with Jim each evening and focus on how well chores are being done.

4. Use the time I used to spend disciplining to do something nice for husband: bake a special dessert; give a back rub.

You may have trouble thinking of concrete behavioral steps. If so, return to brainstorming to develop a list of alternative steps. Then explore the likely consequences of the steps using the same technique you learned for selecting your overall strategy.

Evaluating Consequences—Jane's Goal C

Strategy: *Husband does the disciplining*

Positive Consequences	Score	Negative Consequences	Score
I'll be more relaxed	3	*Husband may be reluctant*	2
Have more time	2		
Better relationship with son	3		
total:	8	total:	2

Strategy: *Check in with Jim once a day; explain problems; ask for help*

Positive Consequences	Score	Negative Consequences	Score
Might understand each other better, feel closer	4	*Still won't do chores consistently*	3
Jim won't feel so pressured	2	*Telling Jim my problems might burden him or make him feel guilty*	3
Have more time	2		
total:	8	total:	6

Strategy: *No matter what, stop yelling*

Positive Consequences	Score	Negative Consequences	Score
It will be quieter	3	*Chores won't get done*	2
Won't hurt Jim's feelings	2	*My frustration will build*	4
total:	5	total:	6

Step 5: Evaluate Your Results

The last step is the hardest since you now have to act. You've selected some new responses to an old situation. It is time to put your decisions into effect.

Once you have tried the new response, observe the consequences. Are things happening as you predicted? Are you *satisfied* with the outcome? Being satisfied means that the new response is helping you reach your goals in a way your old "solution" was not.

If you are still not reaching your goals, return to your alternative strategies list. You can either generate more ideas at this point or select one or more strategies that you passed over before. You may repeat Steps 3, 4, and 5 of the problem-solving procedures.

Example

Al was a travel agent in his late forties. He had become increasingly dissatisfied with his job. He was bored by arranging the same tours and cruises. Six months previously a new computer system had been installed in his office. He was given basic instructions for handling the computer equipment and soon found himself fascinated with computer systems. He hatched the idea of cutting back to half time at work in order to return to school for instruction in programming languages.

Al's boss took a dim view of his plan. They had several confrontations about the issue. Al felt resentful and became inattentive to the detailed travel arrangements that were his responsibility. This provoked still more confrontations with his boss.

Al applied the SOLVE system to his problem like this:

1. **State your problem.** *My job is boring. I want to go to school and switch careers. I have poor relations with my boss. The situation is that I want to take time off to attend school, but my boss won't let me.*

   Al completed his Problem Analysis, spelling out the who, what, where, when, how, and why of his situation. He also looked carefully at his response to the problem:

   - What I do. *Ask the boss for time off, get turned down, complain, and take it out on customers by being rude and forgetting details.*

   - How I feel. *I'm angry, frustrated, feel "dissed" by boss.*

   - What I want. *To feel less bored by what I'm doing.*

2. **Outline your goals.** After looking carefully at his Problem Analysis, Al developed three goals: (1) better relations with boss, (2) to enjoy job more, and (3) to learn more about computers.

3. **List your alternatives.** These are some of the alternative strategies that Al came up with for achieving his goals:
   - Better relations with boss
     Get involved in creating the new Russia tour package.
     Stop complaining and picking fights.
     Quit, go to school, support myself with some mail-order scam.

- To enjoy job more
  Develop more personal relationships with customers.
  Take advantage of travel agent discounts on fares and hotels.

- To learn more about computers
  Experiment with and learn everything about computers at work.
  Take one night class.
  Negotiate with boss for one morning per week off for a class.

4. **View the consequences.** Al crossed off several obviously bad alternatives, such as quitting outright. He considered the consequences in terms of long- versus short-range outcomes and outcomes for himself versus others. This showed him that his best options were to get busy on the new tour package, stop complaining, and concentrate on his customers. His intention was to improve relations with his boss to the point where he could resume negotiations, about getting some time off.

   Al did more brainstorming to develop some concrete steps to follow day by day. He put his plans into effect for five weeks.

5. **Evaluate your results.** As he expected, Al's relationship with his boss improved. Since he was busy and not fighting with the boss, he enjoyed his job more. He showed his boss how he could take a couple of hours off on Tuesday morning and still serve all his customers well. His boss agreed. Al spent that morning taking a computer programming class.

Special Considerations

Some people feel a little overwhelmed by the complex steps involved in problem solving. Their response is, "Do I really have to do all that?" The answer is yes—the first time. You've been stuck for a while in a problematic situation. Your old, habitual solutions haven't worked. You need to follow each step of the technique to identify and then achieve your goals. Later, you can tailor the procedures to fit your particular style, and much of it will have become automatic.

Chapter 15

Testing Core Beliefs

Core beliefs are your most basic assumptions about your identity in the world. For instance, they depict you as beautiful or ugly, worthy or unworthy, lovable or unlovable. These core beliefs are formed mainly during your childhood and affect most of your actions.

From these beliefs or concepts you create rules to regulate your behavior. If the concepts are positive, the rules telling you how to live will be realistic and flexible. The reverse is also true: Negative concepts yield negative rules that are restrictive and fear-driven.

For example, Bud is an artist who, as a child, believed his parents when they called him stupid. He formed the negative core belief "I am stupid," which in turn produced these negative rules:

1. Don't apply for grants. Who would want my ideas?

2. Don't do anything mathematical. I don't have the brains.

3. Don't argue. People will know I am dumb.

4. Don't say too much. People will see how little I know.

Core beliefs and rules are so fundamental to personality that few people are aware of them. Yet every part of your life is dictated by these beliefs and rules. They have enormous influence on your automatic thoughts. Bud's automatic thoughts, in any interaction, remind him of his stupidity. They lead him to expect negative judgments and rejection: "Boy, was that dumb. . . . What a stupid remark. . . . They're wondering if you can even read. . . . Idiot. . . . Shut up, you're making a fool of yourself."

In summary, core beliefs are the foundation of your personality: They largely dictate what you can and cannot do (rules), and how you interpret events in your world (automatic thoughts).

You can change negative core concepts. This chapter teaches how to identify, test, and modify these beliefs based on work by Aaron Beck and Arthur Freeman (1990), Donald Meichenbaum (1988), Jeffrey Young (1990), and Matthew McKay and Patrick Fanning (1991).

Symptom Effectiveness

Techniques in this chapter can help you identify your core beliefs or concepts, test the veracity of these concepts, and begin the process of changing them. This process can relieve worry, depression, perfectionism, social phobia, low self-esteem, shame, and guilt.

People who are victims of child abuse, are in crisis, are addicted, or lack self-motivation should work on core beliefs only with the guidance of a mental health professional.

Time for Mastery

It will take eight to twelve weeks for you to identify, test for validity, and change one core belief and its rules.

Instructions

Step 1: Identifying Your Core Beliefs

You are probably aware of one or two of your core beliefs. But many of them may not be conscious. Core beliefs determine to what degree you believe you are worthy, safe, competent, powerful, autonomous, and loved; they also establish your sense of belonging and a basic picture of how you are treated by others.

Keep a Thought Journal for one week. You can use it to identify unknown core beliefs.

Thought Journal

The Thought Journal tracks negative core beliefs by recording your thoughts whenever you experience negative feelings. At the end of the day, remember or visualize situations where you felt anxious, sad, hurt, guilty, and so on. Note the automatic thoughts that stimulated your uncomfortable feelings.

On the next page is an entry from Janet's journal. Janet is a teacher and single parent.

Whenever you can't remember your automatic thoughts, use visualization to help recall details. To visualize, relax your muscles and then picture the event you wish to remember. See the situation, feel the sadness, anxiety, or anger. In your mind, smell, hear, taste, touch the situation. Then listen carefully to your automatic thoughts and write them in your journal.

Laddering

Laddering uncovers core beliefs by working down, rung by rung, through the meanings of a statement in your Thought Journal until you reach the core belief underpinning the statement. To search for a core belief through laddering, select a statement from your

	Janet's Thought Journal	
Situation	**Feeling**	**Thoughts**
I need to start writing my paper.	anxiety	I can't write well. What makes me think I can do this?
Electric screwdriver is lost when I need it.	anger	Every time I go to do something, I screw it up by losing a tool. I need to be more orderly.
I am cooking and I can't find the pot holder when I need it.	anxiety	This house is a rat's nest. It wouldn't take long to straighten it up. I just put off doing things.
Balancing checkbook and there is not enough money.	anxiety	I need to stop spending so much on restaurants or I won't have any money. I have no control over my spending.
Gave in and took Brad to the movies after I had told him I wouldn't because he wasn't helping around the house.	anger	I'm not a good mother. (Image of my mom upset, telling me I'm too soft.)

Thought Journal. Now write, "What if ___(your thought)___ is true? What does this mean?"

Answer these questions with beliefs about yourself, not your feelings. Feelings do not lead to core beliefs, but self-statements do.

Janet wrote the following exercise using the statement "I have no control over my spending" from her journal:

I have no control over my spending.
What if I just can't stop spending money? What does this mean?
It means I'll go broke.
What if I go broke? What does this mean?
It means my life will fall apart.
What if my life falls apart? What does this mean?
It means I can't control my life.
What if I can't control my life? What does this mean?
It means I am helpless.

Here Janet discovered a negative core belief. Later she could challenge the belief "I am helpless" to see if it was true.

Now select one statement from your journal and write your laddering exercise.

Theme Analysis

Theme analysis is another method to unearth core beliefs. Review the problematic situations listed in your Thought Journal, searching for a particular theme or common thread running through these situations. For instance, Janet reviewed her situations and realized many of them had to do with her son. She recognized a core belief that she was incompetent—a bad mother.

- Bud, the artist, read his list of situations:

- Applying for a grant.

- Arranging a show.

- Being asked to speak in front of the PTA.

- Friend asks for advice.

- Driving on the freeway.

- He realized that, except for driving on the freeway, he was anxious about exposing himself to judgment. He discovered a basic belief that he would not measure up to others' expectations. He felt unworthy.

Automatic thoughts can also be analyzed for themes. Janet reviewed her Thought Journal and saw she was chastising herself in terms such as "I need to be more orderly . . . rat's nest . . . I just put off doing things." She discovered that one of her core beliefs was that she was lazy.

Right now analyze your journal to find your core beliefs. Look for themes that pervade the problematic situations or your thoughts, and write them down.

Step 2: Assessing the Negative Impact

If you've identified two or more core beliefs, rank them by negative impact on your work, mood, relationships, health, and ability to enjoy life. Unless there is a compelling reason not to, begin working on the belief that has the greatest negative impact.

Step 3: Finding Testable Assumptions

Now that you have identified a core belief that has a strong negative impact on your life, it's time to explore its veracity. Because it is so subjective, you cannot test a core belief directly. But you can test the rules for living that derive from your belief.

Identify the Rules for Your Core Belief

Flowing from each core belief is a set of rules, a behavioral blueprint, for how you need to act in the world to avoid pain and catastrophe. For example, if you have a core belief that you are unworthy, typical rules might include "Never ask for anything; never say no; never get angry at anyone; always be supportive and giving; never make a mistake; never be an inconvenience."

Identify the rules derived from your core beliefs by completing the following exercise.

Exploring Your Basic Rules

A. On the top of a sheet of paper write the core belief you wish to explore and question.

B. Read the Basic Rules Checklist carefully. For each item ask, "If my core belief is true, what must I do or not do in this situation?" Be honest and open. Ask yourself, "What do I really do to cope with my belief? How do I protect myself? What do I avoid? How am I supposed to act? What are my limits?" On the left-hand side of your paper write your rules.

Basic Rules Checklist*

- Dealing with other people's . . .
  - Anger
  - Needs/desires/requests
  - Disappointment/sadness
  - Withdrawal
  - Praise/support
  - Criticism

- Dealing with mistakes

- Dealing with stress/problems/losses

- Risk taking/trying new things/challenges

- Conversation

- Expressing your . . .
  - Needs
  - Feelings
  - Opinions
  - Pain
  - Hope/wishes/dreams
  - Limits/saying no

- Asking for support/help

- Being . . .
  - Alone
  - With strangers
  - With friends
  - With family

- Trusting others

- Making friends
  - Whom to seek
  - How to act

---

* Adapted from *Prisoners of Belief* by Matthew McKay and Patrick Fanning (1991).

- Finding a sexual partner
  - Whom to seek
  - How to act

- Ongoing romantic relationships

- Sex

- Work/career

- Dealing with children

- Health/illness

- Recreational activities

- Traveling

- Maintaining your environment/self-care

Using the Basic Rules Checklist for her core belief "I am helpless," Janet discovered these rules:

1. I walk on eggshells to keep George in a good mood.

2. I won't buy a house.

3. I don't start conversations at parties.

4. I don't trust myself with a credit card.

5. I don't make independent decisions.

6. I don't try to solve problems.

Step 4: Generating Catastrophic Predictions

Consider the consequences of breaking each rule. Behind each rule is a catastrophic assumption about how things will turn out if you ignore its mandate. Your core-belief rules are usually based on assumed catastrophic consequences because you developed the rules to cope with real emotional or physical danger. However, these rules may no longer be necessary and the consequences for disobeying them may no longer be catastrophic or even unpleasant.

To the right of each rule you've listed, write the consequences you believe will occur if you disregard it. Remember to include not only your feelings, but objective consequences you can observe and test. For instance, Janet decided the consequences for breaking the rule "Walk on eggshells to keep George in a good mood" would be:

He will leave me.

He will take his anger out on Brad (her son).

I will get upset and he will hurt me.

The consequences she foresaw for breaking "Don't try to solve problems" were:

I won't think of any solutions and I'll get depressed.

My solution will be something stupid that won't work.
George will make fun of what I try.

Step 5: Selecting the Rules You Want to Test

There are five guidelines for selecting rules to test:

First, choose a rule for which it's easy to set up a test situation. Janet can't test her rule "Don't buy a house" because of the time, energy, and money involved. However, she could easily test the effect of being assertive with George.

Second, choose a rule that allows you to test the core belief directly. If Janet tested the rule "Don't start conversations at parties," she would not be testing her core belief that she is helpless. If, however, she tested the rule "Don't return to school" or "Don't make decisions," the outcome could definitely challenge the core belief.

Third, the rule should include a clear prediction of behavioral responses (yours and others'), not just subjective feelings.

Fourth, the outcome should be relatively immediate. If Janet decided to buy a house to dispute her core belief, she would lose her momentum by the time she found, bought, and lived in a new home.

Fifth, choose a relatively low-fear rule to test, or find a rule that can be tested in gradients, from slightly risky to very risky. Janet could check her rule "Don't return to school to learn a new career" by enrolling in one short community college course. If successful, she could move on to more challenging state college courses.

Step 6: Testing Your Rules

A. Identify one relatively low-risk situation in which to make your initial test. Janet decided to enroll in a carpentry class because she wouldn't lose much money or time.

B. Begin a Predictions Log. Write a specific, behavioral prediction of what the catastrophic outcome to the situation will be, based on your core belief. Bud's rule "Don't argue" needs to be rewritten as "Don't argue with the plumber over the hot-water-heater bill." Then he needs a behavioral prediction of what will happen if he disputes the bill. Bud predicts the plumber will mock him and refuse to do any more plumbing for him. Feelings may be included in your prediction, but only in addition to observable results.

C. Make a contract with yourself to break your rule. Commit to a specific time, place, and situation. Check with a support person if possible, one to whom you can report your test results.

D. Script your new behavior. Visualize what you'll do. Practice an imaginary test with a friend, or tape-record a dry run of your test. To avoid incurring the very consequences you wish to avoid, check that your tone of voice and your body language are not cold, frightened, or otherwise negative.

E. **Test your new behavior and collect data.** In your Predictions Log, write the outcomes of your test. Write which specific parts of your predictions occurred and which did not occur. If you are uncertain about people's reactions to your test, ask them some questions like the following:

- Did you have any reaction to what I said?

- I had the impression that you might be feeling _____ when I said _____. Was there anything to that?

- Is it OK with you that I _____?

In your Prediction Log, write the answers to these questions along with other data collected. How did any others on hand look during the test? What was said? What happened?

F. **Select more situations in which to test your rule, and repeat Steps B through E for each test.** Choose situations that gradually heighten your risk. As you obtain more and more positive outcomes to situations that break your rules, your core belief will be modified.

Bud tested his "Do not argue" rule many times. He discovered that 80 percent of the people listened to his arguments with respect, and 60 percent of them altered their behavior as a result of his argument. Twenty percent became irritated or disregarded his argument. Bud's log listed people's reactions, his responses, and his expectations. He noted that, although some people attacked him personally when he argued with them, his successes helped him be resilient when faced with these few "jerks."

With time, Bud's test situations became more spontaneous. He actively took on situations he previously would have avoided. You too, with time and success, can continue to look for opportunities to break the rules. You will have setbacks, but the data in your Predictions Log will enable you to have an objective view of those setbacks.

Step 7: Rewriting Core Beliefs

After you have tested your rules sufficiently and recorded your data in the Predictions Log, rewrite your core belief. Generalize the information in the log, yet include specific facts that will support your generalization. This becomes your new core belief.

Remember Janet, who held a core belief about being a poor mother? She rewrote it to say, "I am a skillful mother, usually. I am loving and self-disciplined as a mom, especially when I am not tired from work."

A. **Develop New Rules.** Use your positive core beliefs to write new rules. Write the beliefs on the left side of a page, your new rules on the right. Use *I* rather than *you*, and the present rather than the past tense to compose these rules. Write them as affirmations instead of commands or restrictions. If possible, include predictions with the rules. Here you may use the future tense.

Bud's page looked like this:

Bud's New Rules

Core Belief	New Rules
I am smart enough and can interact with people well. Most people respond with respect when I assert my ideas.	I am able to argue my position well, especially if I think before I speak.
	I can accept criticism from people I respect without feeling stupid.
	I can think about their objections and decide for myself what is correct.
	I am able to brainstorm ideas with Terry and Sandy and feel accepted.

When you write your new rules, they may seem to belong to another person, a more positive person than you once were. Core-belief work can change you dramatically. For this reason, you may not be sure of the validity of your new rules. This is OK. You will confirm them with your Evidence Log.

B. Keep an Evidence Log. To strengthen your new core beliefs, keep a log of interactions, events, conversations—anything that will support your new rules and core beliefs. To start your Evidence Log, write on the left side of a page "What Happened," on the right side, "What It Means."

Here's an example from Bud's Evidence Log:

Bud's Evidence Log

What Happened	What It Means
I played a trivia game at a party, and although I didn't win, I answered as many questions as George and Cindy.	I can hold my own in games that require thinking.
I asked Sal for more advertising for my show. I prepared what I was going to say, and I said it. I sounded knowledgeable, and Sal budgeted more money for the show.	If I script difficult tasks in advance, I can do as well as the next person.

If you don't remember to write in your log, try setting an alarm to go off every three hours as a reminder. Keep notebooks in your car, or wherever else you may have writing time. Before going to sleep, review your day for contributions to your Evidence Log.

Actively try to verify and therefore strengthen your new belief by testing its rules in a specific arena. Select a low-risk arena at first. Perhaps you might test the rules just with your mom, or just in the morning, or just at the office. Later, when the consequences become less threatening and you are more comfortable with your new belief, you may extend the risk and widen the arena.

Example

Sandra, an emergency dispatcher, wanted a higher-paying job in the same field, but she was afraid to train and apply for another position. She decided to try core-belief techniques to overcome her reticence.

She kept a Thought Journal and explored its meaning through laddering and theme analysis. She discovered that she felt incompetent and unsafe. She decided that her lack of security ("I'm not safe") had the greatest negative impact on her life, and that she would attack this core belief first.

She generated several rules from this core belief, including one she wished to test: "Don't ever question your boss, because you will lose your job." She scripted her first test of this rule with help from her husband, then she told her boss she needed relief during the busiest hours of the evening.

She got the relief and proceeded to riskier tests. Finally, she rewrote her core belief to say, "I am reasonably safe at work because I am skillful and apparently appreciated to the point that they'll do things for me."

Sandra searched for opportunities to test her new core belief and its rules. Eventually she took special training and requested a transfer within her department. She plans to attend nursing school later.

Chapter 16

Changing Core Beliefs
with Visualization

After working through chapter 2, "Uncovering Automatic Thoughts," you have probably identified several hot thoughts that reflect some of your deeply held core beliefs. Core beliefs have their roots in childhood. You can probably remember thinking that way since you were four or seven or twelve years old. This chapter teaches a powerful technique for changing those core beliefs by visualizing your inner child. It is taken in large part from our previous book, *Prisoners of Belief* (1991).

Psychologically speaking, it is not true that you can't change the past. Although you can't alter what happened to you or what you did, you can use visualization to restructure your memories so that they cause you less pain and interfere less with your present life.

Symptom Effectiveness

Inner-child visualizations can alter negative core beliefs, reduce depression, raise low self-esteem, and relieve pervasive feelings of shame and guilt. However, while there are abundant case reports of effectiveness, no major study has been undertaken to date on the effectiveness of inner-child visualizations.

Time for Mastery

For maximum effectiveness, practice visualization exercises two or three times a day for ten to twenty minutes a day. If you concentrate on one age level a day, it will take you about a week to tape-record guided imagery tailored to your core beliefs and memories. You will start to experience a shift in awareness from the very start. Significant results will take several weeks, as you listen to your tapes, refine their imagery, and explore different core beliefs.

Instructions

This technique works because your unconscious mind doesn't believe in time. To your unconscious mind, things that happened when you were six months old can be just as important and immediate as things that happened yesterday. Deep inside, your entire infant personality survives in every detail. This inner infant has no knowledge of any older versions of you. It remains an infant, with an infant's needs, abilities, and understanding of the world.

Likewise, you have a two-year-old toddler inside of you, with a two-year-old's self-centered and contrary feelings. There are countless versions of you, of all ages from birth to your present age.

The inner child is more than an interesting metaphor. It explains why people act "childishly" or "immaturely." Some stressful event reminds them of a childhood trauma and awakens a younger version of themselves. They react as if they were still two or five or ten years old.

Painful feelings that you experienced as a child can return to haunt you in the form of negative thoughts about yourself. Unmet needs from early times may still drive you to this day.

In the past few years, techniques have been developed for "reparenting" your inner child in order to resolve old painful feelings and meet old needs symbolically. This work is often done in twelve-step recovery programs by adult children of alcoholics or by victims of childhood sexual or physical abuse. These powerful techniques also work very well for those who struggle with longstanding negative core beliefs about themselves and the world.

When you visualize your inner child, you imagine that you, a wise, experienced adult, are visiting yourself as a child during a particularly hard time—a specific scene that you have already identified as contributing to one of your negative beliefs about yourself. You impart to your younger self the wisdom you have acquired and the skills you've developed to deal with hard times. Specifically, you counter the negative belief that is being formed in that early-childhood scene with a more positive, more accurate belief. You actually become, in your imagination, the perfect parent and friend that you needed at the time but didn't have.

Your unconscious mind doesn't believe in reality any more than it believes in time. That is, it doesn't distinguish between actual experience and dreams or fantasies. The good advice and support that you give your inner child in your imagination, years after the fact, can be processed and stored and used by your unconscious just as if you had received it at the time of the trauma in question. The fact that you have two contradictory versions of the same memory doesn't bother your unconscious because it doesn't insist that things make the kind of logical sense that your conscious mind requires.

Exercise

Different core beliefs are formed at different times. The exercise that follows is divided into developmental stages recommended by John Bradshaw (1990). But no two people's experiences are identical, and your experience may not match the stages presented here. If you find this to be the case, simply adjust the visualization to match the ages that correspond to your early traumas.

It will work best to tape-record the visualization instructions, altering them to fit your history and hot thoughts. Speak slowly and clearly, with frequent pauses.

This visualization exercise can be a very powerful emotional experience. If you begin to feel overwhelmed by your feelings at any time during the exercise, you should open your eyes and stop at once. Don't continue until you have talked it over with someone. If you have a history of serious mental illness, and especially if you were physically, sexually, or emotionally abused as a child, you should consult with a mental-health professional before doing inner-child work.

Don't try to do the entire visualization in one session. You'll probably want to cover one age level at a time, then take a break or wait until the next day to go on.

Your Infant Visualization

Lie down on your back with your legs and arms uncrossed. Close your eyes and relax, using your favorite relaxation method from chapter 5, "Relaxation."

Imagine that within you is a parklike landscape, with paths, woods, meadows, buildings, streams, and fountains. Within this park you can find all the times of your life, all the selves that you have been at all ages and in all places. Your inner world contains all that has ever happened to you and all that you have ever thought or dreamed about.

Imagine that you are walking down a path in your park. This path cuts through time. You can visit any time of your past just by strolling along this path. As you saunter along, you notice a structure off in the distance. You approach and realize that it is the house, apartment, or trailer that you lived in when you were born. If you have never actually seen the home of your birth, just make it up to look any way that seems right.

Enter the home and go to the room where you slept as an infant. Again, if you don't know what it really looked like, that's OK. Go into the room and find a crib or bed. Go to it and see a sleeping baby. This is you as an infant. Study your tiny fingers, your little mouth, and your wispy baby hair. Notice the color and texture of the blanket. What kind of diaper or sleeper does the baby have on? The more details you add, the more real this moment will become for you.

Imagine that the baby wakes up and starts crying. See your mother, father, or whoever took care of you coming into the room. They can't see the adult you—you're invisible. Watch your mother or other caretaker coping poorly with your needs—being cross and angry, being rough or not cuddling your infant self, trying to feed you when you really need to be changed, trying to change you when you just want company, and so on. See and hear your infant self fretting and fussing.

Now have your caretaker leave the room. Your infant self starts crying again. This time, pick your infant self up. Cuddle and hug your infant self. Offer some milk from a bottle.

Talk to your infant self as the crying stops and is replaced by calm and contentment. Say to your infant self:

Welcome to the world.
I'm glad you're here.
I'm glad you are a girl (or boy).
You're special and unique.
I love you.
I'll never leave you.
You're doing the best you can to survive.
_____ (Your own alternative thoughts)

Next, change point of view and experience the whole bedroom scene again, this time imagining that you are your infant self: Imagine you are sleeping, you wake up crying, your caretaker comes in and fails to help; then feel more calm as your adult self comforts you.

Take just as much time and lavish an equal amount of detail on this second scene. When you are finished and you're ready, open your eyes and take a break. This is a good visualization to do when you are feeling overwhelmed, helpless, or insecure.

Your Toddler Visualization

Find yourself once again on the path that leads to your inner child. This time, spend a few moments fixing details in your mind: the smells, sights, sounds, and tactile feelings of your inner world. Notice what kind of trees there are and what kind of soil is underfoot.

Now you are going to visualize one of the earliest scenes you can remember. Pick a time when you were one to three years old. If you have no memories from that time, you can make up a scene from stories family members have told you or from snapshots you may have. Imagine a time when you were unhappy, when something happened that hurt you.

See yourself in that situation. How are you dressed? What color is your hair? How long is it? Notice the expression on the face of your inner toddler child.

Watch the painful scene begin—when you broke something, when someone abandoned or lost you, when something was taken away, when you were spanked or scolded. See how upset your inner child becomes, noticing all the details.

When the scene is over, take your toddler self aside, into another room or some other safe place. Introduce yourself and comfort your inner child:

I am you. I'm from the future when you're all grown up.
I've come to help you, to be with you whenever you need me.
I love you.
There's never been another kid like you.
I like you just the way you are.
I'll never leave you.
You're acting normally for a child your age.
It's not your fault. You have no choice in the matter.
It's perfectly all right to explore.
I'll protect you while you learn about the world.

You have a right to say no.

It's OK to be angry or scared or sad.

_____ (Your own alternative thoughts)

Hug your younger self and say goodbye. Promise to return whenever needed. Turn and leave the room.

Now switch your point of view. Relive the scene, pretending to be yourself at age two or three. Include all the actions, sights, sounds, and smells. Listen to your older, wiser self and be comforted.

End the session when you are ready and take a break. This is a good visualization to do whenever you are feeling confused, abandoned, put down, or shamed.

Your Preschooler Visualization

Get relaxed in a quiet place and once again sink into your inner world. Explore the path back through time until you come to your home, the place you lived when you were four, five, or six, before you entered the first grade.

Pick a time when you were frightened and unhappy—the fight with your cousin, the scary time daddy came home drunk, the time your mom just lost it and got hysterical, the time you got lost at the county fair, the time the bully at day care threatened or attacked you.

See your preschool self in that scene. Watch without being seen. How tall are you? Skinny or plump? What are you wearing? Are there any favorite toys around? What color are your eyes? How is your skin tone? Are you fresh and rosy from a bath or hot and dusty from playing outdoors?

As the traumatic scene unfolds, notice how scared or confused your preschool self is. Notice how your inner child tries to understand and make things right, even though the skills and knowledge aren't yet available.

When the painful scene is over, take your inner child to a safe place and sit down together. Tell your younger self that you are visiting from the future, that you can be the kind, attentive parent that is missing, and that your younger self can count on you. Put your arm around your inner child and say:

I love you.

I'm glad you're a boy (or a girl).

You're the only one like you in the world, and I like you just the way you are.

You're doing your very best.

You just don't have much power to change what's going on.

It's not your fault.

I'll help you figure out how to protect yourself.

It's OK to cry.

You're good at thinking for yourself.

You're good at imagining things.

I'll help you separate what's real from what's imaginary.

You can ask for what you want.

It's OK to ask me any questions.

_____ (Your own alternative thoughts)

Try to sense how your inner child is interpreting the event that just happened. What does the child believe is going on? What does it mean to the child about his or her worth, lovability, safety, belonging, and so on? The child is confused and trying to make sense of things. Offer an explanation to your inner child that leaves him or her innocent and blameless for what happened. If there is a positive way to interpret the child's behavior, offer that now. Hug your inner child; say you will see him or her again soon, and leave.

Now change your point of view and relive the painful scene as if you were four, five, or six years old. Really experience the shame, the anger, the confusion, or the fear. Without experiencing the feeling you won't get the full benefit of the visualization. Listen carefully to your older self and know that you were not to blame—you were doing your best.

This next part is a new step that you haven't done before. Relive the painful scene once again from your child's point of view. This time, experience it as if you know your future self and already understand the positive messages your future self has given. You will know this time what you didn't know before: That it's all going to turn out OK; that you will survive; that it's not your fault, and so on.

This time, feel less pain in the scene. If it feels right, you can change the memory and react differently than you did in real life. For example, if you were lost at the fair, instead of sitting down and crying, you might find an adult and ask for help. Or if you were scared and alone in your room listening to your parents fight, you might imagine yourself singing songs to drown out their words.

Whatever you do, don't blame yourself for not reacting differently at the time. You really were doing the best you could. Also, don't change the actions of others in your scene. Even in imagination it's important to remember that you can't change other people's behavior, only your own.

When you are ready, end the scene and take a break. You can repeat this visualization several times, covering all the difficult memories you have from this time in your life. This is also a good exercise to do whenever you are feeling dependent, ashamed, or guilty.

Your School-Age Child Visualization

This visualization follows the same pattern as the previous one. Get relaxed and imagine a scene from ages seven through ten: the time you were humiliated in front of the whole second grade, the time your father didn't show up for the soccer championship, the time you were made to feel stupid or clumsy or inadequate. Relive the painful memory, first from the point of view of your future self.

At the end of the scene, take your school-age self aside. Tell yourself the following statements in your own words. Add any alternative-thought statements that you have found particularly useful in the earlier chapters of this book.

The way you are at school is OK.

I'll stand up for you.

It's fine to try out new ideas and ways of doing things.

You can make your own decisions.
It's OK to disagree.
You can trust your feelings.
It's OK to be afraid.
We can talk about anything.
You can choose your own friends.
How you dress is your business.
You're acting normally for your age.
You have no real choice in this matter—there's nothing else you could do.
You are doing the best you can to survive.
_____ (Your own alternative thoughts)

As you did during the last visit, try to sense how your inner child is interpreting the event. Understand what it means to your child in terms of his or her lovability, control, safety, and so on. Again, offer an explanation that leaves your inner child innocent and blameless for the event. And if there is a positive way to interpret the child's behavior, offer that now.

Repeat the scene two more times, first from the point of view of your school-age self, feeling all the old painful feelings but having the help and support of your future self at the end of the scene. Finally, relive the scene as your school-age self but with your future skills and knowledge. The last time through, you can change how you reacted in the scene if you wish.

Congratulate yourself for bringing your inner child to life—for renewing yourself. End the exercise as you have done before and take a break. Repeat this visualization for all the school-age memories that you have identified as contributing to your present negative beliefs and hot thoughts. This is a good exercise to use whenever you are feeling discouraged about your own competence.

Your Adolescent Visualization

This visualization follows the previous one, step for step. This time, get relaxed, enter your past, and visit a painful event from your adolescence—roughly ages eleven through fifteen. For most people, this is an era with plenty of turmoil—rebellion against parents, conflicts at school, intense and stormy peer relationships, new and powerful sexual feelings—and related painful events to choose from.

First observe, from your adult point of view, the memory you have chosen. Then take your adolescent self into a safe place and relate the following statements in your own words. Afterwards, share your adult, resonable beliefs with your adolescent inner child.

You can find the right person to love.
You can find something meaningful to do in life.
It's OK to disagree with your parents.
You are becoming an independent person.
You can safely experiment with sex.
It's OK to feel confused and lonely.

You have lots of new and exciting ideas about life.

It's OK to be wrapped up in yourself now.

It's normal to be ambivalent.

It's all right to feel embarrassed and awkward.

It's fine to masturbate.

No matter how far out you go, I'll be here for you.

You're acting normally for your age.

Often you have no real choice in the matter.

You're doing the best you can to survive.

_____ (Your own alternative thoughts)

Again, offer an explanation that leaves the child blameless for the events. Look for a positive way to interpret the adolescent's behavior.

As before, relive the scene from your adolescent point of view twice: Once to feel the original pain with your future self there; and once as an adolescent with your future skills and knowledge, perhaps changing your behavior from what actually happened.

Take a break when you're done. You can repeat this exercise to heal all the painful memories you have earmarked from your adolescent years. You can return to your adolescent inner child any time, especially if you are feeling confused about sex or in conflict with authority.

Your Young-Adult Visualization

Following the same steps as in the last exercise, visit a painful scene from your young adulthood. After viewing the scene, confer with your young-adult self and convey the following:

You will learn how to love and be loved.

I know you will make a difference in the world.

You can be a success on your own terms.

You're acting normally for your age.

You're doing the best you can to survive.

Often you have no choice in the matter.

_____ (Your own alternative thoughts)

Again, offer an explanation for the events that takes a compassionate view of your young-adult self. Look for a positive way to interpret your young-adult behavior.

Then experience the hard time from your young-adult point of view, with all the frustrations and pain you can remember, but with your future self there to help. Finish by reliving the scene again as your young-adult self, but with your future skills and knowledge. Let yourself act differently if you wish.

Come back to the present knowing that you can handle adult life on your own terms. Revisit scenes from your young-adult life until you have healed all the memories that have contributed to your current hot thoughts. This is a good visualization to repeat any time you have those familiar feelings of confusion over work, money, or love.

Example

Pam was a clerk in a grocery store who was in therapy because of persistent depression, low self-esteem, and a pervasive sense of shame. Some of her key hot thoughts were "I'm a failure," "Scatterbrain," and "Wimp," usually accompanied by an image of herself as a skinny, short, insignificant little girl.

She did inner-child visualizations off and on for several weeks. A couple of scenes were particularly powerful. In the first scene, she visited her school-age inner child on a day in late July. She was eight, playing in the back yard with strict instructions from her mom not to leave the area. She snuck into the front yard to get the sprinkler, leaving the gate open. At that moment, her mom let out Sandy, the dog, who dashed out of the gate and into the street. Pam started chasing the dog, almost getting hit by a passing car.

Her mother dragged Pam out of the street, into the house, and threw her in a closet, screaming all the way: "I thought I told you to stay in the back. What the hell are you thinking of? You stupid idiot, you let the dog out and nearly got the both of you killed. You stay in there and don't move a muscle." Her mom left to catch the dog.

Pam's adult self came into the closet and said, "Calm down, Pammy. It's going to be all right. I'm your future self. I've helped you before and I'll help you again. I love you. You were doing your best. You just forgot to close the gate. That's normal for someone your age."

She reinterpreted her school-age self's behavior: "You were just trying to get the sprinkler and cool off. It's good to try to help yourself." She also explained her mother's agitation: "Mom isn't really mad at you because you're stupid. She was really afraid. She thought you were going to get run over, and it scared her."

Pam relived the scene again, from her younger self's point of view, feeling the fear and shame intensely. Then she felt very comforted by her older self.

Pam's other powerful scene was from her adolescent years. When she was sixteen a popular boy gave her a lift home. On the way he pulled over near the cemetery, a notorious spot for parking and necking. Pam was afraid to rebuff him and allowed him to kiss her and fondle her breasts. When he tried to go further, she started crying. He drove recklessly away in silence and dropped her at her house. The next day the boy acted as if he didn't even know who she was and called her a "skinny little stick" in front of his in-group friends.

Pam visualized her adult self taking her adolescent self aside. "Listen," she told herself, "you're not what other people call you. It's OK to be a virgin. It's OK to be afraid and take it slow. I'm here to tell you that you will survive. This guy isn't important—you are. Soon you'll feel more comfortable and confident."

When Pam relived the scene from her adolescent's point of view, she felt strong waves of shame and humiliation. She wanted to hear her adult's words over and over—that it was OK; that she wouldn't be a frightened virgin forever; that she would have friends; that it was OK to be different. She also changed the plot by telling the guy to keep his creepy hands off her, getting out of the car and taking a bus home. When he taunted her on the schoolyard, she smiled and gave him the finger.

Talking Back

If your childhood trauma includes parents or other caretakers who abused or neglected you, you can talk back to them as part of your inner-child visualizations. This is a visualized version of a two-chair role-playing exercise developed by Jeffrey Young (1990).

You can talk back in two ways. First, you can visualize yourself as a child, talking back to adults who mistreated you:

> You're not treating me right.
> You have no right to do this.
> This is your problem, not mine.
> It's not my fault.
> You're asking too much from me.

The second way to talk back is to visualize your adult self stepping into a scene to address the abuser or neglecter:

> You're mistreating your child.
> This is wrong.
> It's your fault, not the child's.
> Back off.

You can create an alternative scenario in which your adult self rescues your inner child from the scene, stops the abuse, hits or chases the abuser away, or in some other way intervenes directly in the situation.

Special Considerations

If you have difficulty visualizing, try the following simple exercise: Close your eyes and recall something (your bedroom, a pleasant recent or childhood experience, or what you had for breakfast this morning) in as much detail as possible. Pay attention to shapes, colors, and lighting as well as smells, tastes, textures, temperature, sounds, physical sensations, and feelings. If you can't "feel" these sense impressions in your mind, just describe them verbally to yourself. By practicing the mental description of something very familiar to you, you will gradually improve your powers of imagery.

If you have trouble creating strong visual images, you probably have a well-developed memory which favors another sense, such as smell, touch, or hearing. If this is true for you, recall an experience by tuning into whatever sense is easiest for you. Impressions of the other senses will gradually arise if you keep practicing with your favored sense.

Chapter 17

Stress Inoculation for
Anger Control

Anger is one of the most devastating and physically harmful emotions. Stress inoculation training was extended to the treatment of anger by Raymond Novaco in 1975. In his book *Anger Control: The Development and Evaluation of an Experimental Treatment*, Novaco says, "Anger is fomented, maintained, and influenced by the self statements that are made in provocative situations." He makes a strong case for the proposition that the source of all anger is what you think about a situation.

Provocations don't make you angry; hurtful, attacking statements don't make you angry; stressful and overwhelming situations do not make you angry. What turn painful and stressful situations into anger are trigger thoughts. Trigger thoughts (1) blame others for deliberately, needlessly causing you pain, and (2) see others as breaking rules of appropriate or reasonable behavior. If you decide that people are deliberately harming or attacking you, that you are a victim of their unreasonable behavior, then your trigger thoughts act like a match to gasoline.

You aren't helpless when provocations occur. Anger is not automatic. Stress inoculation teaches you how to relax away your physical tension while developing effective coping thoughts to replace the old anger triggers.

There are five steps in stress inoculation for anger control: (1) mastering relaxation skills, (2) developing an anger hierarchy, (3) developing coping thoughts for items in your hierarchy, (4) applying anger-coping skills during visualized hierarchy scenes, and (5) practicing anger-coping skills in real life.

Symptom Effectiveness

Both Raymond Novaco and Jerry Deffenbacher (1987) have demonstrated in numerous studies the effectiveness of stress inoculation for anger control. Hazaleus and Deffenbacher (1986) have shown that relaxation skills, combined with coping thoughts, provide an effective anger management treatment.

Time for Mastery

Developing the key relaxation skills for stress inoculation will take from two to four weeks. Once the relaxation skills are in place, you could successfully complete a visualized anger hierarchy in a week or less.

Applying your new coping skills to real-life anger provocations takes longer. You'll need to take advantage of spontaneous situations when they arise, using them as a laboratory to experiment with relaxation skills and coping thoughts. Real-life anger management may require two to six months of hard work before your new skills become automatic and can be used reliably whenever you're provoked.

Instructions

Step 1: Mastering Relaxation Skills

You will need to master four skills described in chapter 5, "Relaxation": Progressive muscle relaxation, relaxation without tension, cue-controlled relaxation, and special-place visualization. Don't proceed past Step 3 until you have learned and practiced each of these procedures.

Step 2: Developing an Anger Hierarchy

Get a blank piece of paper and begin writing down as many anger situations as you can think of. Think of the full range of provocations, from minor irritations to things that make you blow your top. This list should include at least twenty-five or thirty situations. If you can't think of that many, try breaking some of your anger episodes into steps—how things escalated between you and the other participant(s).

Once your list is complete, write at the top of a fresh piece of paper the least anger-evoking item on your hierarchy. At the bottom of the page, write the item that makes you angriest.

Fill In the Middle Scenes

Now it's time to select from six to eighteen items of graduated intensity that you can fill in between your lowest and highest anger scenes. You can use the list you developed in Step 2, or even come up with some new items, to build your hierarchy.

Once you have enough items, go through the scenes in your hierarchy to make sure that the increments of anger between each item are approximately equal throughout. If some increments are larger than others, you may need to fill in these "holes" with additional scenes. Keep working on it until the steps of your hierarchy are close to even.

As an example, the following hierarchy was constructed by Celeste, a retired legal secretary:

Rank	Item
1	Cleaning lady bangs into hardwood baseboards with vacuum.
2	Reading about the national debt.
3	A friend is very bossy and demanding, and hurries me while eating just because she's through with her meal.
4	Watching people speed in their automobiles/upset about the possibility of being hit.
5	Telephoning city offices and being shifted from one person to another, and finally being cut off.
6	Husband stores old car in garage, blocking cabinets I want to use. The car collects dust and gets piled with junk.
7	A friend gets angry when anyone is late. She withdraws and pouts.
8	Husband makes me repeat questions many times before answering. Seems to deliberately tune me out.
9	Sister prods to know too much about personal affairs and then blabs to others.
10	Read article in paper about government giving away money to other countries and spending on pork barrel legislation while taxes keep going up.
11	Husband goes to a party in an old sport shirt when I have gone to the trouble to get really nicely dressed for the occasion.
12	In-laws demand help with elderly relative while I'm rushed and in the middle of planning a dinner party.
13	Husband leaves things lying around living room every day, and I have to clean them up.
14	Elderly sister eats continually and keeps gaining weight against doctor's orders. Get worried and angry when watching her gluttony.
15	Husband spends money to buy steak for "the boys" but won't take me out to a nice restaurant.
16	A part-time employer is cool and gives no commitment about the availability of future work.

17	Husband splurges on fine liquors and crazy gadgets for his camera while things need fixing around the house.
18	Husband stays up late with TV and then doesn't want to do anything the next day.
19	Expected to cook an elaborate meal at the end of the day when I feel tired. Treated coolly if I refuse.
20	Husband spends his first day off until 3:00 a.m. each week at in-laws' house, then sleeps all the next day. We spend no time together during his days off. No rides or trips because he's always at the in-laws'.

Finalizing Your Hierarchy

Once you've ranked your hierarchy items from 1 (lowest anger item) to X (highest anger item), photocopy the hierarchy form on the next page and fill in the items you've developed.

Step 3: Developing Coping Thoughts

You should develop two or more coping thoughts as you get ready to visualize each new scene in your hierarchy. Here's how you do it: Briefly visualize the scene, making it as real as possible. Notice what you see, what you hear, and even what you feel physically. Now listen to your trigger thoughts. Are you blaming the other person or people involved for deliberately harming or hurting you? Do you see their behavior as wrong and bad, as violating basic rules of conduct?

If your trigger thoughts fall into the category of blame, here are some suggested coping responses to control your anger:

- I may not like it, but they're doing the best they can.

- I'm not helpless—I can take care of myself in this situation.

- Blaming just upsets me—there's no point in getting mad. Don't assume the worst or jump to conclusions.

- I don't like what they're doing, but I can cope with it.

If your triggers fall into the "broken rules" category, where the provocative party seems to be violating standards of reasonable behavior, some of the following coping thoughts may be helpful:

- Forget shoulds—they only upset me.

- People do what *they* want to do, not what *I* think they should do.

- No one is right, no one is wrong. We just have different needs.

- People change only when *they* want to.

- No one's bad; people do the best they can.

Rank	Item	Coping Thoughts
1		
2		
3		
4		
5		
6		
7		
8		
9		
10		
11		
12		
13		
14		
15		
16		
17		
18		

Hierarchy Worksheet

Some of the best coping thoughts simply remind you not to get upset. They affirm that you can stay calm and relaxed in the face of irritation. Here are some general coping thoughts for dealing with anger:

- Take a deep breath and relax.

- Getting upset won't help.

- Just as long as I keep my cool, I'm in control.

- Easy does it—there's nothing to be gained by getting mad.

- I'm not going to let them get to me.

- I can't change them with anger; I'll just upset myself.

- I can find a way to say what I want to without anger.

- Stay calm—no sarcasm, no attacks.

- I can stay calm and relaxed.

- Stay cool, make no judgments.

- No matter what is said, I know I'm a good person.

- I'll stay rational—anger won't solve anything.

- Their opinion isn't important—I won't be pushed into losing my cool.

- It's just not worth it to get so angry.

- This is funny if you look at it that way.

- Anger means it's time to relax and cope.

- Maybe they want me to get angry. I'm going to disappoint them.

- I can't expect people to act the way I want them to.

- Stay cool; take it easy.

- I can manage this; I'm in control.

- I don't have to take this so seriously.

- I have a plan to relax and cope.

If none of the coping thoughts from these lists feels right to you, you can make your own. Or you can combine elements from different coping thoughts into something that feels more useful. Some of the best coping thoughts involve a specific plan for handling a situation: stating your wants clearly, saying no, finding an alternative way to meet your needs, and so on. A good plan in a problematic situation can make you feel less helpless. And when you experience yourself having more control, you often feel less angry.

Now it's time to distill the two or three best coping thoughts for the first scene in your hierarchy. Write them in the space provided on the Hierarchy Worksheet. You'll do the identical process for each succeeding scene you come to.

Example

Here are some coping thoughts from Celeste's Hierarchy Worksheet:

Rank	Item	Coping Thoughts
	Celeste's Hierarchy Worksheet	
3	A friend is very bossy and demanding, and hurries me while eating just because she's through with her meal.	• Don't take her too seriously. • It's a shame she acts this way; I can relax even if she can't. • Easy does it—there's no point in getting mad.
8	Husband makes me repeat questions many times before answering. Seems to deliberately tune me out.	• No one's bad; people do the best they can. • I don't know why he's like that—but I won't let it upset me. • Getting upset is bad for my health.
13	Husband leaves things lying around living room every day, and I have to clean them up.	• I'm not helpless—I can take care of myself. • I'll have him pick them up before we sit down to watch television. • Stay calm—it's no big deal.
18	Husband stays up late with TV and then doesn't want to do anything the next day.	• I'll do something with a friend—he can stay home. • No one is right or wrong—we just have different needs. • Let it go, that's just him.

Step 4: Applying Anger-Coping Skills

Here's the sequence for using stress inoculation in anger control:

A. **Take ten to fifteen minutes to get relaxed.** Go through progressive muscle relaxation, cue-controlled relaxation (which includes deep breathing), and a special-place visualization to feel calm and safe.

   Now briefly review your coping statements with the first (or next) scene.

B. **Visualize the first (or next) item of your hierarchy.** Try to bring the scene alive. See the situation, hear what's going on, feel the growing tension on a physical level. Remember your trigger thoughts. Remind yourself of the unfairness, the wrongness, the outrageousness of the offense. When you really feel the anger, go on to Step C.

C. **Start to cope.** Once the visualized scene is clear in your mind, immediately begin relaxing and using coping thoughts. It's recommended that you use cue-controlled relaxation during hierarchy scenes because this is the quickest stress-reduction strategy. All you have to do is take a few deep breaths and use your cue word or phrase.

As you cope physically using cued relaxation, try to recall your coping thoughts. Say them to yourself while continuing to visualize the scene. Keep coping and visualizing the provocative situation for about sixty seconds.

D. **Rate your anger.** On a ten-point scale ranging from 0 (no anger) all the way to 10 (the worst rage you've ever felt), rate the anger you experienced in the scene *just before you shut it off*. If your anger is rated 1 or 0, you can relax and move on to the next scene. If your anger is 2 or above, go through the relaxation sequence and revisit the *same* scene.

This is a good time to spend a moment evaluating your coping thoughts. If any have proved ineffective, stop using them. If none of them works, go back to the general list of coping responses and experiment with one or two others. If you've been using suggested coping thoughts from the lists and they haven't worked, perhaps you can write a few of your own coping thoughts. The ones you develop yourself are likely to be a better fit for you.

E. **Always do deep relaxation between scenes.** Typically, you might use cue-controlled relaxation and spend time calming yourself in your special place. If a particular anger scene really upsets you, or you're having difficulty reducing your anger during a scene, you might wish to do progressive muscle relaxation or relaxation without tension before re-entering the scene.

Continue visualizing and coping with scenes until you have finished the highest-ranked item in your hierarchy. Best results come from daily practice. Your first practice session should last fifteen to twenty minutes. Later you can extend stress inoculation sessions to as much as thirty minutes. The main limiting factor is fatigue. If you are getting tired and having difficulty visualizing a scene, it's best to postpone practice until you're more alert.

Expect to master from one to three hierarchy items during each practice session. Always go back to the last scene you successfully completed when starting a new practice session. This helps you consolidate your gains before facing more anger-evoking items.

Step 5: Practicing Anger-Coping Skills in Real Life

Since anger situations tend to be spontaneous, it's hard to schedule real-life practice for your new anger skills. If your hierarchy includes items that occur frequently or predictably, you'll find many opportunities to practice. The key to real-life practice of your relaxation and anger-coping thoughts is to recognize the first signs of anger. The earlier you intervene with cue-controlled relaxation and some helpful coping thoughts, the more likely you are to maintain control.

If you are entering a situation where you can predict a likely anger response, prepare your coping thoughts in advance and commit yourself to using cue-controlled relaxation at the first touch of anger. By now, with all your practice in the hierarchy scenes, cue-controlled relaxation has hopefully become "overlearned." It should be getting easier and easier to do, more and more automatic. If you have difficulty remembering to use relaxation and coping thoughts during a particular provocative situation, visualize the scene and practice coping later (using the same procedure as when you worked the hierarchy). Extra practice with an imagined scene can make you more prepared and better able to remember your skills when it next shows up in real life.

Example

Sam had a longstanding anger problem that was affecting both his marriage and his job. Most upsetting were situations where he felt treated with disrespect.

While learning his relaxation skills, Sam also began developing his hierarchy. He started by listing as many anger situations as possible, trying to include slightly annoying items as well as middle range and "blowup" items. Out of this list, he identified the scene that produced the least anger: "Jill doesn't get up for the phone; I have to drop what I'm doing and get it." He also found a recent anger situation that had absolutely enraged him: "Student tells me my class is full of 'unnecessary rhetoric'".

With the extremes in place, Sam filled in eight middle items on his hierarchy. It was hard sometimes to tell which of the items was more annoying, and he sometimes had to adjust his arrangement.

The creation of a hierarchy itself proved upsetting, and Sam threw it in the trash; then he had to retrieve it and wipe off some unfortunately placed coffee grounds.

On the following page is Sam's hierarchy, including a final list of the coping thoughts he developed for each scene.

Sam mostly used coping thoughts from the recommended list, but sometimes he made a plan of his own for coping with the situation and included that among his coping responses. Sam often used reminders to relax during scenes because tension in his body seemed to be a major trigger for anger. When coping thoughts proved ineffective, he replaced them with something new from the list or wrote one of his own.

Sam followed the stress inoculation procedure carefully, beginning each session with progressive muscle relaxation, cue-controlled relaxation, and his special-place visualization. During scenes he used cue-controlled relaxation to achieve quick muscle release.

Sam worked hard at visualizing the items on his hierarchy until he felt truly angry, then he initiated his coping responses. The scene that proved to be the worst problem was item 9, "Jill says you fucked up. . . ." He had to repeat the scene five times before he was able to reduce his anger to 1 (on the ten-point scale). When he started practicing the next day, Sam found that he was back up to level 5 with the scene. He had to visualize and cope in the scene three more times before he was finally able to achieve zero anger.

In real-life anger management, Sam used cue-controlled relaxation and several general coping thoughts to handle the most provocative situations. If these proved inadequate and he relapsed into an anger response, he rehearsed the scene by visualizing it and practicing more specific coping thoughts.

Special Considerations

Please see items 1 and 2 of Special Considerations in chapter 11, "Stress Inoculation." If you repeatedly struggle with an anger-provoking situation that involves a familiar sequence of responses (i.e., fights about money with your spouse, homework with your children), you're encouraged to read chapter 18, "Covert Modeling." This is an excellent technique to help you develop and rehearse new behavior patterns.

	Sam's Hierarchy Worksheet	
Rank	**Item**	**Coping Thoughts**
1	Jill doesn't get up for the phone; I have to drop what I'm doing and get it.	• Forget shoulds—they only upset me. • Easy does it—take a big breath. • If I don't want to get up, I'll let the answering machine take the call.
2	Jill complains that "we never talk."	• No one is right or wrong—we just have different needs. • I can't fix this with anger. • I'm doing the best I can.
3	Jill tells me to drive faster because we're late.	• Stay calm—no attacks. • Easy does it—take a big breath. • She's embarrassed when she's late, that's all.
4	The department head assigns me to a classroom that's in one of the temporary bungalows.	• I can cope with this. • The actual room is OK. • People do what *they* want, not what *I* want.
5	Jill tells me the last minute about social events. No planning or consideration for my schedule.	• Stay calm—no attacks. • State my position clearly—that I won't go if I hear about it at the last minute. • I don't like it, but she's doing her best.
6	Department head gets a complaint and pressures me to raise a student's grade.	• Breathe, stay calm. • Forget shoulds—we just have different needs. • He has pressure from above. He's in a bind.
7	They give me two students who barely speak English—what is this?	• Breathe, stay calm. • I can cope with this—send them to tutoring. • Forget the damned shoulds.
8	Jill doesn't like something I say; turns her back and holes up in her office.	• Breathe and relax. • She's doing the best she can. • This will blow over like always. Don't take it so seriously.
9	Jill says, "You fucked up," pointing her finger at me.	• Breathe and relax. • I can't change this with anger—I'll just make it worse. • Tell her we'll talk later when we're calm.
10	Student tells me my class is full of "unnecessary rhetoric."	• Say nothing you'll regret. • I can't fix this with anger. • Breathe, relax, answer rationally.

Chapter 18

Covert Modeling

Covert modeling is an effective way of altering an existing negative sequence of behavior and thinking—of learning a new pattern. You can probably think of a number of behavior patterns that you find unsatisfactory and want to change. You may want to improve your performance at work, in a personal relationship, or in school. You might have fallen into some routine that you don't like, such as sitting in front of the TV with a can of beer instead of playing with your kids. Or you may find yourself repeatedly coming home tired at the end of a long work day and getting into an argument with your spouse. You might feel bored and uncommunicative every time you go to visit your in-laws. Some situations may be so anxiety-provoking for you that you avoid them entirely: academic tests, doctor visits, enclosed or crowded rooms, being alone, novelty, speaking before others, and so on.

Likewise, there are probably some new patterns of behavior that you would like to add to your repertoire that might not require any change in your existing behavior. You may want to learn assertiveness skills to aid you in looking for a new job, asking for a raise, or returning to the dating scene after a divorce. Covert modeling can be useful for learning such new behavior patterns.

One of the most important ways you learn to perform a new behavior is to observe and imitate someone else doing it successfully. A young musician may learn to perform on stage by watching his favorite artists on television or at concerts, and then modeling his own act on theirs. In social-skills training, shy individuals often watch videotapes of people who initiate and maintain conversations, and then imitate these videotaped models.

Unfortunately, good models are not always readily available when you need them. In 1971 Joseph Cautela found that you can learn new behavior sequences by *imagining* people, including yourself, performing the desired behavior successfully. He called his technique *covert modeling.* Covert modeling enables you to identify, refine, and practice in your mind the necessary steps for completing a desired behavior. Once you feel confident imagining yourself doing a particular activity, you can more effectively perform it in real life.

Cautela's classic covert modeling method is to first imagine someone very different from yourself performing the desired behavior. Then you imagine someone similar to yourself, and finally visualize yourself in action. In actual practice, most people skip the dissimilar and similar models and spend all their time imagining themselves.

Cautela stressed the importance of seeing your models struggling with and eventually overcoming difficulties, rather than succeeding perfectly on the first try. This advice has stood the test of time. Recent practitioners have added the practice of analyzing the negative automatic thoughts associated with your unsuccessful behavior, and composing new, more positive thoughts to go with the new behavior.

Symptom Effectiveness

Covert modeling can be used to improve any already existing behavior sequence, or to learn a new behavior sequence that is a major departure from the usual way you act. It is helpful in reducing avoidance behavior associated with phobias and test anxiety, and in increasing assertive behavior. Covert modeling can be used to reduce depression, resentment, and procrastination associated with the failure to perform desired behavior or solve problems adequately.

If you are unable to create clear and detailed mental images, covert modeling will probably be of little help to you. However, vivid *visual* images are not absolutely necessary. You may be able to form strong physical or auditory impressions that will allow you to use this technique with success.

Psychologists Thase and Moss found in 1976 that guided behavior rehearsal was more effective than covert modeling in reducing avoidance behavior. Unfortunately, avoidance behavior does not always lend itself to rehearsing in real life, making covert modeling a useful alternative.

Time for Mastery

You should get results after four fifteen-minute sessions. Personal preference will determine how quickly you change over from covert modeling to practice in real life.

Instructions

Step 1: Imagery Practice

Sit down in a comfortable, quiet place where you won't be interrupted for about fifteen minutes. Close your eyes and scan your body for tension, using your favorite relaxation exercise. After you have let go of the tension in your body, take a few deep breaths, focusing on your breathing and allowing yourself to become more and more relaxed.

With your eyes closed, practice recalling what the room you are sitting in looks like. What are the major furnishings in the room? How are they positioned? What are their colors, textures, shapes? What are the walls, ceiling, and floor like? What are the decorations? What's on the tables or desks?

After imagining the room, open your eyes and see how much detail you captured. Repeat this exercise until you are satisfied with your imagery of the room. You may want to try this exercise in a variety of settings to develop your ability further.

Next, imagine a nature spot in your mind's eye. Notice the green trees rustling in the gentle, warm breeze. Notice the rough, mottled bark of the trees, and their shining leaves. Feel the earth beneath you, paying attention to its color and texture. Listen to the water flowing nearby and to the birds as they flit from branch to branch. Smell the various scents that fill this natural place. Feel the pleasantly warm sun through the trees. Allow yourself to fantasize what your eyes, ears, nose, and skin would tell you about the spot in as much detail as possible. Then imagine that an old friend walks up to you through the trees and greets you. What does he or she look like? What does he or she have to say? What does the voice sound like? What do you have to say?

Once you have developed some facility in imagining scenes using sight, sound, smell, and feeling, you are ready to begin covert modeling proper. It is not necessary for your images to be as clear as a motion picture or a tape recording, but they should be as vivid as practice can make them.

Step 2: Writing Out Problem Behavior

Write out your problem behavior and thoughts as a sequence of separate steps. (If you are learning an entirely new behavior, start with step 3 below.)

Example: My critical, defensive remarks when my ex-husband brings my seven-year-old son home on Sunday nights after their weekend together:

A. I start looking out the window and watching the clock around six, thinking, "I know he'll be late, he's so inconsiderate."

B. At 7:30 they drive up, half an hour late. I'm seething, thinking, "Danny will be tired and all wound up. I'll never get him to bathe and get to bed on time."

C. I open the door before they get to it and say, "You're late."

D. Jerry explains why they're late, why he hasn't given Danny any dinner—whatever the excuse is.

E. I shoo Danny inside and stand on the porch arguing with Jerry about our visitation schedule. I'm thinking what an irresponsible, uncaring jerk he is.

F. I have to ask for money—his share of tuition or dentist bill. I assume that he's going to get mad.

G. He begrudgingly gives me the money and stomps off. I go inside, thinking, "This is awful, this stinks. I hate him." I look and act angry.

H. Danny is inside, looking scared and sad.

I. I feel guilty for arguing in front of him. I think, "I'm a bad mom; I can't manage my life."

Step 3: *Writing Out Desired Behavior*

A. I do the laundry, weeding, or paperwork, keeping busy so I'm not just waiting around watching the clock. I think, "They'll get here when they get here. The important thing is to stay calm."

B. At 7:30 they drive up and I think, "I've really missed Danny. I hope he had a nice time with his dad."

C. I keep doing what I'm doing and wait for them to come in. Then I go to them and give Danny a big hug and say, "Hi, you guys. How was your weekend?"

D. I stand there and smile while they tell me about the weekend. I feel a bit angry, but I think, "Keep smiling. Don't make this an unpleasant transition for Danny."

E. I tell Danny to go unpack his bag and get ready for a bath.

F. I wait for Danny to get out of the room before I talk to Jerry about visitation, money, or whatever. I tell myself to stay calm, just say things clearly and evenly.

G. If we have a serious conflict brewing, I tell Jerry I'll call him tomorrow, and then I say goodbye.

H. When Jerry leaves, I go help Danny with his stuff. I resist the urge to quiz him about what he ate, how late he stayed up Saturday night, and so on. I try to find out what he did that he really liked during the weekend.

Step 4: *Imagining Context*

Practice imagining the context in which the problem behavior occurs. Hold this clear image twice, for fifteen seconds each time.

Example: I imagine the clock on the wall, the deepening twilight, the view out the front window. I feel it getting cooler and hear the neighbor's dog barking and the stereo playing softly in the background.

Step 5: *Imagining Desired Behavior*

Imagine yourself performing the desired sequence of behavior and thoughts, with difficulty at first, then successfully. Visualize the successful sequence at least twice. An option is to record the desired sequence on tape, leaving space between each step for you to visualize yourself performing the new behavior. Then you can listen with your eyes closed, visualizing the desired sequence as often as it takes to feel confident in your ability to actually do it.

Example: I see myself in cutoffs and a T-shirt, sitting at the dining room table sorting papers. I hear them on the porch. The door opens and I run to let them in. I greet them and they tell me about the weekend enthusiastically. When Danny leaves the room, I tell Jerry about the dentist bill. He talks about unnecessary treatment and I start to lose my cool. I tell myself, "We'll solve this eventually. It'll be okay." I calm down and tell him I don't have time to go into it tonight. I'll call him when Danny's at school.

Step 6: Role-Playing

Role-play your desired behavior. This is an optional step. If you are ready to try the desired behavior in real life, go on to step 8.

There are several ways to role-play your desired behavior. You can rehearse it in front of a mirror. Or you can take both parts of a dialog by sitting in a chair and saying what you would say, shifting to another chair and saying what the other person would say, shifting back to your chair to respond, and so on. Another method is to rehearse the scene with friends who act out the parts of significant characters while you play yourself. Make the scene as realistic as possible. Finally, you can tape-record yourself and practice what you want to say, playing it back to get used to hearing yourself say assertive things.

Example: I practice saying key statements in front of a mirror:

> *Hi, how was your weekend?*
> *Why don't you two say goodbye while I make some tea?*
> *Sweetie, go unpack your bag and get ready for your bath.*
> *Jerry, October's child support was due Friday.*
> *I paid this dentist bill. Your half is forty-five dollars.*
> *I really have to insist on Danny getting back by seven. He needs a predictable routine so*
> *he can settle in, get a bath, and get to bed in time to be fresh for the new school week.*
> *This isn't a good time to talk. I'll call you tomorrow around twelve.*

Step 7: Preparing Coping Statements

Even after practicing your desired behavior and positive thoughts, you might experience some pessimistic thoughts that could inhibit you from applying what you have learned to real-life situations. That's why you need to compose a couple of all-purpose coping statements that you can memorize or write down on an index card to have handy.

In your own words, make up two short coping statements that remind you to relax and instruct you to follow your plan.

Examples:

Relaxation:
> *Stay calm.*
> *Just breathe slowly.*
> *Keep cool.*
> *I can relax and refocus.*

Self-Instruction:
> *Take one step at a time.*
> *I've prepared for this.*
> *Just follow the plan.*
> *I can do this.*

Step 8: Performing Desired Behavior in Real Life

Perform the desired behavior sequence in real life.

Example: Last Sunday was better. Even though Jerry brought Danny home forty-five minutes late, full of junk food and exhausted, I didn't lose my cool. I stayed focused on making it a smooth transition for Danny. I held off on my critical remarks until my son was out of earshot. Then I calmly made my point and took care of business without the usual bitterness and rage. What could have been a screaming match was a relatively quiet negotiation. Danny and I had a nice evening and he got to bed on time.

Examples

Frank and Sharon

Frank and his twelve-year-old daughter, Sharon, had had a good relationship until recently when they began to quarrel over her math homework. Frank resolved to use covert modeling to change this problem behavior.

Step 1. Frank practiced creating imagery in his mind. He chose calming scenes from nature for their added relaxation value.

Step 2. Frank described his and his daughter's problem behavior and his thoughts in sequential order:

A. I'm watching television while Sharon is playing in her room.

B. At 9:30 she asks for help with a math problem.

C. I say "Sure," and we sit down at her desk together.

D. I have to read the whole chapter in order to understand the problem.

E. It's after 10:00 (her bedtime) before we figure out the first problem, and there are four equally hard problems to go.

F. I think, "This isn't fair."

G. I start to feel testy and ask her why she didn't start earlier, and she says that I don't want to help her anyway.

H. I think, "She's totally irresponsible, dumping it all on me."

I. I start to get loud and she starts to cry.

J. Her crying gets worse and I tell her I'm going to figure out the other four problems by myself.

K. She stays up for half an hour while I am trying to do the problems, and I finally insist that she go to bed.

Step 3. Frank rewrote the behavior for the following items:

A. I will check in with her at intervals during the evening to see how she is doing on her homework.

B. I will set up a rule that she cannot ask for help with her homework after 9:00.

E. I will make another rule that she cannot count on help after 10:00 and if the homework is not finished by 10:00, she goes to school with it incomplete.

F&H. When I think she's being unfair and irresponsible, I'll remind myself that she's only twelve, that it's my job to set limits and help her structure her evening.

G. I'll tell her I'm feeling pressured and will only do one more problem. Also I'll joke with her about not wanting to burn the midnight oil with her again.

I. I will take a deep breath when I notice that I'm getting loud and quiet my voice down. I will get some punch and cool off in the kitchen.

J&K. I will give her a hug when she cries, tuck her into bed, and remind her that we do not do homework after her bedtime.

Step 4. Frank imagined the context as being his daughter's desk in her room. He clearly visualized this twice for fifteen seconds each time.

Step 5. Frank chose to practice covert modeling on the sofa in the living room after Sharon went to bed. He made a point of relaxing before he started imagining. He would take three slow breaths, telling himself to relax and noticing the tension drain out of his body. He ran through the desired behavioral sequences in his mind, seeing and hearing himself succeed only after struggling through the usual problems.

Step 6. After practicing step 5 for about fifteen minutes a day for four days, Frank decided to role-play the desired behavior. He practiced with his wife, letting her play his daughter's part.

Step 7. Frank made up the following coping statements to be used when he talked to his daughter:

Relaxation:

Breathe and relax.

Self-instruction:

Keep it simple and sensible.
Use a gentle voice.

Step 8. Satisfied with his role-playing and coping statements, Frank proceeded to carry out the desired behavior sequence in real life.

Sandra and Her Boss

It had never occurred to Sandra to ask for a raise until her friend Jan, who held the same level clerical position in another department, asked for and got a substantial salary increase. Since this was an entirely new behavior for Sandra, she started with step 3, writing out her desired behavior. It was a long script because there were at least two confrontations involved, and several different ways her boss might react. After several revisions, this is what she wrote:

A. I approach my boss in the staff lounge during the coffee break.

B. I have difficulty getting his attention, but finally do.

C. I ask for fifteen minutes of his time in the next couple of days to discuss a raise.

D. He tries to put me off on his secretary, and I have to repeatedly ask for and finally get his cooperation.

E. I tell myself, "Be persistent."

F. At the appointed time I walk into his office and greet him.

G. I sit in the blue chair he reserves for guests.

H. We make some small talk about the weather and how busy the office has been.

I. I explain that I'm here to request a 10 percent raise.

J. I mention my good performance record and how long I've been working at the same salary level.

K. He looks displeased and replies that in these days the department is not doing well and we all have to learn to live with less.

L. I think, "I deserve this. Don't give up."

M. I point out that it would be more cost-effective to give me a raise than to train a new employee to take over my responsibilities.

N. He continues to be negative.

O. I take a deep breath and remind myself to be strong and calm, and that I deserve the raise.

P. I say that if I can't get the raise I deserve, I'll have to start looking for a new job.

Q. He offers a 5 percent raise.

R. I stick to my demand, reminding myself and him that I'm competent and experienced.

S. He eventually agrees, after seeing that I won't be budged.

T. I thank him, make sure to ask when the raise goes into effect, and walk out of his office feeling elated.

Sandra practiced visualizing the staff lounge and her boss's office until she could clearly imagine the sights and sounds. She visualized herself going through all the steps of asking for and getting a 10 percent raise.

Sandra role-played the desired behavioral sequence with her husband playing the role of her boss. Her husband made a point of being a particularly tough boss to talk to.

Because she was still very nervous about asking for the raise, Sandra made up some coping statements. She wrote them on a card and kept it in the middle drawer of her desk at the office, referring to it frequently to counteract negative thoughts about asking for a raise.

Armed with her coping statements, Sandra made her appointment and presented her case. Her boss was a tough negotiator, but they eventually settled on an 8 percent raise.

Chapter 19

Covert Sensitization

Among the greatest sources of painful emotions are destructive habits. These are your vices, the things you have learned to do that feel good for the moment and for which you later pay dearly. There is pleasure, for example, in a three-hour martini lunch. It's a nice way to blot out tension, unwind, and socialize. Unfortunately, a habit of martini lunches wastes time and may leave you quite dysfunctional for the rest of the afternoon. As a consequence you suffer *more* stress trying to catch up on missed work while wrestling with alcohol-induced weariness.

The hallmark of destructive habits is short-term gain coupled with long-term loss. You nightly gorge yourself right up to and including the chocolate mousse, and over the months you are sad to observe your slow evolution into a blimp. You love to shop at your favorite department stores. It's always fun, but you have those ever-mounting credit-card balances and finance charges.

Covert sensitization was developed and popularized by Joseph Cautela (1967) as a treatment for destructive habits. It is called "covert" because the basic treatment takes place inside your mind. The theory behind covert sensitization is that behaviors that become strong habits are learned because they are consistently reinforced by a great deal of pleasure. One way to eliminate the habit is to begin associating your habitual behavior with some very unpleasant, imagined stimulus. As a result, your old habit no longer evokes images of enjoyment, but becomes associated with something noxious and repulsive. This association is formed by pairing the pleasurable images of your habit with painful images of nausea, physical injury, social ostracism, or some other unpleasant experience. Covert sensitization can help the old habit lose most, if not all, of its appeal.

Once your old pleasurable habit has become painful to you, you can escape its un-pleasantness by imagining doing something more appropriate that is associated with enjoyable feelings. For example, the image of nightly gorging, now connected with nausea, is replaced with the image of enjoying lighter, healthier food, which is paired with feelings of strength, well-being, and relaxation.

Symptom Effectiveness

Covert sensitization has had significant success in the treatment of sexual deviations such as sadistic fantasies, pedophilia, transvestism, and exhibitionism. It has also been used to reduce stealing, fingernail biting, compulsive gambling, compulsive lying, and compulsive shopping. It has been helpful in curtailing use of nonaddictive drugs such as marijuana.

Covert sensitization has been used with mixed results on alcohol, obesity, and smoking problems. The weight of research evidence indicates that it is not particularly effective with smoking. It's not effective in treating alcoholism per se, but has been used to treat a habit of alcohol indulgence on particular occasions and in particular environments. The previously discussed martini lunch at a favorite watering hole can lose its appeal with covert sensitization. Although it is not the final answer to obesity, covert sensitization can be used to treat a weight problem that is exacerbated by a few particular foods or by a certain eating environment.

In short, covert sensitization is effective when the habit is confined to a particular substance, setting, or situation. It is not very effective with generalized habits such as smoking and compulsive eating or drinking. The reason appears to lie in the word *sensitization*. You become sensitized to something unpleasant, which you associate with your habit in particular settings and situations. A sensitization to one particular food, drink, or setting does not seem to generalize. It is nearly impossible to become sensitized to all food, all drink, or all situations associated with compulsive eating, drinking, and smoking. And thus the technique has diminished effectiveness with such pervasive habits.

Time for Mastery

It will take four days to master progressive relaxation and an additional two weeks to begin getting results from the covert sensitization procedure.

Instructions

Step 1: Learning Progressive Relaxation

The first step in covert sensitization is to become relaxed. Progressive muscle relaxation, outlined in chapter 5, "Relaxation," is the quickest and most effective way to let go of your muscular tension. Practice progressive muscle relaxation in two fifteen-minute sessions daily. Once you have mastered the four-step shorthand procedure, you will be capable of deep muscle relaxation throughout your entire body in less than two minutes.

Step 2: Analyzing Your Destructive Habit

What environment are you typically in? Who is with you? How did you set the situation up? What's the first thing you do as you prepare to launch into your old habit?

A housepainter who was becoming too stout to climb scaffolding analyzed the conditions under which he tended to gorge himself. He shopped once a week, and usually spent that evening watching television and making endless raids on the icebox. He continued eating until he had polished off the cinnamon bread, ice cream, and fruit pies—his favorite snacks. He also gorged himself at an Italian restaurant a block from his house, and at a McDonald's that was on the way home. He noticed that he was always alone on these occasions because he was embarrassed about friends observing his binging. He usually had skipped lunch and felt terribly hungry. The first thing he did before gorging himself was to think of all the wonderful foods he had in the icebox, or to peruse the menu with a sense of excitement as he searched for the most filling meal.

Step 3: Creating a Pleasure Hierarchy

Make a short list of five to ten scenes in which you enjoy your destructive habit. Rank them from the least to the most pleasurable, and assign pleasure ratings on a scale from one to ten. If your destructive habit is overeating, you could base your hierarchy on a few of your favorite foods, always being certain to include the settings in which they are consumed. The stout housepainter listed these items on his pleasure hierarchy:

Item	Pleasure rating
Leaving work and thinking about a big dinner.	1
Shopping for favorite snacks.	3
Snacking on fruit pies while at home watching TV.	5
Snacking on ice cream while at home watching TV.	6
Snacking on cinnamon bread while at home watching TV.	7
Huge, spicy meal at favorite Italian restaurant. Feeling very hungry.	10

Other hierarchies are more complex and contain items revolving around anticipation of or preparation for the destructive habit. A compulsive shopper created the following hierarchy:

Item	Pleasure rating
Depositing paycheck and thinking about a favorite department store. Imagining the clothes racks and display cases.	1
Looking through catalogs for "ideas."	2
Fantasizing about some new clothes while making dinner.	5
Walking around Macy's.	5
Selecting clothes to try on.	6
Impulsively splurging on a gift.	7
Getting something really exciting, like a new stereo or TV.	9
Getting it home to be tried out or tried on.	10

Still other hierarchies focus on various elements of a particular pleasurable situation. A teacher found himself smoking prodigious amounts of marijuana in the hour after he got home from his last class. His hierarchy consisted of the routine steps he took in preparing a joint:

Item	Pleasure rating
Get stashbox, papers, and matches out of bookcase.	1
Sit in reclining chair and spread out newspaper to catch excess.	3
Put on earphones and roll joint.	5
Light up and take first hit.	7
Put last of joint in roach clip, feeling stoned.	9
Smoking, spacing out, forgetting about everything.	10

Now it's your turn. When developing your pleasure hierarchy, write it out completely. The items in the examples are abbreviated, but yours should be much more detailed. You might include where you are, who is with you, what you are doing, what you are thinking, and what is going on inside your body. A typical item in your hierarchy might read like this:

> "The cards are dealt and I pick each one up. I am excited and nervous. Green felt over the kitchen table at Jack's house. A couple of strangers, but mostly the same crowd. The fifth card goes around and we're ready for the first bets. I'm to the left of dealer, I bet a buck."

The more detail you have, the easier it will be to imagine the scene. If you have difficulty getting a mental image of an item in your hierarchy, spice it up with a variety of sense impressions. In addition to what you see, notice how it smells, what you hear, whether you feel warm or cold, and so on.

While creating the hierarchy, make sure your first item is no more than a 1 or 2 on the ten-point pleasure scale. In other words, select something barely pleasurable to start off with, and then work your way up to the intensely delightful aspects of your habit. Try not to let more than two points separate consecutive items.

Use the following form to create your hierarchy.

Pleasure Hierarchy	
Item	**Pleasure rating (1 to 10)**

Step 4: Creating an Aversion Scene

Find something the *thought* of which deeply repulses or frightens you. Rate the following for degree of repulsion or fear experienced when *imagining* the item:

Open wounds	Crawling insects
Dead people	Raging fire
Getting teeth drilled	Nausea, throwing up
Thunder	Throwing up in public
Looking down from high places	Heart attack
Falling	Physical injury
Injection, having blood drawn	Fainting
Huge, open places	Looking foolish
Closed spaces	Snakes
Dead animals	Spiders
Rejection, ostracism by friends	Blood
Rejection, ostracism by strangers	Severe criticism

Select the two or three items that distress you most when you think about them. Nausea is the most commonly used aversive item for covert sensitization. Social ostracism and rejection have also been used extensively. The aversive item should be sufficiently repulsive so that thinking about it generates a very explicit bodily sensation. Your really *feeling* the repulsion or fear bodily will be very important to the success of this procedure. For example, the thought of nausea should be accompanied by a very specific memory of something that really nauseated you—until you begin to feel a little of the old nausea returning.

Step 5: Combining Pleasurable and Aversive Scenes

Once you are able to clearly imagine and experience the aversive scene, you are ready to begin pairing it with items on your pleasure hierarchy. The following example shows how it is done. A young man who privately enjoyed certain rituals of transvestism was concerned that it was sapping his motivation to meet women and have a sexual relationship with another person. Here is one of the items from his hierarchy combined with the aversive feeling of nausea:

> "Slowly pulling up the green panties, watching everything in the full-length mirror. Feeling very turned on. The room is warm, the panties cool and smooth. Then suddenly that sick feeling starts and a bad smell. I get really turned off as my stomach turns over and over, and pieces of lunch catch in my throat. I try to gag it back but I can't. I start to vomit all over myself. I quickly pull off the panties and begin feeling better. I run into the bathroom for a cool shower, and begin to feel much more comfortable and relaxed."

Pair each item of your pleasure hierarchy with the aversive scene in just this manner:

A. Start with a detailed description of that particular item on the hierarchy.

B. Introduce the aversive scene so that you feel turned off to whatever you were just enjoying.

C. Imagine yourself feeling better as soon as you stop whatever you were doing.

Write out this three-step scenario for each item on your hierarchy. The aversive scene should be as disgusting as possible, full of detail, and completely eradicate any experience of pleasure. Be sure to turn off the aversive scene *as soon as* you cease the destructive habitual behavior. Let yourself have immediate feelings of relief, comfort, and relaxation.

When you have rewritten your hierarchy to include the aversive scene, you can begin practicing covert sensitization. Read over the first item of your hierarchy until you have it clearly in mind. Close your eyes and relax using progressive relaxation. Relaxation helps you form clearer images. When the tension is out of your body, imagine the first item. Notice what you see, smell, and hear. Notice everything you are doing. Then move right into the aversive scene until you feel uncomfortable and repulsed.

The stout housepainter sat in his favorite chair and used the shorthand procedure to progressively relax all his muscles. When he felt relaxed, he began relishing the thought of snacking on cinnamon bread, the fifth item in his hierarchy:

> "The TV is on. There's a blue glow. I'm slumped in my chair and I think of getting a little something to eat. I go into the kitchen and butter five pieces of cinnamon bread. It looks delicious. As I bring the first slice to my mouth I start to feel queasy. It's like that time I ate the bad crab. Just like that and I feel sick to my stomach. I start to take a bite but everything comes up—all over me. I throw the bread in the garbage and open a window. Immediately I feel relief. While I'm breathing the fresh air, the nausea goes away."

Using this procedure, go through each item in your hierarchy three to five times. Limit yourself to one or two items a day so that over a period of approximately one week you can complete the entire hierarchy.

Step 6: Altering the Aversive Scene

Now change the scene so that you avoid vomiting, being ostracized, or whatever you have chosen for an aversion. Avoid the aversion by avoiding your destructive habit. At the first sign of feeling queasy you put the food down, get up and leave the bar, quit the card game, etc. and start to feel better. For example, the stout housepainter rewrote the fifth item of his hierarchy to reflect this change:

> "I'm relaxed. The TV is on. There's a blue glow. I'm slumped in the chair and I think of getting a little something to eat. I go into the kitchen and butter five pieces of cinnamon bread. I start to bring a piece to my mouth, but I have that queasy feeling and put it down right away. I immediately feel relieved and relaxed again."

Go through your hierarchy again, avoiding rather than experiencing the aversive scene. As you did initially, limit yourself to one or two items a day, practicing each item three to five times before going on to the next one.

Step 7: Practicing Covert Sensitization in Real Life

Once you have mastered covert sensitization with imagined scenes, practice the procedure in the presence of tempting objects or situations when your desire for them is low. As you become more confident about controlling a destructive habit, you can begin using covert sensitization when the temptation is stronger. For example, if you have been working on controlling pastry cravings, you might pass by a bakery window when you aren't very hungry and practice covert sensitization while you look in. Later, when you are more sure of yourself, you can go down to the bakery just before breakfast and repeat the procedure.

Covert Sensitization of Hot Thoughts

Covert sensitization can be used not only to inhibit destructive habits but also to reduce the frequency of negative "hot thoughts" that precipitate painful emotions. You simply pair a recurrent negative thought or irrational belief with an an aversive covert stimulus such as an image of spiders, vomiting, or being socially ostracized. If the stimulus is aversive enough and it is paired with the hot thought frequently enough, the hot thought is eventually experienced as unpleasant and it is less likely to recur. For instance, when the belief "I can't cope with life on my own; I need someone to help me" is paired with sufficiently vivid images of having a tooth drilled, it becomes aversive and is less likely to occur.

McMullin (1986) calls this use of covert sensitization *cognitive aversive conditioning*. He recommends combining it with *cognitive escape conditioning*, in which you "escape" the aversive image by replacing it with a positive alternative thought, followed by images of relief. For example, you would replace the image of a tooth being drilled with the alternative thoughts, "I can take care of myself, I can solve my own problems" and images of yourself successfully handling your problems and feeling relieved, free of pain, relaxed, and competent.

Instructions

Step 1. Lie down, close your eyes, and relax.

Step 2. From material you developed in chapter 2, "Uncovering Automatic Thoughts," imagine a typical problem situation in which your negative automatic thoughts typically occur. See the people involved, the setting, the sounds, smells, and textures.

Step 3. Think your hot thought. Use the words and images that typically present themselves.

Step 4. Immediately "punish" the hot thought by an aversive image. Use the same kind of aversive images described earlier in this chapter: vomiting, social ostracism, and so on.

Step 5. Repeat Steps 3 and 4 several times, alternating your hot thought with increasingly aversive images.

Step 6. Escape from the final and worst aversive image by thinking an alternative, more balanced thought. It's important that you not remove the aversive image until you have your alternative thought firmly in mind.

Step 7. Immediately "reward" the alternative thought with a pleasurable image of yourself successfully coping with the situation.

To assist your practice, you can tape-record the description of your scene, the hot thought, aversive images, alternative thought, and pleasant image. Listen to your tape two or three times a day for about a week.

Example

Daryl was a sixty-two-year-old woman who wanted to work on the hot thought "Without the assistance of my family, I can't cope with something going wrong when I go out." She came from a closely knit family and relied heavily on her mother, sister, and husband when they were alive. Now that these family members were no longer available, Daryl rarely went out on her own and only with the reassurance that she could call her daughter on her cellular phone. Typical situations in which this hot thought caused her anxiety were going to the mall, the grocery store, any new social activity, and driving alone, especially on the freeway.

Here is a script that Daryl recorded to help her practice covert sensitization:

"I want to go grocery shopping, but I don't want to go alone. Something might go wrong that I couldn't cope with on my own: I might get sick, something might go wrong with the car, I might have an accident or get mugged. I'd better call my daughter and arrange to go with her. As I continue to think these thoughts, I smell rotten, uncooked hamburger wafting from a container in the back of my refrigerator and I feel a little queasy. If she can't go, I want to be sure that she is available for me to call on the cellular phone in case I have a problem. The putrid stench of rotten, uncooked hamburger fills my whole apartment and I feel nauseated. If she isn't going to be available by phone, I can find out when she will be and postpone my shopping trip until then. As I think this, I envision the apartment air so weighted down with the putrid smell of the decomposing hamburger that I begin to gag. As I contemplate postponing my shopping, I think that I might as well wait for a time when she can go with me, and I envision opening up the container of green, slimy hamburger. I am overwhelmed by the sight as well as odor, and I retch. I can feel food coming back up my throat and a burning taste in my mouth. I force it back down. I think that maybe I shouldn't go shopping at all, and instead maybe I should ask my daughter to shop for me and have dinner with me when she drops off the groceries. As I think about this option, I notice that the smell of rotten hamburger is unbearable. My stomach is turning, my eyes are watering, my nose is running. I think again about how important it is for my daughter to be with me in case I have a problem that I can't deal with on my own. I am overwhelmed by the sight and smell of putrid meat and I start to vomit all down my dress, nylons, shoes, and onto the white rug. I think about how much more secure I feel when my daughter drives me to the store, especially over that new stretch of freeway. The sight and smell of vomit causes me vomit again and again. I start dry heaving. I can't stop. It feels like I'm about to vomit up my whole stomach.

"I still feel nauseous. I'm about to heave again when I start thinking that I can drive myself to the store without my daughter. I imagine myself cleaning up and getting ready to go shopping by myself. I immediately begin to feel better. I take a deep breath, and my lungs and stomach relax and clear. I take an enjoyable shower and put on clean clothes. I go out into the fresh air, feeling a gentle clean breeze, and look up at the pleasantly warm sun twinkling through the dark green trees. I walk through the cool grass, continuing to breathe slowly and deeply, relaxing as I think about my own inner strength and how I have coped with so many unexpected problems on my own. I drive myself to the grocery store without calling my daughter. I enjoy shopping alone. On the way home, I imagine handling a fender bender on my own, exchanging information with the other driver. I call AAA when my car won't start. The tow truck comes quickly, and the driver explains that the little accident must have loosened a wire on the battery. He is able to reconnect it, and I drive home feeling relieved, relaxed, and confident in myself."

Daryl scheduled five practice sessions a week. She listened to her script all the way through three times during each practice session. She found by the end of five sessions that she had fewer avoidance thoughts, was even looking forward to going places on her own, and felt less pressure to call her daughter for reassurance. When she came back from a vacation with her daughter, she found that she needed to give herself two booster sessions in order to feel comfortable going out on her own again without calling her daughter.

Special Considerations

1. If you have difficulty visualizing or feeling an aversive stimulus, you can provide yourself with an actual aversive stimulus by smelling real rotten meat, rotten eggs, or ammonia. You can also try holding your breath, doing pushups, or making harsh, unpleasant sounds.

2. Always time the nausea or other aversive stimulus to coincide exactly with the moment you begin to engage in the destructive habit. Cut off the aversion as soon as you abandon the destructive habit.

3. The effects of covert sensitization can be strengthened with booster sessions. When you feel stronger or more frequent impulses to engage in your destructive habit, go through your hierarchy again and resensitize yourself to the aversive scenes.

Chapter 20

When It Doesn't Come Easy

Each of the techniques in this book is designed to change the way you habitually react to things. But your old way of reacting has been with you a long time. It's familiar and therefore difficult to change. This chapter takes a look at why old habits are hard to part with, even when they are clearly contributing to your pain.

Cognitive behavioral therapy is not a "talking cure" like traditional psychoanalysis. Change does not come about from a series of insights gained during analysis, conversation, rumination, or merely reading about your problem. Change in cognitive therapy happens because you do something. You must actually fill out the worksheets in this book and diligently practice the various visualization exercises.

If you find yourself skipping exercise sessions or find that you are just going through the motions in a halfhearted manner, ask yourself some of the following questions:

Why am I doing these exercises?
Are they really important to me?
What am I doing or what would I like to be doing instead of these exercises?
Is this alternative activity more important to me than doing the exercises?
Can I schedule my life so that I can do both?
If I do not do the exercises now, exactly when and where will I do them next?
What would I have to give up if I succeeded with my exercises?
What would I have to confront if I succeeded with my exercises?

Common Difficulties

A common roadblock to successful use of cognitive behavioral techniques is an untrained imagination. To strengthen your ability to imagine, you can:

1. Focus on senses other than sight when you do visualizations. Create mental sense impressions of sound, touch, taste, and smell. For instance, if you are trying to imagine your kitchen, the visual impressions may be very hazy to you. But you can focus your imagination on the smells of food cooking, the taste of a cold soda, the temperature of the room, the texture of the wooden table top, the feel of the tiles on your bare feet, and so on.

2. Tape-record a detailed description of the scene you want to practice imagining.

3. Draw a picture of the scene you want to practice imagining as a way of tuning into the visual details. Notice which objects and details give the scene its unique identity.

Another major obstacle is simply not believing that a technique or exercise will work. Failure to believe is a cognitive problem. You repeat to yourself such discouraging statements as "I'll never get better.... This won't work.... These sorts of things don't help me.... I'm too stupid.... Somebody has to show me how." One of the basic tenets of this book is that you believe what you repeat to yourself. If you say any negative statement often enough, you will act in such a way as to make it true for you. This book will be of little or no value until you overcome the belief that it cannot help you. To work on this issue, commit yourself to a specific time period of focused effort: two weeks, one week, even one day. Then evaluate any change in your problem at that time. If you've made a little progress, if the symptom is less painful or frequent, commit yourself to work for a second period of time.

Boredom is a frequently mentioned barrier to success with cognitive behavioral work. Many of these techniques are boring! But they work. Practicing them becomes a trade-off: a few weeks of occasional boredom in exchange for years of freedom from an unwanted symptom. This is the choice you may have to make every day when you do these exercises.

Another difficulty, often overlooked, is too rapid success. When you recover from a symptom too quickly, you should expect a setback. The danger is that you may say to yourself, "That was a snap to get over—maybe it wasn't a problem after all. I don't have to worry about that anymore." By minimizing a symptom's significance like this, you are laying the groundwork for its recurrence. It may gradually reemerge in your patterns of behavior, perhaps without your immediate awareness, and then you are stuck with it again. To avoid recurrence, continue practicing your exercises for a time after you are free of symptoms. If symptoms should reoccur, immediately resume the exercises for a few "booster" sessions.

Fear of novelty is a well-documented obstacle to treatment success. Just following new directions may be anxiety provoking for you. The directions may not quite fit your needs. They may be too detailed, cumbersome, or rigid. They may be not detailed enough and leave you floundering without sufficient guidance. It is important to remember that the directions are intended to provide a general outline, which you must adjust to fit your individual needs.

Your world view changes when you realize that you have the power to change how you think and therefore how you feel. You are no longer a helpless victim of good and bad fortune, but an active creator of your own experience. When you give up a symptom, your life changes. Many people prefer to hold onto a familiar though painful symptom rather than learn to cope with their new life without it.

Poor time management is a major roadblock to success. People who give up after half-learning a technique often explain that they were overscheduled and didn't have time for doing exercises. The real problem is one of priorities. Everything else had a higher priority than mental and physical health. The after-work drinks came first, the errands came first, the long phone calls came first, the television came first. You need to schedule your exercises just as you do other important parts of your day. Write down the time and place, and keep the commitment just as you would an appointment with a friend.

What's Your Excuse?

When you miss an exercise, how do you justify it to yourself? Typical reasons are "I'm too tired today.... I'm too busy.... Missing once won't hurt.... I'm too bored.... I feel okay today, so I don't need to do the exercise.... My family needs my help.... This isn't going to work anyway."

Many of these excuses are partially true—you do in fact feel busy or tired, somebody may want your help, and missing a single session probably won't hurt. The part that isn't true is the implication that being rushed or tired or feeling the weight of obligations necessarily prevents you from doing the exercise sessions. The complete truth would be "I'm tired, I could do the exercise, but I choose to focus on the needs of my family today."

The important point is that you take responsibility for your decision to choose one activity over another, rather than pretend that you are the passive victim of circumstance. You need to honestly assess your priorities. If your psychological health is not very high on your list, then you are not likely to make sufficient time to master any of these techniques.

Most people fall back on a favorite theme for avoiding the exercises. A common theme is "I'm indispensable—things will fall apart without me." For example, an insurance executive had difficulty delegating responsibility. Her desk was piled with a dozen half-finished tasks and projects. She was nagged by the belief that any time taken for her exercises would make her fall hopelessly behind. After years of compulsive attention to detail and chronic fear of failure, she had become increasingly phobic. She was afraid of driving more than twenty miles from home and had the sweats whenever she deviated from her normal routine. She was a victim of her irrational belief that she could never take the time to take care of her psychological needs. This belief had exhausted her and prevented her from attempting a solution.

The excuses you give yourself for not taking time to master a technique are likely to be the same ones you have used for years to perpetuate old habits. These excuses are based on faulty premises. The executive believed that only she could do the job right, and that the slightest mistake would bring about her downfall. Her priorities were "successful business person first, healthy human being second."

Making a Contract

Often it is not enough to make agreements with yourself to master a particular technique. After a time you slack off and return to old patterns. Your commitment to yourself doesn't have the same power as commitments you make to other people. Nobody else feels disappointed or concerned when you fail yourself. Nobody else knows about it.

If you have a tendency to start and not finish things, make a contract with someone who knows and cares about you. Make sure you select someone whose good opinion you value, someone you will be afraid to let down. Use the contract form that follows, or a similar document to formalize the agreement. Both of you should sign it and keep copies.

If failing a friend isn't a sufficient motivator, write a penalty clause into the contract. For example, failure to keep your commitment might obligate you to donate twenty dollars to the candidate or cause you hate most. Failure might obligate you to clean out the weeds in your back yard or to put off buying your new television set. If your penalty clause includes a donation, have your friend hold the check in a stamped, addressed envelope, to be mailed upon notification of your failure.

Official Contract

I have decided to deal with my problem of _____

by using _____ technique(s).

I am making a commitment to _____ (person's name)

to undertake the following: practice the _____ technique

_____ times per day/week for _____ days/weeks.

I will evaluate my improvement only at the end of this period.

I will immediately notify the above mentioned person of any failure to uphold this commitment.

_____   _____
(signature)   (date)

I commit myself to taking this work seriously, and I will periodically check with

_____ (your name) as a reminder that your progress

is important to me.

_____   _____
(support person's signature)   (date)

When Symptoms Persist

Occasionally you will be unable to rid yourself of an unwanted symptom, even though you have been conscientious and have practiced regularly. There are several reason why this may occur.

Misdiagnosis

It's possible that you're working on anger when your real problem is fear, or treating your depression when your main goal should be quitting alcohol or other drugs. Perhaps you suffer from a subtle underlying physical problem.

Return to the first chapter and spend more time with the assessment process, especially any sections you skipped or skimmed before. If that doesn't suggest any alternative techniques, consider getting a medical checkup and consulting a therapist.

Misplaced Emphasis

There are three broad avenues of approach in cognitive behavioral therapy: the physical, the cognitive, and the behavioral. Physical approaches are progressive muscle relaxation, breathing exercises, and the like. Cognitive approaches include uncovering and restructuring automatic thoughts, visualization, and so on. Behavioral techniques involve problem solving or testing schemas.

If you have been doing mostly cognitive work, try some of the more physical or behavioral techniques. Shift your emphasis to another avenue of approach and see if that provides better symptom control.

Secondary Gain

Oddly enough, many people are attached to their symptoms. These symptoms may serve an important function in their lives. For example, your fears may relieve you of social obligations you find unpleasant, in a way that lets you avoid taking responsibility for disappointing others.

A simple way to determine if you receive such "secondary gain" from your symptoms is to keep a log of when your symptoms occur and what activities (or would-be activities) surround them. For instance, you might find out that you thought you were nervous in all social settings, but are actually nervous only when people are flirtatious with you, and that you have been saying "I'm not available" by being nervous.

Often the secondary gain of a symptom dates back to a specific event or situation. Ask yourself when your symptoms first began. They may have been an appropriate and adaptive response to a stressful situation. How did you learn your symptoms? For example, a young teacher was anxious when being driven in a car. She had experienced the symptom since childhood, when she was frequently driven by her intoxicated father. If she became sufficiently frightened and noisy, her father would quickly take her home.

At times you may share a symptom with an important person in your life as part of your identification with them. For example, you may share with your father a belief that people are victims of circumstances, accompanied by a feeling of depression and helplessness. As a result, any new challenge you encounter includes the expectation of failure and the opportunity to reinforce your world view. Ask yourself who in your family shares your symptoms. Examine their belief system and compare it with your own. The easily seen speck in someone else's eye may help you begin to notice the beam in your own.

Should symptoms persist, consult a professional therapist or counselor. The old patterns and beliefs that produce symptoms are difficult to identify. A professional can help you uncover your psychological culprits. Even when you know that certain patterns and beliefs are maladaptive, it is hard to give them up because they are so familiar. After all, change could make things worse. A professional can help you outline and implement a treatment program and provide support when the going gets tough. Your medical doctor, company health plan, or community health organization are potentailly valuable sources of professional help.

Persistence Pays Off

Persist. Don't give up. Your ability to heal yourself by modifying your thoughts and feelings is a tremendous power. You can control what you think, and therefore what you feel. You can change the structure of your life by altering the structure of your mind. You can take away your pain. "It's supposed to be a professional secret," Albert Schweitzer once said, "but I'll tell you anyway: We doctors do nothing. We only help and encourage the doctor within."

References and Resources

Barlow, D. H. and M. G. Craske. 1989. *Mastery of Your Anxiety and Panic.* Albany, New York: Graywind.

Beck, A. T. 1976. *Cognitive Therapy and the Emotional Disorders.* New York: International Universities Press.

Beck, A. T., A. J. Rush, B. F. Shaw, and G. Emery. 1979. *Cognitive Therapy of Depression.* New York: Guilford Press.

Beck, A. T., G. Emery, and R. Greenberg. 1985. *Anxiety Disorders and Phobias.* New York: Basic Books.

Beck, A. T. and A. Freeman. 1990. *Cognitive Therapy of Personality Disorders.* New York: Guilford Press.

Benson, H. 1975. *The Relaxation Response.* New York: Morrow.

Bourne, Edmund J. 1995. *The Anxiety and Phobia Workbook.* 2nd edition. Oakland, Calif.: New Harbinger.

Bradshaw, J. 1990. *Homecoming.* New York: Bantam.

Brown, T. A., R. M. Hertz, and D. H. Barlow. 1992. New developments in cognitive-behavioral treatment of anxiety disorders. In Vol. 2 of *American Psychiatric Press Review of Psychiatry,* edited by A. Tasman. Washington, D.C.: American Psychiatric Press.

Cautela, J. 1967. Covert sensitization. *Psychological Reports* 20:459–468.

———. 1971. Covert modeling. Paper presented at the fifth annual meeting of the Association for the Advancement of Behavior Therapy, Washington, D.C.

Clark, D. 1989. Anxiety states. In *Cognitive Behavior Therapy for Psychiatric Problems,* edited by K. Hawton, P. M. Salkovskis, J. Kirk, D. Clark. Oxford: Oxford University Press.

Craske, M. G. and D. H. Barlow. 1993. Panic disorder and agoraphobia. In *Clinical Handbook of Psychological Disorders,* edited by D. H. Barlow. New York: Guilford Press.

Davis, M., E. R. Eschelman, and M. McKay. 1995. *The Relaxation and Stress Reduction Workbook.* 4th ed. Oakland, Calif: New Harbinger.

Deffenbacher, J. L., D. A. Story, R. S. Stark, J. A. Hogg, and A. D. Brandon. 1987. Cognitive-relaxation and social skills interventions in the treatment of general anger. *Journal of Counseling Psychology* 34(2):171–176.

D'Zurilla, T. J. and M. R. Goldfried. 1971. Problem solving and behavior modification. *Journal of Abnormal Psychology* 78:107–126.

Ellis, A. and R. Harper. 1961. *A Guide to Rational Living*. North Hollywood, Calif.: Wilshire Books.

Emmelkamp, P. M. G. 1982. *Phobic and Obsessive-Compulsive Disorders: Theory, Research, and Practice*. New York: Plenum.

Freeman, A., J. Pretzer, B. Fleming, and K. Simon. 1990. *Clinical Applications of Cognitive Therapy*. New York: Plenum.

Greenberger, D. and C. Padesky. 1995. *Mind Over Mood*. New York: Guilford Press.

Hackmann, A., D. Clark, P. M. Salkovskis, A. Well, and M. Gelder. 1992. Making cognitive therapy for panic more efficient: Preliminary results with a four-session version of the treatment. Paper presented at World Congress of Cognitive Therapy, Toronto.

Hazaleus, S. and J. L. Deffenbacher. 1986. Relaxation and cognitive treatments of anger. *Journal of Consulting and Clinical Psychology* 54:222–226.

Homme, L. E. 1965. Perspectives in psychology XXIV: Control of coverants, the operants of the mind. *Psychological Record.* 15:501–511.

Horan, J. J. and R. G. Johnson. 1971. Coverant conditioning through self-management application of the Premack principal: its effect on weight reduction. *Journal of Behavior Therapy and Experimental Psychiatry* 2:243–249.

Horney, K. 1939. *New Ways of Psychoanalysis*. New York: Norton.

Jacobson, Edmund. 1974. *Progressive Relaxation*. Chicago: The University of Chicago Press, Midway Reprint.

Jannoun, L., M. Munby, J. Catalan, and M. Gelder. 1980. A home-based treatment program for agoraphobia: replication and controlled evaluation. *Behavior Therapy* 11:294–305.

Karlins, M. and H. M. Schroder. 1967. Discovery learning, creativity and the inductive teaching program. *Psychological Reports* 20:867–76.

Maletzky, B. 1973. Assisted covert sensitization. *Behavior Therapy.* 4:117–119.

———. 1974. Assisted covert sensitization in the treatment of exhibition. *Journal of Consulting and Clinical Psychology* 42:34-40.

Masi, Nick. 1993. *Breath of Life*. Plantation, Florida: Resource Warehouse. Audiotape.

Mathews, A. M., J. Teasdale, M. Munby, D. Johnston, and P. Shaw. 1977. A home-based treatment program for agoraphobia. *Behavior Therapy* 8:915–924.

McGuire, M. T. and P. E. Sifneas. 1970. Problem solving in psychotherapy. *Psychiatric Quarterly* 44:667-673.

McKay, M. and P. Fanning. 1991. *Prisoners of Belief*. Oakland, Calif.: New Harbinger.

———. 1992. *Self-Esteem*. 2nd ed. Oakland, Calif: New Harbinger.

McMullin, Rian E. 1986. *Handbook of Cognitive Therapy Techniques*. New York: W.W. Norton & Co.

Meichenbaum, Donald. 1974. Self-instructional methods. In *Helping People Change,* edited by F. K. Kanfur and A. P. Goldstein. New York: Pergamon.

———. 1977. *Cognitive Behavior Modification*. New York: Plenum.

———. 1988. Cognitive behavior modification with adults. Workshop for the First Annual Conference on Advances in the Cognitive Therapies: Helping People Change, San Francisco.

Novaco, R. 1975. *Anger Control: The Development and Evaluation of an Experimental Treatment*. Lexington, Mass.: D.C. Health.

O'Leary, T. A., T. A. Brown, and D. H. Barlow. 1992. The efficacy of worry control treatment in generalized anxiety disorder: a multiple baseline analysis. Paper presented at the Meeting of the Association for Advancement of Behavior Therapy, Boston.

Osborn, A. F. 1963. *Applied Imagination: Principles and Procedures of Creative Problem Solving.* 3d ed. New York: Scribner.

Perlman, H. H. 1975. In quest of coping. *Social Casework.* 20:213–225.

Rackman, S. J., M. Craske, K. Tallman, and C. Solyom. 1986. Does escape behavior strengthen agoraphobic avoidance? A replication. *Behavior Therapy* 17:366–384.

Salkovskis, P. M. and J. Kirk. 1989. Obsessional disorders. In *Cognitive Behavior Therapy for Psychiatric Problems,* edited by K. Hawton, P. M. Salkovskis, J. Kirk, and D. Clark. Oxford: Oxford University Press.

Stampfl, T. G. and D. G. Levis. 1967. Essentials of implosion therapy: A learning-based psychodynamic behavior therapy. *Journal of Abnormal Psychology* 72:496–503.

Thase, M. E. and M. K. Moss. 1976. The relative efficacy of covert modeling procedures and guided participant modeling on the reduction of avoidance behavior. *Journal of Behavior Therapy and Experimental Psychiatry* 7(1): 7–12.

Wanderer, Zev. 1991. *Acquiring Courage.* Oakland, Calif.: New Harbinger. Audiotape.

Weeks, C. 1978. *Peace from Nervous Suffering.* New York: Bantam.

Wolpe, J. 1958. *Psychotherapy by Reciprocal Inhibition.* Stanford, Calif.: Stanford University Press.

———. 1969. *The Practice of Behavior Therapy.* Oxford: Pergamon Press.

Young, J. 1990. *Cognitive Therapy for Personality Disorders: A Schema-Focused Approach.* Sarasota, Fla.: Professional Resource Exchange.

Index

Some Other
New Harbinger Titles

Depressed and Anxious, Item 3635 $19.95

Angry All the Time, Item 3929 $13.95

Handbook of Clinical Psychopharmacology for Therapists, 4th edition, Item 3996 $55.95

Writing For Emotional Balance, Item 3821 $14.95

Surviving Your Borderline Parent, Item 3287 $14.95

When Anger Hurts, 2nd edition, Item 3449 $16.95

Calming Your Anxious Mind, Item 3384 $12.95

Ending the Depression Cycle, Item 3333 $17.95

Your Surviving Spirit, Item 3570 $18.95

Coping with Anxiety, Item 3201 $10.95

The Agoraphobia Workbook, Item 3236 $19.95

Loving the Self-Absorbed, Item 3546 $14.95

Transforming Anger, Item 352X $10.95

Don't Let Your Emotions Run Your Life, Item 3090 $17.95

Why Can't I Ever Be Good Enough, Item 3147 $13.95

Your Depression Map, Item 3007 $19.95

Successful Problem Solving, Item 3023 $17.95

Working with the Self-Absorbed, Item 2922 $14.95

The Procrastination Workbook, Item 2957 $17.95

Coping with Uncertainty, Item 2965 $11.95

The BDD Workbook, Item 2930 $18.95

You, Your Relationship, and Your ADD, Item 299X $17.95

The Stop Walking on Eggshells Workbook, Item 2760 $18.95

Conquer Your Critical Inner Voice, Item 2876 $15.95

The PTSD Workbook, Item 2825 $17.95

Hypnotize Yourself Out of Pain Now!, Item 2809 $14.95

The Depression Workbook, 2nd edition, Item 268X $19.95

Beating the Senior Blues, Item 2728 $17.95

Shared Confinement, Item 2663 $15.95

Handbook of Clinical Psychopharmacology for Therapists, 3rd edition, Item 2698 $55.95

Getting Your Life Back Together When You Have Schizophrenia, Item 2736 $14.95

Do-It-Yourself Eye Movement Technique for Emotional Healing, Item 2566 $13.95

Call **toll free, 1-800-748-6273,** or log on to our online bookstore at **www.newharbinger.com** to order. Have your Visa or Mastercard number ready. Or send a check for the titles you want to New Harbinger Publications, Inc., 5674 Shattuck Ave., Oakland, CA 94609. Include $4.50 for the first book and 75¢ for each additional book, to cover shipping and handling. (California residents please include appropriate sales tax.) Allow two to five weeks for delivery.

Prices subject to change without notice.